THE FACILITY MANAGER'S GUIDE TO INFORMATION TECHNOLOGY

GEOFF WILLIAMS   MICHAEL MAY

Edited by Geoff Williams and Michael May

ISBN: 188317693X
ISBN 13: 9781883176938

Table of Contents

6 Facility Management and CAFM

*Michael Marchionini, Dan Rusch-Fischer, Joachim
Hohmann, Bill Jordan, Michael May, Peter Prischl*

7 Applications

Alwin Schauer, Gary Kropp, Alexander Maier

11 CAFM Systems   197

Stefan Koch, Nicole Lobb, Rita Görze, Michael
Marchionini, Michael May, Dirk Ranglack, Geoff Williams

Appendix 2: General Dynamics C4 Systems   325
Patrick Okamura, Deborah Schneiderman

Appendix 3: St. Mary's General Hospital / Grand River Hospital   339
Geoff Williams, Roger Holliss

Preface

Buildings and properties constitute between 25 and 50 percent of balanced fixed assets. Real estate usually is the largest active position on the balance sheet and represents the largest expenditure after human resources. Accordingly, it has a tremendous impact on profit and loss calculations. Therefore it is increasingly understood as a strategic resource and is part of the value chain creation for an enterprise. Now that the core processes of corporations have been restructured and optimized to a large extent, real estate is being called upon to strengthen the corporation's economic position.

The costs of planning, establishing, using, and managing real estate have risen enormously, and therefore these play a tremendous role in the operating results of a corporation. Corporations are looking at both their core and non-core businesses to find potential cost reductions. Facility management (FM) as a profession is relied upon in this manner to improve continuously on its efficiency to support the financial goals of the corporation. However, it is not only concerned with reduction of costs but also with the continuous improvement of the occupied spaces in an effort to improve the comfort and morale of the occupants. Thus, it is not only possible that the FM can improve the corporate bottom line by reducing costs, but there is also a tremendous opportunity to provide spaces that allow employees to work more efficiently and productively. In doing so, the role of the FM can be both considered a cost center and a potential profit center.

This text is a joint effort among members of the German Facility Management Association (GEFMA), IT Working Group, and the Information Technology Council of the International Facility Management Association (IFMA). This is the first book to look from a global perspective at FM and IT, and we hope it is the first of many international collaborations.

Based on the 2006 second edition of the German book *IT im Facility Management erfolgreich einsetzen—Das CAFM-Handbuch*, by Springer Publishing Company, this also represents the first tangible result of an international collaboration between both of these groups with the goal of broadening this effort in the future.

The purpose of the book is to provide an informational text that presents a current, impartial, and comprehensive look at how information technology (IT) and facility management (FM) have become inextricably bound together in the modern workplace.

Exploring the evolving relationship between IT and FM, this book will provide a text that can be used by students, novice facility managers, and experienced facility managers. As a result, the authors intend the text to be used as both a teaching and a reference tool for educational organizations and corporations alike. This text will also cover the latest advancements in FM automation and provide a guide for implementing them successfully.

Traditionally, IT has been the one to ride off into the sunset, while facilities cleaned up after the horses. This is changing now. Facilities are increasingly being recognized as a strategic resource and part of an organization's value chain. They have always played a pivotal role in the success or failure of an enterprise, and the increased use of technology is making this more evident.

For the average facility manager, much of this was invisible, but this was the beginning of facility management's interaction with IT.

Throughout this book, countless ways that FM has grown to use IT will be demonstrated. At each new or reconfigured genesis, a new acronym has been applied to the relationship. There are countless names for this relationship, but they all boil down to facility management and related processes being supported by IT. Therefore, for the purposes of keeping it simple, CAFM (Computer-Aided Facility Management) was chosen as the acronym of choice, with apologies to the countless marketing folks who keep coming up with new ones.

This book examines the interaction of FM and IT in several ways:

- *As IT being a customer of FM.* As technology begins to play a larger role in facility operations, IT increasingly relies on FM to make sure layout, specification, and configuration support IT initiatives.

- *As IT and FM being partners.* Today's facility has become a technology tool, with hundreds of miles of cables, specialized cooling and power requirements, and the need to move technology within the facility to assist in collaboration and functionality.

- *As FM being a customer of IT.* Facility management automation is changing the way facility managers do their jobs, as the use of technology is increasing efficiency and raising the level of service provided to the organization.

This book aims to provide invaluable knowledge to FM professionals, service providers and consultants, as well as lecturers and students.

From the editors' perspective, this has been a very long journey beginning with meetings in San Diego and including New Orleans, Dallas, Manchester, Orlando, Berlin, Philadelphia, Atlanta, and Toronto. We would like to acknowledge and thank all of the following contributors for their dedication and expertise:

- Kevin Janus for his dedication and support in his editorial roles

- GEFMA and IFMA for their support of the project at large

- Springer Publishing Company for transferring the rights of the English translation to the editors

- All of our authors, both German and North American (see the "Authors" section)

- Christy Gotcher from Krystal Blue Design for providing cover artwork and image content

- Jan Ritzmann, a student at University of Applied Sciences Berlin, for his technical assistance in preparing of the book

This book has been a true test of endurance and has facilitated the formation of long-lasting friendships.

Michael May   Geoff Williams
   Berlin   Toronto
Spring 2012

1

THE RELATIONSHIP BETWEEN FM AND IT

Kevin Janus

As stated in the preface, facility management (FM) and information technology (IT) did not always understand their dependence on each other or the value that they could provide each other. Information technology personnel were thought of as highly skilled professionals, and facility managers were thought of as engineers in jumpsuits, residing in basements, running boiler plants, carrying massive key rings, changing light bulbs, and performing janitorial duties.

But as early as the 1980s, FM was being introduced to IT. CAD was getting a foothold in the architecture industry, and construction was still using paper-based drawings, but these drawings were created by a software program. Industrial facilities were seeing automation in manufacturing, and engineers were beginning to use automated building controls to monitor and run mechanical systems. For the average facility manager, much of this was invisible, but this was the beginning of FM's interaction with IT.

Fast forward to the 1990s, when most facility managers were dealing with IT on a daily basis. Most office workers now had a PC, which meant facility management's electrical and IT's telecom and data cabling were starting to share some of the same wireways. Cubicles could no longer be set up with just electrical drops; these now had to make way for their other cable brethren. Data centers were putting demands on facilities that had not been seen before. The need for high concentrations of power and cooling were changing the inherent design of facilities, and desktop PCs and monitors were replacing lighting as the number-one cause of heat in office space. Power was not only in high demand, but it also needed to be conditioned and uninterrupted. Space planners were well down the path of using CAD for new layouts, and hand-drawn blueprints were becoming a lost art.

The way people were doing their work had changed as well. With the mainstreaming of computers, workers were able to collect and connect to large groups of information in ways they had never done before. This information was now being called "data." Savvy facility managers saw this and thought it may be able to help them, but they were too busy changing bulbs, building cubes, and making sure bathrooms functioned properly.

Facility management by nature deals with a tremendous amount of data from multiple sources. Building control systems continued to evolve beyond manufacturing and had entered office, retail, and even some residential space. Email was outpacing the written communication. Requests for service were now coming in via electronic work orders, and budgets were being tracked in spreadsheets.

Much of IT's prowess had come from the PC and an organizations ever-growing reliance upon it, and the use of mainframes to store and utilize rapidly growing amounts of data.

Then came the looming specter of Y2K, and IT departments were growing exponentially, in some corporate offices accounting for as much as 35 percent of the support staff. Information technology budgets grew by leaps and bounds, and FM was left in the dust as people forgot the importance of a properly running facility. Information technology was clearly the focus at the turn of the millennium. Y2K came to pass, and planes did not fall from the sky, power plants did not go dark, and accounting data made the transition without much trouble. To be fair, this was in part due to the countless hours and dollars IT groups put into prep, but once the "crisis" passed, corporations started to look at IT departments with a new scrutiny. No longer could they just dictate needs and have them carried out based on fear of the unknown. Information technology was going to have to take its place alongside the other organizational support groups like Human Resources, Finance, and even FM.

This leveled the playing field and the use of IT and FM had a chance to catch up. This involved not just the pioneering building automation and design groups, but the ability of FM to take advantage of some of the data processing that other groups (IT, Sales, Finance) had been using for some time. This gave FM the ability to quantify their work and hopefully show some of their value. It also provided an opportunity for FM to take advantage of additional information and automated building system monitoring, asset management, work distribution scheduling of preventative maintenance, and predictive failure analysis, to name a few. It also provided better reporting tools for a facility manager to show how his work affects the bottom line and to help better align this work with organizational goals. This, if used effectively, is IT's greatest gift to FM. With the onset of ever more sophisticated technology, both for the FM to use and for the FM to support, this trend should continue to provide a synergistic partnership between FM and IT for the foreseeable future.

2

TECHNOLOGIES AND THEIR IMPACT ON FM

Julie Knudson

2.1 INTRODUCTION

There is little doubt that the impact of technology on the facility management industry has been prodigious and profound. Every facet of our industry has felt some degree of change from the technologies that surround us. From controlling building access to minimizing energy usage, advances in technology have allowed us to do more, to know more, and to accomplish many tasks faster.

But technology was not easily embraced by the FM crowd. While other groups quickly began leveraging new technologies to address their business needs, facility managers (FMs) were more pragmatic. Trading in a working (though cumbersome) access control system such as the lock and key for a more sophisticated card reader, or later for biometrics, meant risking system errors, downtime, and unhappy end users. But while FMs may have taken a little extra time to warm up to technology, it is now an expected—and largely trusted—part of the job.

2.2 FACTORS FOR CHANGE

The implementation of technology by facility professionals has been an incremental process. The FM industry as a whole did not start out as an early adopter, instead choosing to monitor and analyze new developments prior to implementing them. In the construction industry, even with the increasing availability of automation, many tasks are still done by hand. But even in areas where humans continue to be the main engine, technology is still able to augment our ability to impact cost, schedules, results, and communication. The pace at which new technologies are adopted has increased, spurred on by a wide range of factors, from costs to world events to environmental concerns.

We have seen a change in how some aspects of FM are viewed and managed as a result of events such as 9/11, the availability of technologies like Wi-Fi and the Internet, and the extent to which mobile devices have permeated our culture. The range of people and processes affected by new technologies is growing rapidly. Of course, the ever-evolving nature of user needs and expectations is also having a sizeable effect on how quickly new technologies are adopted.

2.2.1 ADVANCES IN TECHNOLOGY

The interconnected nature of the facility industry means that an advancement in one technology will often prompt innovations in another dependent on or otherwise linked to technology. Sometimes the simple fact that a particular technology has advanced creates a new or increased set of needs and expectations.

Advances in technology frequently also spell reductions in consumer prices for that technology, making it more widely available. As prices fall within reach, more FMs are able to incorporate new technologies into their existing programs. The increased level of use of a technology brings about even more adopters, as data regarding the technology's security, stability, and ease of use becomes widely available.

2.2.2 VIOLENCE AND TERRORISM

Along with our progression into the twenty-first century has come a rise in acts of violence and terrorism that affect our daily lives. The attacks of 9/11, a sharp uptick in school shootings, and an increase in various kinds of domestic terrorism are among the factors behind many of the past decade's process and system changes.

A more complete discussion surrounding the changes brought about by violence and terrorism is far outside the scope of this chapter. But a sampling of implications shows widespread changes in procedures, practices, regulations, and expectations. Existing technologies have been more widely adopted, and many new technologies have been created to support these changes.

2.2.2.1 COMMUNICATION NEEDS

The need to communicate across functional groups and even across disciplines—buildings managers, building users, law enforcement, first responders, utility crews, and vendors—was brought into sharp relief by the events of 9/11. Existing communication platforms were not designed to integrate easily, and very quickly it became critical to bridge the communication gaps we had previously accepted as the status quo. An immediate search began for platforms that allowed us to share information, coordinate activities, and provide timely notification to end users and co-workers.

Interoperability problems in the existing communication infrastructure also illuminated the need for a wider range of communication methods that did not rely on any single technology platform. Walkie-talkies and mobile phones could not do the job alone—we needed to find a way to join the myriad ways in which people communicated into a single umbrella that could be activated at a moment's notice. The potential to target these communications by geographic region—a school campus, a particular city, or even a multi-state area—was also a factor in designing new, more comprehensive systems.

2.2.2.2 SECURITY NEEDS

The focus on security in the built environment shifted from protecting occupants against outside threats to protecting occupants and assets (buildings, etc.) from all threats, both those originating from within a facility and those coming from the outside. New technologies (see Anderson 2008) were needed to give FMs and first responders better access to security information and video surveillance footage. And rather than focus on the ability to view historical information such as the previous day's security video footage, it became critical that real-time images were available, often from a remote location.

Building operations previously assumed to be safe and predictable needed to be reviewed. Companies that considered themselves potentially at a high risk for terrorism began to ponder how effective their building systems would be if confronted with a threat. More FMs installed compact X-ray scanners to ensure the safety of their mail and parcel programs. Rooms previously secured by conventional locks were upgraded to card readers (or biometrics) for more controlled access and better reporting on entry/exit data. Security cameras were installed in greater numbers, with remote operator access, better resolution, and increased storage capacity.

2.2.3 THE INTERNET

Once seen as unsecure and maybe even unreliable by FMs, the Internet has grown into a platform that now supports and facilitates a wide variety of safe, trusted technology tools. It allows multiple systems to more easily interact, and it enables us to access and broadcast information, as well as access systems.

The Internet and other technologies allow companies to provide software as a service (SaaS). Providers are responsible for maintaining current software versions, for updating secure access methods, and for bearing the cost of the equipment needed to run the system. This shift in how programs are deployed, maintained, and accessed allows FMs to leverage technology while keeping costs down. User access can often be enabled from any Internet-connected device, further supporting today's "work anywhere" model.

2.2.4 MOBILE DEVICES

No longer restricted to the realm of voice communications, mobile devices—smartphones, laptops, handheld computers and their brethren—give us an unprecedented ability to retrieve, broadcast, and receive information. Even the most basic cell phones are capable of sending and receiving text messages. More advanced devices can access the Internet and exchange information with encrypted systems (see Johnson 2011).

The various technologies used by mobile devices make us connected, no matter where we happen to be. Access to building and security systems is no longer restricted to onsite members of the facility team. End users are able to receive immediate information regarding building disruptions and emergencies, even if they are away from their desk. And vendors or other business partners can lend their expertise and assistance at a moment's notice.

Management of physical space itself has been impacted by the evolution of mobile devices. Some companies are moving away from conventional infrastructure cabling, opting instead to install wireless hubs to support computers and telephones. We now have the ability to support personnel independent of their location.

2.2.5 EXPECTATIONS

Intertwined with these other factors is the marked change in the expectations of end users, building occupants, co-workers, and senior staff. Immediate notification of building disruptions has become standard practice; emergency information can now be broadcast to members of the facility team and end users simultaneously; building information and surveillance video can be accessed from anywhere; and top decision makers have the ability to review real-time usage, system data, and project deliverables.

In some instances, user needs and expectations have driven advances in technology. But in some cases, the reverse may be true. Once a technology is available, users and developers often discover new ways to employ it. Have students taken to carrying cell phones because that is how they can most easily receive broadcasts from their school's mass notification system, or have mass notification systems grown to include text messaging because students carry cell phones? Using this oversimplified but still relevant example, it is easy to see how technologies, industry needs, and user expectations are inextricably linked.

2.3 TYPES OF TECHNOLOGY

The technologies impacting the facility industry span a wide variety of software, hardware, processes, and systems.

2.3.1 SOFTWARE

In general, software impacting the facility industry falls into two major categories.

2.3.1.1 GENERAL

A variety of general-use programs are regularly applied in support of facility management. These include personal information management (PIM) applications for managing contacts, calendars, and task lists, among other things; spreadsheet and word-processing programs; accounting and reporting software; project management applications; database programs; and email or other communication platforms.

In some instances, these general programs are leveraged for FM-specific tasks, such as monitoring detailed capital project timelines. In other cases, they are used to manage the daily flow of work that is relatively universal among industries, professions, and reporting levels. Even though much of this software is not designed or used expressly for the facility industry, many of these programs are considered critical pieces of our technology infrastructure.

2.3.1.2 FACILITY-SPECIFIC

A number of software applications exist to address specific needs within the facility industry. They include spatial design and rendering programs; Computer Aided Facility Management (CAFM) programs that track space usage, cable pathways, and employee locations, among a host of other metrics; security, access control, and biometric software; life-cycle analysis programs; databases to track the environmental impacts of building activities; and utility management systems that allow for real-time monitoring and trend analysis.

Early software platforms have been joined by newer entries, though many of the earliest technologies are still used in some form. In some instances, technologies are simply evolving to incorporate the best features of early version with innovations made possible by the latest available technology. Conventional CAFM programs, relied upon by FMs for so many years, are slowly evolving into Integrated Workplace Management

Systems (IWMS). While relying on the solid foundation of CAFM, IWMS offers a broader range of features and capabilities.

Asset tracking was once easily managed in spreadsheet form, but the scope of assets is growing. While a number of programs exist to track more conventional assets such as furniture and equipment, Information Technology Service Management (ITSM) programs are designed to track new types of "softer" assets—e.g., computer memory and software licensing—commonly related to IT functions.

2.3.2 BEYOND SOFTWARE

Technologies used in FM stretch beyond software, and the offerings are vast and diverse. Just a brief sample of the wide variety of technologies and their impact on the built environment follows.

2.3.2.1 ACOUSTICS

Improved sound-masking systems help FMs manage intruding noise and privacy. New fabrics offer better acoustical properties while being more environmentally friendly. And an increasing range of materials and surface treatments gives FMs the opportunity to more cleanly incorporate aesthetics when designing new or remodeled spaces.

2.3.2.2 CABLING

Advances in cabling technology mean all sorts of devices and systems can be supported by cabling once thought of as only computer cabling. Security cameras can reside on the corporate network, providing secure and remote access, while also providing for on-network storage that is vast, easily indexed, and less susceptible to degradation than conventional video tape.

2.3.2.3 SECURITY CAMERAS

Cameras have pan-zoom-tilt features that allow a remote operator to focus on a particular person or area to record an event, analyze behavior, and evaluate a situation. The days of grainy, black-and-white, or jerky video are fast disappearing. Today's cameras have better hardware, are supported by much-improved software (some of which is capable of recognizing individual faces), and provide significantly better image quality.

2.3.2.4 FLOORING

A variety of flooring technologies are increasing in popularity due to their sustainability and reduced maintenance costs. While some of the materials used in today's flooring may not be new, the technology to manufacture and dispose of them often results in a more environmentally friendly product.

2.3.2.5 LIGHTING

Many advances in lighting technologies are focused on reducing energy consumption. Occupancy sensors are growing in popularity as a way to fine-tune how much—and how often—lighting is used. New lamp and ballast technologies deliver better-quality light along with greater light output, while also lowering utility, maintenance, and relamping costs.

2.3.2.6 VIDEOCONFERENCING

The combination of advancing technology and globalization has made videoconferencing common in many organizations. Facility managers must now consider the needs of videoconferencing systems when setting up or retrofitting meeting spaces. Conference areas designs need to be fine-tuned to limit the amount of background noise and motion that can be a distraction when many people or locations are involved, and video-capable cabling must be used.

2.3.2.7 RECYCLING AND DISPOSAL

More efficient methods and processes used during recycling and disposal have affected how FMs manage the disposition of materials and equipment. As an industry, we are keen to minimize how much we add to our already-burgeoning landfills. We have more and better recycling options;

vendors and manufacturers are eager to participate in environmentally friendly disposal programs; and new processes allow for a greater reuse of material that would normally have been thrown away.

2.4 INCREASING RESPONSIBILITIES

Facility professionals have a much more diverse set of responsibilities on their plate than even a decade ago. Depending on the specific industry, company size, and geographic region (among many other factors), many FMs oversee security, intrabuilding technology links, business continuity planning, energy reduction plans, space planning, trip reduction, tele-commuting, emergency preparedness, life safety, and environmental stewardship, along with technology implementation in each of these areas.

To make the best decisions and meet corporate goals, FMs must now be technology experts in their own right. Determining specifications for a new system often requires a solid understanding of the underlying technology and its capabilities and shortcomings. Evaluating the best storage and access methods for existing technologies means FMs must be informed about the options and advantages of each. Even if IT is able to assist with the more technical aspects of a technology implementation, they are usually just as understaffed as any facility group, and ongoing administration or troubleshooting often defaults back to the FM.

2.5 REVENUE AND EFFICIENCY

Saving money and time are among the goals—spoken or unspoken—of every employee. The increased responsibilities now firmly under the jurisdiction of many FMs do not usually bring with them a comparable increase in budget. FMs are employing technology to help balance their ever-growing goals and ever-decreasing budgets, with impressive results.

Communication technologies are enabling FMs to look outside their organizations for the best sources of labor to meet a particular need—expertise, cost reduction, quick lead time, etc. Outsourcing and offshoring have become valid choices for many organizations. Advancements in technology mean proximity to vendors and suppliers is now less important, though fuel costs and environmental impacts sometimes continue to make location a prime factor when making purchasing decisions.

Radio-frequency identification (RFID) technology is moving asset tracking and management to a new level (see Brown 2006). FMs are able to minimize expenditures when they know exactly which supplies they have on hand, how many are available, and where those supplies are located. (How many times have you uttered the phrase, "Hey, here's another box of those filters we thought we were out of"?) It is easier than ever to ensure that products do not sit around past their expiration dates, and asset tracking can even be used to deliver products using the most cost-effective method. Assets can be tracked geographically, allowing FMs to plan for the most efficient use of resources in each location.

Building Information Modeling (BIM) systems allow facility teams to manage budgets on design and construction projects more closely by reducing change orders. They can also work with contractors to create detailed trade schedules that maximize resources and minimize costs. Depending on the project, it may also be possible to shorten the overall project timeline.

Technology is allowing some companies the flexibility and resources to improve efficiency by conducting preventive maintenance (PM) activities based more closely on need than on time alone. UPS is a good example; they are working to implement a program to replace vehicle components based on usage (miles driven, number of vehicle starts, etc.), rather than on the amount of time since a vehicle's last maintenance visit.

CAFM and related technologies enable a smaller FM staff to make prudent and efficient decisions for much larger facilities. Previously, facilities consisting of multiple buildings in different geographic areas would have likely operated in a fairly autonomous manner, both fiscally and from an overall decision-making standpoint. This required more staff and often did not allow for aggressive price discounts for services and supplies based on company-wide volume. Now nationwide and even global purchasing and labor decisions can more easily encompass the real-world needs of the users occupying and the resources available at multiple facilities.

2.6 INFORMATION MANAGEMENT

Gathering and managing vast amounts of information is at the root of many technologies today, and many of the advances we are seeing are driven by growing needs for information storage, access, updates, and system interlinks with multiple programs. Facility managers are managing much of that information, along with an IT partnership that allows un-fettered (but secure) access to information in all its forms: building draw-ings, energy usage data, surveillance video footage, etc.

Computer Aided Design (CAD) and Computerized Maintenance Management Software/Systems (CMMS) have been around for a long time. But it has been in more recent times that CAFM and other systems have come to the forefront. CMMS platforms of today can not only man-age preventive maintenance activities (see Bagadia 2006), they also have the ability to help decrease the time from task request to task comple-tion, increase the speed and accuracy of information related to each task, and provide improved cost and trend analyses.

First-generation web-based tools carried a higher risk of hackers and viruses, and thus were not considered viable information management solutions for FMs. Initially, many IT departments were not willing to open up the secure areas of their networks to facilities or other groups outside the core IT team. Improvements in IT technology such as virtual private networks (VPNs), more secure server software, and other security improvements have largely removed concerns about the security and in-tegrity of critical systems.

New technologies frequently help us to manage the same types of information in a much more efficient way. For example, security cameras relied on low-resolution images and tape storage, which were subject to degradation and bulky. Today's devices capture images at 10 megapixels and more; they store images and videos digitally; and the media is avail-able remotely.

2.7 EVOLVING RELATIONSHIPS AND EXPECTATIONS

The very nature of our interactions with end users, other departments, and vendors is evolving. As technologies are linking people, systems, and information, we are finding we need to change some of the fundamental methods of communication and support.

2.7.1 CUSTOMER RELATIONSHIP MANAGEMENT

Years ago, it was not uncommon for end users to have very little interac-tion with the facility team. Other than small-scale (overflowing toilets) and large-scale (fire) emergencies, the groups rarely communicated. Today, we have moved to the other end of the spectrum. Many end users are active participants in energy-reduction programs; recycling and sustainability are corporate-wide initiatives; and FMs have a more in-depth understanding of exactly how the built environment affects and supports users. While this shift in the relationship between users and FMs has not been entirely influenced by technology, there are many aspects being directly affected by available and emerging technologies.

The very process of receiving requests from end users has undergone an evolution. Users can now enter requests directly into corporate-wide databases. Rather than waiting to be manually logged, evaluated, and delegated, those requests are automatically assigned a unique identifier and routed to the correct member of the FM team for further action. Users, facility team members, and senior staff can track the status of each request at any moment. For budgeting and workflow management purposes, these request systems can quickly produce reports showing the total amount of time dedicated to completed requests, how the quantity of requests compares to historical data, and what resources—time, parts, etc.—were required to complete each request. PM and CMMS systems can incorporate recurring tasks into the general workflow schedule, too, so the FM is able to view a more complete picture of the demands on their team.

2.7.2 ALERTS

If there is one key word swirling around customer relationships in today's climate, it is *alerts*. Customer expectations regarding information sharing have surely changed as a result of technology. End users are now accustomed to receiving information relevant to their lives immediately—weather alerts, traffic alerts, building alerts, life safety alerts, flight alerts. Today's cars are even capable of sending alerts when it is time for an oil change or when something is amiss. (I guess this means one day soon we might receive spam from our cars.)

End users now expect immediate notification of potential building disruptions and emergencies. They also expect information to be readily accessible in any number of ways—via email, over the phone, on the Internet, and even on their handheld devices. There are advantages as well as disadvantages to providing all this information in such a diverse and global way. Advantages include the ability to provide targeted information to users based on time of day, type of alert, and perhaps the user's specific location. Downsides include the added layer of customer notification during what may be an already busy time (emergencies, etc.), as well as the possibility that users may miss alerts for various reasons. There is also the potential that sensitive information could reach unauthorized users, through glitches, inaccurate or outdated programming, or user error/action.

2.7.3 INFORMATION SHARING

FMs have long needed the ability to more quickly and easily share information—such as building layouts, surveillance video, and card key access records—with first responders, investigative agencies, and departments within the company. Technology now makes what was once a potentially cumbersome task fairly straightforward. Rather than providing bulky computer printouts or unwieldy architectural drawings, we have the ability to email reports, to transfer large datasets between systems, and to post information and documents on secure web pages.

2.7.4 COLLABORATION WITH IT GROUPS

Facility and IT departments once viewed each other only as end users in need of support. Now we have formed alliances and partnerships between the two groups that function and enable progress on multiple levels. Both the FM and IT teams are tasked with supporting the needs of today's workforce, and combining resources and expertise is often advantageous.

Facility managers are quickly coming up to speed on the various information technologies available. They are relying heavily on corporate IT groups for guidance and historical data. Implementation of most systems requires some level of support from IT, either for training, administration, or recommendations on hardware and software. Smooth system interoperability and secure access to stored information typically requires IT oversight.

For IT's part, they are now tasked with managing an increasingly robust and diverse set of cabling standards, software, and hardware devices to support the FM environment. They are learning about operating costs associated with data centers, energy management techniques, security practices, and building management—all at a furious pace.

Efficient data centers have become a major focus for FM and IT groups. Teams are working together to decrease power usage, maximize cooling resources, make the best use of available space, support 24/7 critical operations, and provide the right level of security. In companies with extremely large or complex data centers, there may be very little distinction between some of the FM and IT tasks, and the groups work in close cooperation.

2.8 IMPACT ON FM PROFESSIONALS

Technology affects not only the facility industry as a whole, but individuals within FM are also impacted on more a personal level.

2.8.1 COLLABORATION AMONG FMS, PARTNERS, VENDORS, AND OTHER RESOURCES

Networking and collaboration among FMs and their partners now happens in the blink of an eye. Advice can be requested and dispensed from anywhere. Business partners can weigh in on projects without ever visiting the physical plant. Vendors can remotely access systems to troubleshoot, make repairs, and implement upgrades. Equipment and systems are able to send out distress signals when there is a problem or supplies are running low.

Local FM organizations are still instrumental in supporting our ability to learn and to network, but FMs have quick and easy access to mentors and colleagues around the globe. Through email, webinars, and video conferences, we can collaborate with professionals in other areas in an interactive and engaging environment. We are no longer limited in our ability to learn from each other just because we are not in the same geographic area. We have access to experts and leaders like never before.

User groups exist to provide support on every program, system, and process in the FM world. Technology that may not have existed in a recognizable form twenty years ago, such as BIM, now has a robust collection of user groups poised to provide advice, expertise, and other support to FMs looking for information and guidance.

2.8.2 FACILITY MANAGEMENT EDUCATION

A huge amount of learning still happens on the job. But technology has allowed FMs unprecedented access to additional educational tools. Conventional college courses and degree/certification programs can often be completed almost entirely online. Assignments are posted on a class website, study materials are downloaded from online storefronts, and class participants often work together over the phone or Internet.

Within the facility industry, FMs are able to remain abreast of current trends, news, and technologies. They can also advance their careers, grow their areas of expertise, and maintain the knowledge level of their teams without spending time and money to travel each time. Seminars, workshops, symposiums, and conventions are held to discuss and analyze everything impacting the facility industry, from emerging trends in technology to pending legislation, changes to industry standards, and updates to best practices. Not all of these events happen in the physical world—many are conducted via web broadcast or over the telephone. For those interested in learning a new skill, there are also a wide variety of how-to videos available on the Internet.

2.9 ISSUES AND HURDLES

No matter how many technologies emerge to make us more productive, there are always problems to work out and obstacles to overcome. Interoperability, competing standards, and general user acceptance are all common issues. Budget limitations and affordability also affect the rate of new technology adoption, as well as the overall effectiveness of any particular technology.

If a new technology falls under the jurisdiction of a regulating body, then that technology needs to overcome the hurdle of complying with applicable regulatory standards and practices before it can be used. Any number of issues may crop up that must be addressed before a new (or revised, improved, or expanded) technology can be fully implemented. The technology's methodology of use; the training of its users; the accuracy, integrity, and reliability of its data; and the impact on other already accepted systems or processes must all be demonstrated and validated in a way that meets the requirements of the regulating body.

Another issue that usually comes up when you are least prepared to tackle it is a need to upgrade one system that require upgrades to separate but linked systems, each with its own impact on project costs, downtime, and user inconvenience. Rather than enabling FMs to move forward, sometimes the connected nature of these systems is a hindrance.

Along the same lines, the proprietary nature of some systems occasionally creates a stumbling block. Implementations may require more vendor involvement than anticipated, along with increased training for system users. The very nature of our interconnected world means that even a single malfunctioning system could hinder other processes.

Sometimes technology companies are proactive in addressing potential problems through extensive user testing, increased support of beta products, and a variety of other forward-thinking business practices. In many instances, the users themselves find workarounds through creative use of supporting technologies, clever leveraging of more conventional technologies, or the simple use of a new technology in a way unanticipated by the designer.

2.10 SUMMARY

The implementation of technology by facility professionals has been an incremental process. The FM industry as a whole did not start out as an early adopter, instead choosing to monitor and analyze new developments prior to implementing them. However, the pace at which new technologies are adopted has increased, spurred on by a wide range of factors, from costs to world events to environmental concerns.

A number of software applications address specific needs within the facility industry. They include spatial design and rendering programs; Computer Aided Facility Management (CAFM) programs that track space usage, cable pathways, and employee locations, among a host of other metrics; security, access control, and biometric software; life-cycle analysis programs; databases to track the environmental impacts of building activities; and utility management systems that allow for real-time monitoring and trend analysis.

Both the FM and IT teams are tasked with supporting the needs of today's workforce, and combining resources and expertise is often advantageous.

3

IT BASICS FOR FACILITY MANAGERS

Marco Jedlitzke, Joachim Hohmann, Michael Marchionini, Michael May, Marko Opić, Geoff Williams

3.1 THE MEANING OF IT FOR FACILITY MANAGEMENT

Effective, holistic facility management can be realized only when there is a tight integration between FM and relevant primary enterprise processes (see chapter 9). Since this type of integration raises the bar of complexity, through the organization of and the use of dependency-based processes, there is no option but to seek the assistance of IT solutions.

When considering a CAFM solution, as with any cost burden on the organization, the facility manager must carefully weigh the Value Proposition of the solution under consideration. The easiest way to assess value is to place it under the microscope of simple dollars and cents. Consider how the implementation of the solution will save time and resources, reduce costs, and improve the competitive position and the services of the business.

Remember that with any CAFM solution (or any IT solution), you are essentially speaking of data that can be processed, manipulated, and shared by a machine. Therefore, when assessing your data needs, you must consider what and how much data you need to deliver value. For instance, if you consider the life cycle of a building, only focus on data that is actually needed in the individual life-cycle phases. Then consider if a specific dataset is even necessary, since not all data is easy to update at a later phase in the life cycle. If the data cannot be easily updated, there is a chance that it may not be kept up-to-date and therefore is not useful and/or may be used in error when taken as correct.

A solution must also ensure the ability to exchange data not only within the enterprise but also with business partners and customers. For example, it is necessary to consider external data exchange formats and interfaces and not just your corporate data exchange protocols.

A solution also needs to consider the support infrastructure both internally and externally for hardware and software. The tools that constitute the CAFM solution will represent an increase in value only if they lead to the appropriate quantitative and/or qualitative effects. These effects can be leveraged only with the proper support mechanisms in place for training, technical support, and implementation. If you cannot dedicate the support required by a CAFM solution, it will not succeed.

The IT aspects that support a CAFM solution include networks, software, databases, graphics solutions, application integration, and software management. The next several sections of this chapter are dedicated to both educating the facility manager in the above aspects of IT and also examining them from a CAFM perspective.

3.2 NETWORKS

3.2.1 GENERAL DESCRIPTION OF COMPUTER NETWORKS

A *computer network* is the connection of several different and usually spatially separated computers. It has the task of making applications available for use and communication. Simply put, it makes the transmission of messages between the computers possible. Transferable information comes in the form of text, data, pictures, audio, video, or a combination of these types (multimedia).

Since facility management is a general term, when considering CAFM solutions, there are often a number of departments involved as stakeholders. These departments rely on and leverage the abilities of networking to distribute large volumes of data and other IT resources (hardware and software) throughout the organization to satisfy a common objective. Therefore, when FM data is shared across a network, the expenditure is reduced because the costs associated with data duplication are eliminated. Furthermore, the "compound effects" of having multiple users attached to the same data resources can be described as follows (Stahlknecht 1998):

- Data aggregate

- Load sharing (capacity group and safety group)

- Device sharing (resource interlocking),

- Resource sharing (program group)

- Communication sharing (message group)

A further advantage exists in improvement of shared business processes through the support of IT solutions. These are "routine procedures" that are well structured and arise cyclically, including the following:

- Work sequencing

- Work orders

- Resource planning

Other improvements include the following:

- Scheduling

- Common treatment of documents

- Fast conveyance of results

- Collaboration

These group tasks can be completed in a more ad-hoc manner (such as through telecommuting), because they do not rely on the spatial proximity of the group to one another, nor do they rely on a structured timeline (allowing flexible working hours). Therefore, the flexibility of the personnel is increased.

3.2.2 STRUCTURE OF NETWORKS

The structure of a computer network is usually referred to as its topology. Graphically, one can represent the *network topology* with computers as junctions and the network connections as lines. Depending on which structure is selected, the efficiency (kind and speed of the information transmission) and/or the stability (reliability) of the network will be affected. The following network topologies (see figure 3.1) are frequently used (Disterer et al. 2003):

- *Star structure:* A central mediator (router or switch) controls the transmission of all messages sent on the network. The loss of a connected computer does not influence the network's stability, but the loss of the router or switch causes the complete failure of the network.

- *Ring structure:* Without a central mediator, the computers are circularly, unidirectionally interconnected. The loss of a knot leads to the total failure of the network (this can be prevented only by double wiring in opposite direction).

- *Bus structure:* The computers in the network are interconnected by a common bus (channel). Since individual stations request the transmission here, the loss of a station does not influence the network stability.

- *Tree structure:* Several central, partial mediators take over message transport over the subnodes. A tree structure can be understood as a hierarchical connection of bus structures. The loss of a mediator entails the loss of the subnetworks behind it.

- *Mixed structures:* These result from the connection of the single structures to a total network.

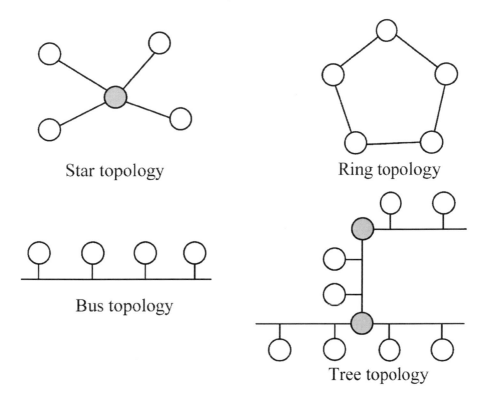

Fig. 3.1: Topologies of computer networks

3.2.3 DATA COMMUNICATION IN NETWORKS

There are two basic conditions of information exchange: the hardware, or physical connection of the computers, and a guarantee that the conveyed message will be understood as it was intended. For this, the operating system of the computer must make the appropriate services available, and there must be many different *transmission protocols*, that have been developed to accommodate different network topologies and manufacturers requirements. The most important transmission protocol in use today is TCP/IP (Transmission Control Protocol/Internet Protocol), because it is what the Internet is built on. The basis of communication between components of different manufacturers forms a generally respected standard: the ISO/OSI *reference model* (International Standards Organization (ISO), Open Systems Interconnection (OSI). It defines the capacity and the communication interfaces of the assigned components by the partitioning of the necessary tasks into individual layers (levels).

3.2.4 EXPANSION OF NETWORKS

Networks are not only named after the structure or transmission mechanisms, but also the way the network is used. The following names are commonly used to describe networks based on their use:

- Local area networks (LAN—local area network; WLAN—wireless local area network)—a single floor or office network

- Urban networks (MAN—metropolitan area network)

- Long-distance networks (WAN—wide area network)—a network connecting multiple offices

- Global networks (GAN—global area network)—the Internet

However, an exact demarcation between the different uses of networks is difficult to delineate, since the borders are not firmly defined and can (and will) change over time. The term LAN is here usually used to identify a local, not publicly accessible, network. Through this network, the IT department administers and supplies information services.

The terms WAN and/or GAN are receiving increased meaning within FM as a result of the Internet. Through a connection to the Internet, almost any enterprise or individual can communicate easily with others across the planet. This global connection has led to the creation of purely electronic businesses that interact only with their customers via the Internet. Value is added through a connection to both the customer (e.g., tenants) and business partners (e.g., supplier).

3.2.5 INTERNET, INTRANET, AND EXTRANET

The *Internet* was developed by a group of state, public, and private institutions by building on the functionality and ideas of a network used by the American Department of Defense (ARPANET), which was the largest computer network in the world. While many believe the Internet is a new phenomenon, ARPANET sent its first transmission in 1949. The graphical Internet as we know it today was first introduced to the public

1993, and by late 1994 it began to have a following that was previously mostly academic. The Internet at its core is just a shared network that allows almost any service to run on it. The most popular services on the Internet are currently the World Wide Web ("www") and email. Due to the fact the World Wide Web is so popular and the fact that it is the most visible portion of the Internet, the terms are often confused. The Internet is just a network, and the World Wide Web is only a service available on the Internet. Many other services run over the Internet, such as chat, newsgroups, Peer to Peer, Voice-over IP (VoIP) and video conferencing.

The services and standards of the public Internet are often used within the private network, or *intranet* of an enterprise. Large corporations often run their own internal websites and email services as a service to their company. These are used for much of the same reasons as the public Internet but also include company-specific, often confidential information. Some corporations blur the line between the private intranet and the public intranet by using one common system to host both services and controlling access to sensitive information via permissions control and user names and passwords.

The less well-known term *extranet* is used to describe the connection of separate private intranets between enterprises. This is used to facilitate communication between the enterprises for the benefit of both enterprises involved. When an *extranet* is used, the types of information that may be exchanged must be carefully defined.

3.3 DATABASES

Database systems are used for storage of extensive and complex structured volumes of data. A large advantage of database systems is the various query options, which permit the user to generate different views of the contained data. The data contained within the database can be queried by any criteria relevant to the data contained in the database and can also be filtered by the permissions of the user.

Database systems (DBS) can consist of several *databases* (DB), which are administered through an integrated *database management system* (DBMS). The DBMS supervises all the commands interacting with the database and permits only the procedures that are allowed via the user permissions. Also, the DBMS maintains a log of every transaction so that they can be reverted or reconstructed in case of failure.

The data structure within a database system can be either centralized or distributed. With a centralized structure, all of the information is held on one computer (or a cluster of computers). This is usually a dedicated server, which all authenticated users can access via either the internal intranet or over the public Internet. With a distributed structure, the databases are stored on many different computers. All these individual databases are considered by the DBMS as a single logical unit and can be treated as one large, singular database. A distributed structure provides data redundancy as well as lowers the computer hardware requirements. One downside to a distributed structure is that a lot of work must be done to synchronize the data to ensure the results are consistent.

A common way to classify database systems is by their *database model*, which specifies the database syntax and semantics. The following DBS are differentiated by their database model (Lassmann et al. 2001):

- *Hierarchical DBS* store data in a tree structure. Here the data can be subdivided into multiple levels. Every item in the database is described in terms of its predecessor or parent (with exception of the top most item) and its successors or children (again, with exception of the bottom items). Due to the difficulty in recording the dependency between neighboring levels (items with several predecessors), these DBS are limited in their usefulness and are used only in certain key roles.

- *Network-oriented DBS* store data in a network structure describing items by their connections to the other items in the database. Relations can be illustrated by the connections between items, and items can have multiple predecessors. These types of databases are not used anymore.

- *Relational DBS* store data in tables that are connected by relationships. This model can also be used to illustrate network structures. Relational databases are usually designed so that data duplication is minimized through a process called normalization. This process separates any common or redundant data into separate tables within the database and retains the structure and meaning of the data by relating the tables to one another. This greatly reduces the size of the data stored, because common elements are stored only once, which allows the data to be queried easily by any criteria. Relational database systems are the most common of all database systems and are used in almost every business and enterprise.

■ *Object-oriented DBS* store information in the form of objects as used in object-oriented programming. Apart from the extended possibilities of transmitting data as objects, there is also the potential for storing object-specific executables and, in so doing, allows the separation of these executables from the programming of the application. Although object-oriented database systems have not become generally accepted, they are currently being used successfully for niche commercial applications.

■ *Object-relational DBS* combine the advantages of the two different database models, and therefore are not new in principle. The advantages of these DBS lie in a flexible data-type extension, so that these are used in specialized applications such as the administration of multimedia data (documents, pictures, audio).

■ *Post-relational DBS* place data in unstructured and dynamic fields. These DBS also use existing database models. Their advantages arise as a result of the efficient administration of complex data structures.

Communication with database systems is accomplished using special database languages. These are commonly known as the data definition (DDL—Data Definition Language) and data manipulation and/or inquiry (DML—Data Manipulation Language). The most common database language for relational databases is SQL (Structured Query Language). SQL can be used over the available operators both of DDL and DML.

Object-oriented databases can be differentiated by their languages for data definition and data manipulation, while ODL (Object Definition Language) serves the definition of attributes. For example, data can be queried and changed using OQL (Object Query Language). OQL is similar to SQL and permits a similar approach to the querying of data as SQL in relational databases. The object-relational and post office-relational databases primarily use well-known database languages. These types of databases are selected specifically for the application purpose of the respective database. Most current CAFM software is built on relational and object-relational DBS; however, some systems are also built on object-oriented DBS.

3.4 GRAPHIC DATA PROCESSING AND CAD

Much of a building's information can be represented better in graphics than in text and data. Examples are sketches, conceptual drawings, shop drawings, floor plans, damage photos, etc. As a result, CAFM software packages usually have integrated *graphic editors*. A characteristic is thereby a linkage of graphic information with individual data records of the CAFM database. This linkage can take place on the document level (shop drawing to maintenance task) or on the level of individual graphic objects (symbol in plan to inventory entry). In a perfect world, the graphic editor is based on a building model (BIM) with a database structure including geometry, so that the linkage is obtained by simple relations of the individual data records without redundancies.

The relevant graphic systems available on the market for CAFM can be divided in four groups with different technical foundations:

■ Raster-oriented diagram programs

■ Vector-based drawing systems

■ 3-D modeling

■ Building Information Model (BIM) editors

The raster-oriented programs are used for the scaled representation of graphic contents. Typical examples are digital photos such as those used for the representation of damage or inventory documentation. Typical file formats are BMP (bit-map), tiff (Tagged Image File Format), and JPEG/JPG (Joint Photographic Experts Group). Usually these files are linked at the document level with data records in the CAFM software.

So-called Computer Aided Architectural Design (CAAD) systems can be based on either of the following techniques. What they have in common are special functions to create building components such as walls, windows, doors, etc.

Vector-based drawings use point data to group simple and complex lines and other graphical primitives. These grouped elements can be provided with attributes, which give them logical connections to data.

For example, two lines can be grouped to represent a wall. The usual file formats for these are DWG (DraWinG file by Autodesk) or DXF (Drawing eXchange File by Autodesk), as well as DGN (Microstation Design file, originally by Intergraph) in particular in the automobile and equipment construction. With DWG there are grouping functions such as Layer for organizing objects (walls, doors, windows) and blocks for objects that are referenced several times in the same drawing (chair, light, symbols). Blocks can have attributes attached to them (arbitrary text in predefined fields), which can be referenced and updated with the data records from the CAFM database. Furthermore, modern architecture applications based on DWG allow the user to embed custom objects such as walls or doors with geometry. This technology represents a step toward the building model and BIM. Besides using 2-D representations, DWG also has been supplemented with some objects of the classic 3-D modeling tools. However, for all intents and purposes, the DWG format is still used for entity-based drawing/modeling and lacks the object-oriented tools of BIM. Project-based work on complex buildings with large teams can be achieved only by means of the combination of several files (rather than a single model) and is supported by what Autodesk calls External References (XREF).

A strong characteristic of vector formats is their optimization (small file size compared to raster) for transmission across networks. These are compressed files mainly used for viewing rather than editing. Typical "view-only" formats are the public SVG (Scalable Vector Graphics), which is based on XML as well as the DWF (Design Web Format) developed by Autodesk. Web-enabled and web-based CAFM programs use these formats frequently for publishing full-scale building plans on the Internet and/or intranet. Both formats support grouping functions for displaying and/or hiding certain information, whereby DWF is suitable for very large datasets. For simple, compound documents from text, raster, and unstructured vector diagrams, Adobe's PDF (Portable Document Format) is commonly used.

3-D modeling is used particularly in the design process. There are also special applications for the building industry with numerous libraries of three-dimensional parts such as furniture and lights. These tools are based on technologies such as NURBS (Non-Uniform Rationally B-Spline) for the description of free-form surfaces or ACIS (3-D modeling kernel from Spatial Technology). Frequently the 3-D modeling tool is equipped with matured rendering technologies for photo-realistic representation. Hardware supported drivers, such as OpenGL, supply a fast screen representation and regeneration.

Building Information Model editors. State-of-the-art *CAD programs* are based on a Building Information Model. As in CAFM databases, the structures of a building and their individual elements are stored (such as envelopes and structure as well as the equipment) in a file and/or a database. In this structure, complete geometry and the relations between the elements are recorded. Examples of this are the format PLN (ArchiCAD solo file) for the storage of a building model and/or a GDL (Geometric Description Language from Graphisoft) for the description of parametric construction units.

The software should be able to permit editing and viewing of the building from different sightlines (typically from any viewpoint). So a window can be shifted both in plan and in elevation. Likewise, in all views the same data record should be represented (i.e., Plans, Sections, Elevations, Perspectives, etc., are all views of the same model and do not have to be drawn separately). A further function can be context-dependent representation in the ground plan. Thus the working drawing will have more detail than the layout plan. Building modeling software must not necessarily dispose of 3-D views. In CAFM, the 2-D aspects of a building model also have substantial advantages in relation to a classical graphic editor with attributes.

The only problem with the building models has been *data exchange.* Similar to relational databases, the data must be transferred using the *logic of the model*, so that the receiving system is able to translate and understand all information. If we consider the exchange between DWG and DXF formats, inevitably redundancies develop and data gets bloated. Therefore prominent software houses, as well as the International Alliance for Interoperability (IAI) have developed *Industry Foundation Classes (IFC)*, which transmit all substantial information of a building model.

Some modern CAAD and CAFM systems use a combination of all four graphic techniques. The basis here is a building model, whose geometry can be provided with a 3-D-modeling tool, can be linked over reference technology with vector graphics, and can contain layers with raster data. So there is always a fall-back on classical procedures for data exchange in addition to the modern redundancy-free BIM technologies.

3.5 SOFTWARE

3.5.1 SOFTWARE LIFE CYCLE

Software is a generic term used to describe any and all computer programs. Software can be separated into two groups: system and application software, where *system software* is for the controlling of the hardware components and application software is used to solve specialized tasks (Stahlknecht 1998).

An example of system software is the operating system of your computer, be it Windows, Mac OS, or Linux. Application software could be CAFM software, ERP software (Enterprise Resource Planning), or office productivity products (e.g., word processing).

Software can be understood as a *product*; however, there are some criteria/specifics/differences:

- Software is immaterial; it cannot be easily represented physically.

- Software can be duplicated for zero cost; it must be treated differently, because products typically have some cost to duplicate. There is a lot of work being done to enforce duplication costs, because software is often duplicated in violation of its license agreement and of copyright laws (called software piracy).

- Software has a high potential for errors. Due to the complexity of software and the environment it is run in, there is a very high potential for unforeseen errors and bugs in the application. Much work must be put into software to reduce the number of bugs, and it is very hard to create software without bugs.

- Software is subject to "decay." Due to the continuing advances in hardware and the need to maintain software, it will eventually become impossible to use.

As figure 3.2 shows, software possesses a *product life cycle* similar to any other products. As a result, decisions made in each of the individual phases have a strong influence on the expense, quality, and maintenance related to the life expectancy of the software.

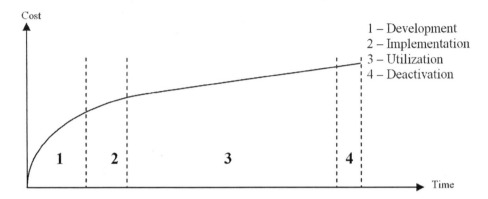

Fig. 3.2: Life cycle of a CAFM software

Using the example of CAFM software, a life cycle can be easily represented. *Phase 1, "Development of the Software,"* accounts for a very high expenditure due to the cost of the software. Thus it is necessary to have a strong modularity as well as a good basis for functionality and ease of use. The technical abilities of the software to be integrated into the IT environment of the enterprise are realized, and customization is assessed and completed.

In *Phase 2, "Implementation and Introduction of the Software,"* adjustments are made by tweaking parameters, user interface customization, or working through the software's API. Some customization requirements may also arise at this point, based on the customers' needs that would require programming to be provided by the software vendor. If necessary the integration must be made possible in the enterprise and/or the binding of external business partners over interfaces.

Phase 3, "Use of the Software," can range from a few years to several decades. Apart from the initial costs of the software, the expenditures of software maintenance and the permanent data administration are relevant for the duration of the amortization. Also, a good adaptability of the software is necessary to keep pace with the changes of the organization without having to procure new software.

Phase 4, "Deactivation of the Software," can come about as a result of the "decay" we described earlier in this chapter when the ease of use is no longer there or by way of technical deficiencies (errors, integration issues). To deactivate software, a complete data transfer to a new system is desirable, since the data represents the most important monetary investment in the old software. For this reason, it is important to choose software that is built on standard data formats (see chapter 10).

3.5.2 INFLUENCE OF THE SOFTWARE ARCHITECTURE

As already briefly discussed, the design of software specifies not only its abilities but also its limitations. These abilities not only include the specific functions embedded in the software but also the possibilities of its integration into the existing IT of an enterprise. Also, if necessary, some large requirements can be programmed separately. These types of abilities and limitations of a selected software combined with any customization requirements begin to outline the parameters that will set the stage for the overall expenditure on the CAFM solution. Please keep in mind that heavy customization is not always a onetime cost, as it most likely will need to be updated as the software itself is updated with new versions.

When considering the architecture of a solution, there are distinct options to consider:

- Hardware-based solution,

- Standalone solution

- Client/server solution

- Web-based and/or web-enabled applications

Hardware-based solutions are software solutions that are implemented exclusively on one type of hardware to create a single-purpose computer. Usually these applications run under special operating systems and depend strongly on the hardware/software manufacturer. These types of solutions are not typically used in FM.

Standalone solutions are single place systems, which do not rely on network connections for their ability to work. However, the value of data used within the CAFM solution is limited to a single machine and/or a single user. Standalone solutions include smaller asset management products, which are typically used to support FM sub-functions but are neither shared nor able to share with the enterprise. Caution should be taken when placing the entire implementation value of the software on a single user, since staff turnover could lead the project to fail at any time.

Client-server applications designate software solutions where clients with a common need share components on a central server. This does not only refer to data storage but also to the fact that some of the processing power can also be offloaded onto the server from the client. This in effect creates a streamlined process whereby multiple client machines are not storing redundant and possibly dated information, and it preserves the hardware resources of the client machines. Most of today's CAFM applications were primarily developed as client/server solutions. What has become clear is that in the dynamic world of facility management, FMs are looking for even more from their CAFM solutions. Therefore client/server applications form the foundation for something larger.

Web-based and/or web-enabled applications extend this client/server foundation. Here the components of the software are distributed as objects over the World Wide Web according to the IT requirements of the individual enterprises. These objects no longer rely on special operating systems and thus can be used "platform-independently" and accessed by any web browser. This facilitates a much easier maintenance and expansion of the solution as the application is hosted on the server exclusively and changes that are made at a server level are immediately experienced at the client level. However, this also can increase demands on the network infrastructure, so care must be taken to ensure bandwidth availability. Most CAFM applications (client/server based) have become web-enabled to address the growing needs of FMs in this format. However, there have been some struggles to overcome the bandwidth bottlenecks in order to deliver the feature-rich experience that a client-server application can offer. As a result, there are few applications on the market that can claim to be web-based, in that they are not built on the foundation of a client-server application. Technologies such as AJAX (Asynchronous JavaScript and XML) and Web 2.0 seek to bridge the bandwidth gap along with much easier access to higher bandwidth.

Many CAFM users are bearing witness to a paradigm shift whereby the success of their organizations is no longer marked by the development and optimization of rigid processes, but rather by their ability to be flexible to the changing business as dictated by market conditions. As a result, software has a crucial role to play in facilitating this level of flexibility. It has to be adaptable—able to change to illustrate new business processes in even shorter cycles. And upon changes of the firm's structure, the application landscape must be flexibly transformed.

Service Oriented Architecture (SOA) presents the ability to quickly develop and integrate solutions around business processes using interoperable services. If applied, SOA would dissolve the dilemma of how organizations could be adapted as needed in today's marketplace (see figure 3.3, adopted from NN 2002).

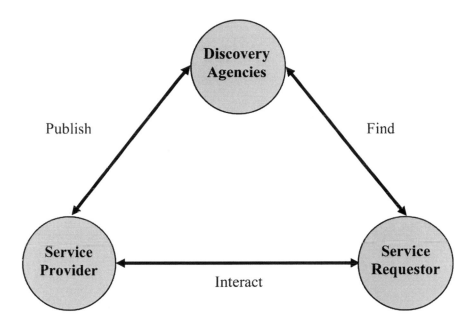

Fig. 3.3: Service Oriented Architecture (SOA)

The term SOA (NN 2002) is not new, as it was defined in 1997, but only now is its practical relevance being realized.

Usually CAFM software is part of an IT landscape characterized by a multiplicity of heterogeneous systems. Frequently ERP software forms the dominant enterprise application system; consequently specific implementations of SOA for ERP systems directly impact the integration of CAFM systems. SAP is a prime example of a technical realization of SOA using ESA (Enterprise Services Architecture).

3.5.3 WEB SERVICES AS A PLATFORM FOR THE REALIZATION OF DISTRIBUTED OBJECTS

Just referring to web services generally may not do justice to the impact they are having and will have on the CAFM market. As a result, this section will deal with the underlying concepts in greater detail. The idea of *service-oriented software architectures* is to build whole functionalities in a distributed manner—thus not only data from different software products but also functions. These can range from the care to administration to analysis of datasets to custom-made processes.

The automobile industry has been a model for this procedure for some time. The large manufacturers are limited essentially to the design and assembly of vehicles. They in turn rely on suppliers who not only produce headlamps for a specific automobile manufacturer, for example, but also supply many of their competitors. If we compare the automobile industry in this regard with the management of facilities, then we can see that by dissecting primary and secondary facilities processes, we establish the goals of FM automation software (as it compares to the automotive assembly line). Digging deeper, we will find that only ideally will the facility manager find the optimal solution for everything in the product of a single manufacturer. Usually the system choice is a more or less painful compromise for the individuals involved in the processes to be supported. This suggests a CAFM system without the equivalent of headlamps or, at the very least, with headlamps that do not illuminate the road properly.

However, if one were able to choose the "Best of Breed'" functionalities from a variety of products, solutions could be implemented in combination with functionalities of other systems in place of the compromise practiced at present. In the automobile industry, this is the case, since parts are sourced, combined, and deleted from packages to suit not only the overall design intent of the vehicle but also the demands of the consumer. In contrast is the world of CAFM: If one wants to use the move management tool of a specific manufacturer, one cannot just deploy it inside an existing work order system, even if it offers more suitable functionality, but especially if no move management feature is available inside the existing software.

If one wanted to transfer the example of the automobile industry into the software industry, consider that the assembler of automobiles does not need to understand the complexities of an injection pump in order to install and mount it. In the same way, software functions are installed without having the experts to the development of both the primary application and third-party feature on hand. Furthermore, once installed, the functionalities, while integrated for each component, remain divided when it comes to the servicing of each.

Unfortunately most program products, despite using client/server architecture, are still viewed as monoliths, and the detailed inner workings of the software are only well known to its developers. We need each of these components to be transformed into services using an agreed upon language for interoperability. The market demand will drive this phase shift rather than the past model, where the proprietary nature of manufacturers dictated the market. With technologies such as DCOM (a substantial cornerstone of the Windows operating system for the integration of its applications) and CORBA (the integration of applications in non-Windows environments), these agreements are set out in the form of an *interface description language*. Unfortunately these concepts are so complex and hardly standardized that their understanding has barely developed beyond the programming community, and therefore only a small market for individual components (report generators, graphic viewers, etc.) has developed.

Nevertheless, many vendors are exposing interfaces to their software called APIs (Application Programming Interfaces), which are primarily used by third-party software houses. These are an indispensable part of the next step to the supply of *mountable components* for the trained final user or the supporting IT department. Keys for this step are the technologies of the Internet, which—after they revolutionized communication between humans and computers through HTML—made communication possible between computers by XML. The Google search engine is an excellent example, because we can use it not only by its address at www. google.com but also on our own web page. These individually mountable components are called *web services*.

Web services are based on the three components of a service-oriented software architecture (see figure 3.3):

- *Messages*: using and communication with services via SOAP

- *Services*: the actual software component, described by its WSDL (described in figure 3.3 as "service")

- *Processes*: publishing and finding suitable services by UDDL and fitting the services into business processes

SOAP means *Simple Object Access Protocol*, or in its more recent meaning, *Service Oriented Architecture Protocol*. SOAP is the technical basis for the triumphant advance of web services. Just as a web browser communicates via HTML with the net, XML is the basis on which programs are able to communicate directly across the network. This communication is not visible to the user. The conversion of the transportable "bits and bytes" of HTML to the graphical display of the web browser follows similar principles as the conversion of XML-based SOAP messages. HTTP plays a crucial role for both HTML and SOAP as a transportation method. However, SOAP does not depend on HTTP for transport since it can use different transports such as SMTP (used for email traffic) or TCP/IP transports.

This flexibility is actually reached by the "packaging" of the data to be transported. This packaging includes an envelope specified as a header with the necessary information to transport and a body that includes all of the data. The *headers* are the key to the success of a message. This arbitrary combination of the headers allows new functionalities to be developed, such as transaction control or improvements to transport security. While the header may specify that the message be forwarded and in so doing modify the header, the message content—the body—remains untouched. Thus web service developers can focus their concentration independently on how a message arrives and on the clarity and presentation of their service. With messages sent as clear text in XML and the transport taken care of using HTTP, for example, the programming model used for the implementation of a web service becomes just as insignificant as the operating system the service runs on.

WSDL (Web Service Description Language) provides the model for describing web services. Here one describes which message a service can receive and which it dispatched.

The WSDL contains concrete definitions for *binding* the message to concrete data format specifications such as SOAP, the transport protocols, and the addresses of the web services (Uniform Resources Identifier—URI).

The abstract part of the WSDL is comparable with the interface and/or Object Description Language from the COM/DCOM and/or CORBA model; the concrete part opens the flexibility and platform independence of the Internet to the web services.

UDDL (Universal Description and Discovery Language) finds suitable web services in the network. By means of UDDL, a registry of the web services described with WSDL is administered. This registry consists of the following:

- White Pages, with the base data for the enterprise

- Yellow Pages for the classification of the business fields of the enterprises

- Green Pages for the description of the IT platforms, of the purchase, and of the terms of delivery of the offered web services

A web service is announced with its WSDL, and the information for the three types of pages (Yellow, White, and Green) at a UDDL registry and can be found there by prospective clients/users. By "downloading" the WSDL, a client can then use the web service, whereby a *contract* can come according to the terms of delivery and of purchase of the Green Pages. Apart from the publication of a web service in public registries, with which the owner decides on the admission of new services, a web service can be seized by engines in a way similar to how Google can be used over the Internet. Based on these two principles, there is also the opportunity to combine search results from various registries with results from index searches.

Apart from the activities for distributing web services over the Internet, efforts are being made toward the *standardization of various application fields* so web services can be developed and used more simply to solve specialized tasks. Such standards already exist within the following industries:

- Architecture and Construction industry (ADML—Architecture Description Markup Language, based on architecture specification language ACME)

- Real Estate Management (RETML—Real Estate Transaction Markup Language)

- Bookkeeping (smbXML—small and medium sized business), finances (XBRL—eXtended Business Reporting Language, FIXED—Financial Information eXchange, IFX—Interactive Financial eXchange)

- Astronomy, chemistry, mathematics, physics

- News, law, insurance, administration, health

The Enterprise Services Architecture (ESA) has been developed by SAP, which supplies framework called NetWeaver to arrange customized business processes from standard services in the form of a web service. Each new release of the NetWeaver Framework is offered with additional functionality, but NetWeaver must be used to connect business processes through SAP. With these, as well as the developments of other manufacturers, a clear direction has been formed to package existing products with so-called adapters to make their services available for incorporation into web services.

Components are already offered today based on web services for, among other things, commercial *real estate management*; these have already been merged as a web service into CAFM systems. However, for move anagement, mentioned above, there are still no well-known web services. We can expect that such components will be developed by specialized manufacturers as demand rises. Not only is the CAFM software developer community affected by these changes, but CAFM strategists are also embroiled in these new challenges. In the future, it will no longer be enough to know the strengths and weaknesses of different systems to select and to introduce a solution that best aligns with customer needs. Rather, it will become necessary to know the CAFM-relevant web services present in the marketplace as well as the technical specifications for their use.

3.6 OPEN-SOURCE SOFTWARE IN FACILITY MANAGEMENT

3.6.1 OPEN SOURCE AS AN IDEA

Open source is primarily a comprehensive term for "free software." This idea is characterized by the following philosophies:

- The software should be rightfully usable without royalties.

- The software is based on a source code, which is freely available to everyone.

- The advancements are permitted and understood as open source.

- A transformation with the intention of making the code more difficult to understand is not permitted.

- Copies may be provided and passed on at will.

Free software in the sense of it being "free of charge" is not the main intention for the development of open source software. The freedom in this context is freedom of spirit and science. However, free availability under the various open-source licenses promotes the emergence and fast spread of developer communities. In this case, the frequently stated prejudice "You get what you pay for" is not always correct. Consider that in a software market where there is bad commercial software, it is likely that good applications can be based on open source.

The list of the successful projects within the worldwide open-source community is lengthy and growing. Many of them are well known and compete directly with their commerce-driven competitors. An example of this is the web server software Apache, which has a market share of almost 50 percent. The product range spans from high-performance server systems to free content-management systems to small but helpful business tools. Below is a list of well-known open-source software:

- GNU, FreeBSD, and Linux

- DNS, bind, and Sendmail

- Apache, Tomcat, and Samba

- PHP, Perl, Python, and Tcl/Tk

- The enterprise content management system Typo3

3.6.2 OPEN SOURCE AND CAFM

Although there are many successful open-source software projects founded on the collective knowhow of a worldwide software developer community, and distributed and motivated by it, CAFM software stands in strict contrast to other applications that have harnessed the power of open source. The positive experiences and profitable results of open-source projects have not yet hit the CAFM market. However, open source quite possibly represents an alternative in the CAFM market.

It is not surprising to note that open-source projects are particularly advanced in the academic field. This is also true within the CAFM market.

3.6.3 AN OPEN-SOURCE CAFM PROJECT

With the project Open.FMgate (Keller and Kruse 2005), a foundation was laid for an open-source CAFM software. Under this project, graduates of the University of Applied Sciences (FHTW) Berlin coordinated a project for the development of a free, web-based CAFM tool and leveraged the role of open-source software developers to drive future development.

The project's scope was to offer a cutting-edge alternative to conventional CAFM. An interested and international development community of distributed knowhow and innovative resources was bundled, with open-source ideals always the center of attention. For the development, the following premises were realized:

- All results are subject to the GPL (General Public License).

- The CAFM software is free of charge and freely usable.

- The source code is open to developers and users alike.

The server platform, Apache Web Server, was chosen in an effort to be consistent with the idea of open source. Likewise, MySQL was chosen as the primary data management solution, but with interfaces to other database systems. The languages for the project core development were the following:

- PHP + SQL

- Javascript

- XML and XHTML

Also, the binding of commercial components, or the integration of non-free software components over defined interfaces to the open-source CAFM software, was not restricted.

The principal purpose of the project is to realize, with the help of the current and typical web and Internet technologies, a complete, expandable application for typical FM uses. The substantial advantages and possibilities of a browser-based solution can be summarized as follows:

- Lowering of transaction costs

- Simpler product differentiation

- Accelerated knowledge dissemination

- Provision of information by credential-driven rights

- Customized, process-driven, and multilingual interface

- Short training period using familiar software (web browser)

- No need for a separate client installation

- High security and encryption standards (HTTPS and SSL)

The software's modular structure ensures the solution meets the demands of users and is inherently flexible, so that it can be used to serve a broad range of CAFM needs. The software offers interfaces and methods that invite a development community to extend the functionality of the software in all directions. A substantial characteristic of the developing software system is its ability to scale itself freely to adapt to changing FM requirements.

The software is based on an advanced, *four-tier architecture* (see figure 3.4). The draft of the CAFM software system is based on a classic MVC (Model View Controller) architecture.

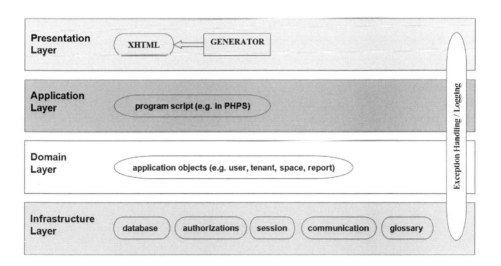

Fig. 3.4: Four-tier architecture of open-source CAFM software

A structural separation between the data and application is also represented in the behavior control of the software by using an event-oriented program logic.

The user interface of the CAFM software is completely web-based. Therefore, to use the system, a generic web browser is needed that can employ current web techniques as well as client-side scripting capabilities such as JavaScript controls. For the visualization of the XHTML-based interface of the CAFM application, a *frameset* is used. Thus the interface of the web application can be subdivided into separate parts that can be interacted with independently.

To ensure maximum openness for other software developers or system requirements that will surely emerge, the entire software system is designed to be modular (Keller, Kruse, and May et al. 2005). It offers the possibility of integrating new functional components for which there is currently no need or possible solution.

These modules are referred to as nuggets by the software developer and are at their disposal for the development of and the advancement of the system. A *nugget* is a firmly defined component of the system that can be accessed using the proper interfaces and methods. For the basic system, there are nuggets for database management, user interface, user and session management, XML tools, glossaries, and monitoring functions, among other things.

Like many software types, if open source becomes more common in CAFM, it could push the boundaries of CAFM development beyond the traditional, packaged product development. At the very least, it will guide traditional CAFM vendors toward a level of interoperability in their APIs.

3.7 SUMMARY

In this chapter we explained the fundamental importance of IT as it relates to the practical work of facility managers. Even though FMs are usually not IT experts, they do need a basic understanding of both IT concepts and technologies. This is one of the key factors in the success of a CAFM project. The knowledge required includes computer networks, databases, and modern software architectures. Additionally, the challenges and opportunities resulting from the development of open-source CAFM software were discussed.

4

MOBILE TECHNOLOGIES AND IT INTERFACES

Marco Jedlitzke, Joachim Hohmann, Michael Marchionini, Michael May, Marko Opić, Geoff Williams

4.1 MOBILE TECHNOLOGIES

The increasing employment of mobile IT technologies in facility management is strongly influenced by, among other things, the constantly rising number of mobile devices such as PDAs (Personal Digital Assistants). In small and large companies, this technology is becoming standard equipment of FM personnel. For example, a PDA can be used by maintenance personnel to perform their work when out in the field.

In principle, the following goals are pursued with the employment of these devices:

- To be able to see on site all up-to-date data for the facility

- To be able to correct recognizable errors or gaps in the documentation by making changes directly to the dataset

- To be able to document and close real-time scheduled and unscheduled work orders (with location and time stamps)

Further typical applications aside from the maintenance of a building include the administration of inventory and taking readings relating to energy consumption for energy management.

4.1.1 IDENTIFICATION BY MEANS OF BAR CODE OR RFID

Both bar codes and *Radio Frequency Identification (RFID)* technology serve predominantly the clear identification of objects. In FM, essentially the application is for recording inventory items and equipment with their location inside the building (among other things, doors, exhaust, fire extinguisher, and electrical meter).

The strengths of bar codes are as follows:

- An extensive selection of labels (broad vendor market)

- Easy and simple attachment and removal

- Possibility of reading without scanners by a combination with parallel imprinting of ID numbers

In RFID, a *transponder* is a microchip with an integrated memory and an antenna, which receives the electromagnetic waves as energy from a reader and, strengthened by this energy, transmits a response. The term *transponder* comes from a combination of the terms *transmitter* and *responder*.

The strengths of transponders are as follows:

- Large variety of types based on the technical parameters of their use

- Sturdy against wear and tear

- Fraud-proof and cannot be duplicated

The variety of ways transponders are used is affected by the variety of the technical parameters, which also determine the technology of the reader.

Transponders can be differentiated with respect to the following technical parameters:

- *Active/passive*
  Passive transponders do not possess their own energy source but instead "get themselves" the necessary energy from the reader. Therefore, they cannot send data without a reader present. The reader distance to transponder is usually small.
  Active transponders possess an integrated battery. Therefore, they send constant data signals. The reader distance to transponder can exceed one hundred meters. Because of the battery, transponders are more expensive and have a maximum life span of five to ten years.

- *Method of storing data*
  - Read-only transponders are writable only once and usually store only bits of data, such as serial number and are sometimes already written with an ID value directly by their manufacturer.
  - Read/write transponders can be written to several times, and the memory is usually larger (up to 2 MBit).

- *Frequencies for the data and/or energy transmission,* including but not limited to
  - *125 kHz for access control, marking of equipment, etc*
  - 13.58 MHz for access control and logistics (post office, trade, etc.)
  - 849/915 MHz for production (e.g., car).

With respect to the working frequencies, there are no international standards for ranges, penetration rate, and transmission rate. Therefore national adjustments according to local regulations must be considered, which concern both the distribution of the frequencies as well as the permitted maximum transmitting power.

4.1.2 MOBILE DEVICES
Mobile terminals can be divided according to their technical and ergonomic characteristics into different categories (See table 4.1).

Table 4.1: Categorization of relevant mobile devices in facility management

Category	Examples
Mobile PC	• Notebook/laptop • Sub-notebook • Tablet PC • Netbook
Handheld	• Pocket PC/PDA • Mobile telephone • Smartphone/communicator
Chip cards/smart cards	• SIM card (Subscriber Identity of Module) • RFID smart card (radio frequency identification)
Embedded device	• Onboard computers • Control systems
Wearables	• Wearable scanner • Head Mounted Display (HMD)

Mobile PCs possess similar technical components and software equipment as usual standalone PCs. However, they are usually designed with specific energy-saving features (special processors, chipset, and display) and with mobile communication functions (WLAN, Bluetooth, and Infrared). The tablet PC possesses a touch-sensitive display capable of recognizing handwriting by means of Optical Character Recognition (OCR) software.

Handhelds, and in particular PDAs and smartphones, are substantially smaller in size than mobile PCs and are less powerful. They use an operating system (Windows Mobile, Palm OS, Symbian OS) tailored to mobile communication (portable radio and/or local networking) and lower requirements. The functional combination of mobile telephone and PDA equipment is called a smartphone. It must be noted that most PDAs also have solid-state design and therefore do not require the lengthy boot time of mobile PCs.

Chip cards (and/or smart cards) can only be regarded as mobile devices when used in connection with a reader. They possess their own processor, which increases data security and flexibility of use. Data exchange can take place using direct contact (SIM) or contactless (RFID).

Embedded devices are computer systems integrated in technical systems, which are used for the measurement, diagnosis, and/or controlling of technical parameters via sensors and actuators.

Wearables are small, hands-free computers that are worn on the body or integrated into clothes and are operable by voice commands. Wearable computers are used in working environments where both hands are required (such as in a repair scenario) or if protective clothes make the conventional operation of computers impossible.

In FM, the selection and configuration of the necessary mobile hardware is determined by the bar-code and/or RFID technologies in use. Typically handhelds are used as terminals. The market offerings are large. Common PC capability characteristics such as processor, memory, display, operating system, and expandability and/or interfaces are crucial to the decision on a model. When choosing a manufacturer and type of device in addition to the availability of appropriate readers (scanners) for bar code and/or transponder (consider frequency), attention must be paid to a sufficient power supply. The best equipment does not pay off if, for example, it is to be used for a large inventory job and it stops operating after just two hours due to a lack of sufficient power.

Traditionally processes of energy management, such as regular readings of the electrical meters and tracking current consumption, are similar to inventory management and usually are based on bar-code technology. The respective objects are thus marked with a bar-code label. A simple PocketPC with an integrated bar-code scanner is usually considered to be a sufficient IT requirement. It is assumed that the respective data is part of a central CAFM database, and it is exchanged in a controlled form.

The requirements of mobile technology become more challenging in the context of a maintenance management solution. Special requirements for this type of use can include the following:

- Extensive volume of data (e.g., plant documentation and maintenance activities), which must be stored and processed on a PDA. This increases the demands on the processor, memory, operating system, and interfaces.

- The more complex the data and processing programs on the PDA are, the more intense are the requirements for the size and resolution of the display.

- With permanent employment in maintenance management, a rugged design is necessary. This includes the ability to resist impact, to function in a dirty environment, to withstand high/low temperatures, and to resist water as site conditions require.

4.1.3 MOBILE TECHNOLOGIES AS A COMPONENT OF A CAFM SOLUTION

With all new technologies, one must very carefully weigh and/or decide whether mobile technologies can generate a benefit and, if so, which technologies can support certain processes best. Saving money and improving quality are the major criteria. When weighing out components against their cost, there is usually a cost saving through improved efficiency and quality improvement (usually more transparent in a manufacturing facility application). If we consider that downtime is the worst-case scenario in a manufacturing facility, then the quality improvement of a more expensive component may be easily justified. Quality improvement may result in a greater ability to control the state of the equipment, improved security (e.g., fire protection), and higher availability of the facilities.

RFID is far more than substitution of the existing bar-code technology. RFID permits new business models and perhaps causes changes in existing processes. When implementing this type of solution, caution must be taken to prevent isolated solutions.

On this basis, a practical example of RFID use for maintenance management is outlined as a process cycle (see figure 4.1). The following emphasis characterizes the process cycle:

- Central CAFM system with database for the documentation of the technical equipment (including maintenance specifications), companies (as bidders and contractors), and contracts

- Labeling of the facilities (rooms, doors, technical equipment with components, etc.) with passive transponders, which contain a unique ID value, which is assigned to the respective component in the database

- Delivery of the maintenance activities as a job (trade/period) in file type to the maintenance company (e.g., transfer of the data to a PDA, smartphone)

- Execution of maintenance according to the defaults, and identification at the transponder locally with date and time, confirmation of the completion, note of deviations

- Close the loop by transmitting data back to the central database, for accounting, reconciliation, and actualization of the central documentation according to the noted references

- Possibility of generating a job for quality control according to a fixed scheme or by random selection methods. The respective transponders are then scanned onsite, and the state is confirmed or deviations are reported.

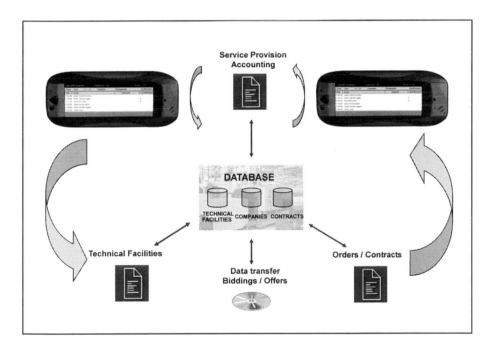

Fig. 4.1: Closed CAFM-based maintenance management cycle using RFID technologies

4.2 INTERFACES

4.2.1 NECESSITY FOR IT INTEGRATION

Software systems are connected and data is distributed and retained over interfaces. Interfaces are not only used for data exchange between the software systems of interest, but they also can serve in the automation of FM processes (see section 11.6.1 and NN 2007a). These FM business processes must be illustrated as a CAFM workflow. Here all process steps are analyzed in enough detail to facilitate the automated flow control possible between the different systems. These software systems must permit external software to further process the transferred data. An example of this would be a sales calculation for an external order and a status change after an external release.

The interfaces serve as a kind of communication layer, which is responsible for the transmission of the source data between the individual software systems. Once a certain complexity and flexibility is reached, these interfaces can be referred to as *middleware* or EAI (Enterprise Application Integration) *solutions*.

Fully automated business processes in most cases will not be possible (or desired). The degree of process integration depends on what extent transactions of FM and business decisions can be illustrated in the software. Progressive networking of enterprises over the Internet leads inevitably to the fact that software is spreading across enterprises, as in a WAN. This intensifies the interface to be highly flexible with respect to the software systems with which it can be used.

4.2.2 CLASSIFICATION OF INTERFACES

Interfaces can be classified according to many different criteria. GEFMA Guideline 410 (NN 2007a) assists in classifying interfaces. The most important classification of interfaces takes place under the temporal viewpoint and differentiates them as off-line and online.

With *off-line interfaces* (also called batch interfaces), data is exchanged at fixed times. The transmission is made by a file format specified beforehand. The source system writes the data at a certain time into a file, which is read in by the receiving system at another time.

With *online interfaces*, the data is written directly into the database of the receiving system. Advantages include a data supply without time delay and the avoidance of data redundancy or synchronization issues. Control of time-critical operational sequences between the systems is realized more easily.

Another important criterion for the classification of interfaces is the *direction* of data exchange. The two distinctions are unidirectional and bidirectional.

With *unidirectional interfaces,* one of the software packages is specified as "dominant" and only in it is the appropriate data updated. The data communication then takes place exclusively with the receiving system.

With *bidirectional interfaces,* data exchange takes place in an arbitrary direction. Here a differentiation can be made between synchronous and asynchronous modes of operation.

A further classification can take place according to the *degree* of the IT-integration (see figure 4.2).

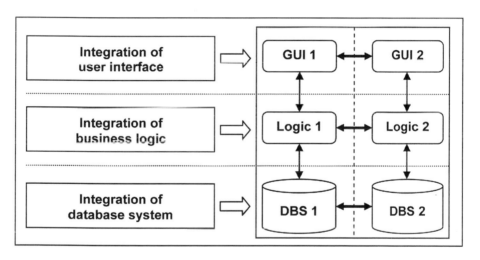

Fig. 4.2: IT integration (according to GEFMA 410)

During *integration at the database level*, direct data exchange is reached by online interfaces. The interface must be adapted on the DBMS and the data structure to exclude unwanted reactions to the receiving system. In particular, when there are changes to the database design of the receiving database, there are also changes that need to be made to the interface.

Integration at the logic level is necessary if a direct database access is not desired (e.g., if data integrity with the receiving database must be guaranteed). Over the interface, the data that can be exchanged is handed over to4.2.3 Organization of Data Exchange the receiving system. The receiving database then examines with its own tools whether manipulations of the data are permissible and what further actions need to be implemented (e.g., error messages and flow control). Therefore, a change in the database design of the receiving system has generally no effects on the assigned interface. If these datasets are produced automatically and/or called up in specified intervals (batch operating), they are commonly referred to as batch interfaces. These are available with most CAFM systems.

During the *integration of the user interface*, by using a uniform appearance, there is effectively no visual distinction that a user can make between different software products. This requires a high integration level from the interfaces involved, since, apart from data retention, all software functionalities must be coordinated with one another.

4.2.3 ORGANIZATION OF DATA EXCHANGE

Since CAFM systems are usually based on existing data and structures, the data to be considered in the CAFM system usually exist in different databases and file formats (alphanumerically and graphically). For data to be used productively later, it must be transferred in a variety of standardized formats and in varying qualities (e.g., CAD). Then the data must be imported into the CAFM software only once (replacing the old system) or multiple times over interfaces in a data exchange cycle.

Therefore the following questions must be answered first in order to clarify the extent of data exchange (NN 2007a):

- Which tasks in the enterprise are to be supported by holistic CAFM systems?

- Which business processes are included and/or affected thereby?

- Which IT systems (in addition to CAFM) are to be used for this (e.g., CMMS—Computerized Maintenance Management System, BMS—Building Management Systems, ERP—Enterprise Resource Planning, etc.)?

- Which datasets are administered for this in the individual systems?

- Which datasets are to be exchanged between which systems?

To achieve a constant FM software solution with low data redundancy, all existing software systems must be examined to see which form of data exchange will be meaningful and/or if it is even possible. Qualitative organizational factors must be considered apart from the pure technical requirements (e.g., incorporation of legacy systems and guarantee of data consistency). Improving customer satisfaction and internal FM organization or avoidance of manual errors are excellent examples.

In contrast to the above are questions concerning legal and operational considerations (data security) as well as efficiency (frequency of data exchange, production expenditure).

Software houses frequently make their interface specifications available, which gives third-party manufactured products access to the source data (through APIs—Application Programming Interface). In building automation, however, many manufacturer and product-dependent specifications exist. A standardization attempt (named BACnet) has been undertaken by ASHRAE so that data can be exchanged independently between different systems. Another example is OPC (OLE for process control) (Mahnke et al. 2009).

Interfaces should be reviewed regularly through a process of critical evaluation. This allows defaults in the course of the project or enterprise to change and/or be revised.

The following questions should be considered both in the development of an interface solution and during the operation of the interface:

- Is the interface solution able to realize an alignment of all tasks required?

- Are the interfaces efficient and effective?

- Does the documentation agree with actual functionality?

- Are the requirements of flexibility and user-friendliness within the interface balanced so that the relevant changes of the operational sequences can be integrated easily?

■ Has the interface undergone sufficient testing with sample data before a change is implemented?

4.3 IT OPERATING CONCEPTS

While CAFM is primarily a database application, there is also a connection to technical and organizational operating concepts. Formal implementation depends substantially on the kind of CAFM modules, the number of users, and the geographical distribution of users accessing the solution. Many CAFM applications still use a client/server configuration over a LAN (or also WLAN) with two to five CAFM workplaces for FM specialists geographically separated with rather low requirements. This requires a substantially lower operating expenditure for one user than for several thousands of users over an enterprise portal. The following deals with the operating concepts that are both technical and organizational. These are separated according to rising IT complexity.

4.3.1 TECHNICAL OPERATING CONCEPTS

Single-user solution. This standalone solution follows the same rules as other professional PC solutions in an enterprise (among other things, virus protection and data protection).

Multiuser solution. A CAFM software as a multiuser solution (see figure 4.3) nearly always consists of a client/server configuration with a LAN (Local Area Network), a WLAN (Wireless LAN), or a combination of the two. Some CAFM systems also permit different operating systems on servers and clients. Also, several servers are possible within one CAFM system (e.g., database and application servers) and even within a distribution of the database (clusters, etc.).

With a multistation CAFM system, a system administrator should be used to assign rights of access, define data protection rules, upgrade and patch the software, oversee the use of the system, and make small system modifications. For a small to midsized organization this system administrator can also be a trained user in the FM department.

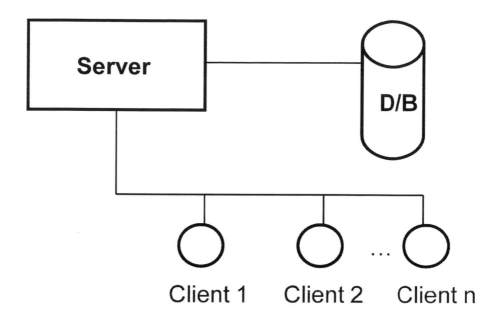

Fig. 4.3: Multiuser system

Internet/intranet portal solution. If a large number of users are to access the CAFM software, a recommended configuration consists of a web server and browser-based clients (see figure 4.4). The most important advantages of this solution are simple access (including portable clients such as PDAs, laptops, mobile telephones), flexibility, and low operating costs (no additional software installations, or plug-ins are necessary for the clients). If a web infrastructure is present already, the CAFM solution can be technically managed and maintained by the web master. The same operating conditions apply as in other Internet, intranet, or portal solutions (firewall, valid access authorization, etc.).

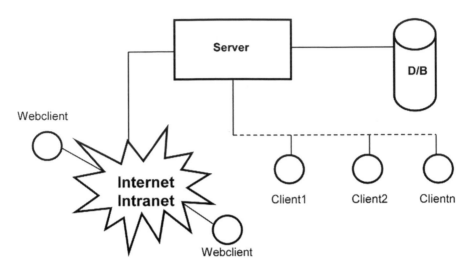

Fig. 4.4: Internet-based system

Modern CAFM software, which is used in a business-critical manner, represents a combination of both the multiuser and the portal solution concepts.

4.3.2 ORGANIZATIONAL OPERATING CONCEPTS

If we refrain from discussing the single place solution, questions arise as with all technical operating concepts. As a rule, there are three groups of questions regarding organizational operating concepts, which are not immediately connected but in the end are connected through their answers:

- Will the solution be hosted in-house or by a third-party IT supplier (ASP—Application Service Provider, or SaaS—Software as a Service)?

- Will the enterprise solution be the technical responsibility of the FM or the IT department?

- Is it an integrated solution, that is, integrated with other application systems such as ERP systems, building automation, and telephone system?

Hosting in-house vs. third party hosting. Most CAFM systems are operated by the organizations that use them. This requires the same organizational conditions as with other business-critical applications. Thereby the maintenance and availability of the data is of critical importance to CAFM. This again shows the advantage of process-oriented CAFM solutions, with which the datasets are updated as part of the operating concept. While CAFM including data maintenance (see chapter 10) is well suited to being provided by a third party (ASP/SaaS), this comfortable service is not yet widely offered and accepted. Especially in medium-size enterprises, this concept could be an attractive alternative.

Operated by FM department or IT department? In many larger organizations, the question frequently leads to turf wars, because the advantages of one alternative over the other are not easily proven. Also, the expenditure and probability of success of a CAFM solution is not clearly evident if one department takes control over the other. The final decision depends on corporate politics and the amount of power IT has over FM. In principle, it can be assumed that when a CAFM solution is tightly integrated with the existing IT landscape of the enterprise, the preferred steward would be the IT department. This is a result of the inherent knowledge of IT standards for the enterprise and how they relate directly to the CAFM solution. This requires the compatibility of the CAFM software with the IT standards established in the organization.

Integration into the existing IT environment. With large CAFM implementations, the integration of software into an existing IT environment (including building automation) is the most critical aspect of IT operation. Attention must be paid in particular to the minimization of interfaces and the guarantee of the overall viability of deployment (applications are still ready for operation after patches and upgrades). As a rule, this only succeeds with the use of accepted standards. To ensure integration into the enterprise environment, a parallel test and production system is required. This is similar to implementations with most ERP systems. Despite the expense of implementing integrated web-based CAFM systems, this operating concept is recommended for delivering the highest added value for an FM organization.

4.4 SUMMARY

In this chapter we discussed the increasing employment of mobile IT technologies in facility management. The number of mobile devices, including PDAs and smartphones, is rising constantly. Interfaces between different hardware and software components from an IT infrastructure perspective is a major challenge for FMs in any CAFM project. This is especially true if CAFM software needs to be integrated with legacy systems and/or proprietary software.

Finally, operating concepts that are both technical and organizational were presented. They were separated according rising complexity.

5

IT SECURITY FOR FACILITY MANAGERS

Marco Jedlitzke, Joachim Hohmann, Michael Marchionini, Michael May, Marko Opić, Geoff Williams

5.1 SECURITY

There are two different types of IT application security:

- The software and/or the application internally
- The application externally, its databases and the network

With application internally, we have assumed that the program will be protected against bad transactions executed by users. The external protection must prevent unrestricted external access.

5.2 DATA AND SECURITY CONCEPTS IN CAFM

With the constant advancement of electronic data processing, ever higher requirements need to be satisfied to safeguard processing, procurement, distribution, etc.—and at the same time new expectations are produced. More and more business processes must be supported by IT. Since a CAFM system represents a large quantity of data, originally from independent datasets, stringent requirements for data security are required. Depending on the objective of the CAFM solution, the quantity of business-relevant data can be very high, and the need for security is compounded by its high value or sensitivity. Typical application areas (see chapter 7) requiring security include the following:

- Inventory documentation (CAD drawings, sketches of buildings)

- Contract management (subject-matters of the contract, achievements, costs)

- Key and lockset asset management (security plans, locking numbers)

- Controlling (business numbers, benchmarks)

- Human resources (personnel data, salaries)

5.3 GENERAL SECURITY ASPECTS

Ensuring the security of datasets means privacy, integrity, and availability. Threats to the security of data can be divided into the following superordinate groups of vulnerability (NN 2006b):

- *Force of nature:* Influences of environment and weather, personnel loss, construction measures, etc.

- *Organizational shortcomings:* Missing resources, missing support by the management, insufficient organizational regulations, incomplete knowledge of existing regulations, etc.

- *Human error:* False estimate, faulty operation, failure, etc.

- *Technical failure:* Disturbances and losses of technical devices and plants, defects in data storage devices, etc.

■   *Deliberate action:* Vandalism, breakdown, theft, data manipulation, unauthorized access, etc.

These are threats to any information system. The following section considers some of the security issues particularly relevant for CAFM.

5.4 AUTHORIZATION CONCEPTS

CAFM systems are usually operated within networks as a tool for the supply of different user groups with different information. Understanding authorization concepts helps to ensure that the data stored within the databases matches the network security rights. To simplify the user administration, both the users and the datasets should be grouped.

User groups: Organization of all users into groups and/or roles (role-based authentication) with a similar need for information. Criteria can be the role (house technician, controller, system administrators) or the position (consultant, department manager, management) of a user.

Datasets: Organization of all data into groups of similar kind, such as the summary of all costs, all data of a hierarchy level (building, floor, room), etc.

When allocating access authorization from user groups to datasets, the definition of the possible rights (such as creation, deletion, listing, read, etc.) are assigned. When adding a new user, he or she must be assigned to a user group so that the rights of the group will automatically be inherited.

While access management is a relatively simple task within CAFM software, it is more difficult in complex CAFM systems (see chapter 11 and NN 2007b), as a result of the increased number of different software components or systems involved. This situation includes the risk that a user could access data from another software package through a single interface.

5.5 DATA COMMUNICATION OUTSIDE OF A LAN

The protection of a building's internal cable system against unauthorized access usually is a standard network administration service and does not need to be discussed further (see section 11.6.1.3).

There are a number of different aspects to consider with recent developments concerning the networking of computers outside of closed cable systems.

5.5.1 INFORMATION DISSEMINATION VIA THE INTERNET

Almost all CAFM products offer the ability to spread arbitrary information across the Internet in an effort to be web-based or web-enabled. In addition, this requires only a single web server, which ascribes its own predefined script languages on the database that is accessed by a large number of clients (see section 4.3.1). On the client machine, only a web browser must be present. However, the simplicity of this solution poses a number of potential security hazards and risks.

To effectively ensure security via the Internet, one must first consider the transmission of data and then the security of the web browser itself. The transmission of web-based data is usually accomplished by Hypertext Transfer Protocol (HTTP), which offers no inherent security, and in each node of the transmission path eavesdropping on the data is possible. Only by using an SSL connection (HTTPS) can a relatively high measure of security be achieved. A further security gap is represented by the web browser. In particular, Internet Explorer is susceptible to security compromises because of its broad install base and because it is a popular goal of hackers searching for safety gaps. Having said this, no web browser is immune to security flaws.

During the transmission of data over HTTP, the transmissions often rely on a practice called caching or the provision of intermediary storage for data. The goal of caching is to be able to serve frequent inquiries directly from these cached buffers in an effort to shorten data paths and to accelerate the data communication. The disadvantage of this technology is the lack of control over which data becomes buffered. As a result of the lack of control over how the buffer is handled, there is a potential that the security of this buffer can be compromised by a hacker.

The web server itself also represents a point of attack in the IT environment of the CAFM solution. The server receives the web inquiries and processes them, connects to the database, places scripts and programs for the request, and requires its own user administration, independent of the CAFM solution.

5.5.2 SECURITY IN WIRELESS LOCAL AREA NETWORKS

Under the terms WLAN (Wireless LAN, see section 3.2.4) and Bluetooth, high-speed techniques for data communication by radio waves were established very rapidly. They facilitate a fast and relatively simple structure for the creation of local networks. Although corporate facilities may utilize WLAN as a method for extending the cable-based infrastructure without a hardwired upgrade, the real power is in extending access to mobile telephones, handheld computers, and notebooks, which are typically WLAN enabled.

Despite of the differences between WLAN and Bluetooth devices, the same security principles remain for both.

Wired networks do not have the additional vulnerability of radio waves. Interception of radio data is very simple compared with cable systems. In fact, if the data is unencrypted and the attacker is able to be within range of the wireless network, much of the data can be read as plain text. Beyond this, hackers can make use of directional antennas to breach networks from a further distance than the functional range of the communicating devices.

As with most new technologies, the first transmission and encoding protocols of the two radio standards IEEE 802.11 (WLAN) and Institution of Electrical Engineers offered to 802.15 (Bluetooth) still had relatively large security vulnerabilities. In the course of the development of these standards, to a large extent, many of these errors were corrected. The current standards are valid with proper configuration and can be applied safely in a corporate environment.

In particular, with Bluetooth, security gaps attributed with certain hardware have become commonplace. These security flaws are usually a result of a poor implementation of the 802.15 standard.

5.5.3 REMOTE ACCESS AND VIRTUAL PRIVATE NETWORKS (VPNS) VIA THE INTERNET

Internal networks have to be protected against unauthorized access from the outside as a result of the growing demand for specialized connections that allow users to be highly mobile. Frequently the request for unrestricted access by staff to the network from any place of work is a demand on the network administration. Here the user using a remote-access service gets access through a telephone connection or the Internet.

The common method for accessing a corporate network is called Virtual Private Networking (VPN), which develops a communication channel fortified by access supervision and encryption over the Internet. Tunneling over VPN or SSH (Secure Shell) creates a special encrypted link between the external client and the tunnel server. The external computer must authenticate itself first with the tunnel server and then separately with the network before data is permitted to transfer. With the help of this method the employee is able to work over the Internet from any ISP by logging in using a software-based VPN client, which is installed on the employee's computer. Once configured, the VPN can be used to access all corporate network resources, just as they would if connected directly to the wired network.

5.5.4 FIREWALL SECURITY BETWEEN NETWORKS

If two differently trustworthy domains border each other, they are usually configured for additional safety requirements and an access control methodology. Consider the safety mechanisms in place in an airport to screen and permit passengers to enter the "secure side" of the airport. Airports are employing a series of tried-and-true tactics to determine if a person is a threat. Similarly, a network firewall is often composed of a combination of hardware and software. This protects the network through a number of different methods, such as authentication, packet filtering, and data flow monitoring from unauthorized access from adjacent domains (in particular, the Internet).

A firewall protects internal files and databases against malicious attempts to read and/or manipulate the data directly and also the applications before they can be manipulated or destroyed (as in the case of a virus). The programs or databases are behind the firewall, which grants access only to authorized users. This *authorization* is validated in different ways:

- By passing a user name and a password

- Based on the IP address of the computer

- By publication of a security key (e.g., private/public key method)

All inquiries that are not authorized are rejected by the firewall. It is important to use only special firewall computers for this service. If it is not a firewall computer, its normal utilization for other services may result in the firewall system no longer being functional, simply due to a depletion of processing power.

5.6 MOBILE DEVICES

PDA (Personal Digital Assistant), PPC (Pocket Personal Computer), smartphones, handheld, or similar devices (see section 4.1.2) served traditionally as organizers for contacts and calendars, which at most could be synchronized with a PC. Today these devices are fully functioning computers that usually have several interfaces for communication with IT systems. Besides Bluetooth, many devices are also equipped with WLAN. Also, a clear trend is to integrate the handheld computer with the mobile telephone; together they are known as a smartphone. Due to their compact design, these small computers also find a use in FM in areas such as maintenance and quality assurance.

The safety aspects that must be considered with their use are, in principle, the same as with notebooks. However, since the operating systems on PDAs are different from those on PCs, it is difficult to apply the same security concepts. While the backup of data from PDAs is not a problem anymore, there are very few anti-virus software packages available. Furthermore, there have been cases of viruses written specifically for PDAs and smartphones, and it is not unreasonable to think that in the near future these devices—like their Windows Mobile counterparts—will be equipped with anti-virus and spyware protection. The short innovation cycles in the development of this computer segment require an attentive observation of the market.

5.7 DATA PROTECTION

As previously mentioned, data forms the central component of a CAFM system. Consequently a routine, complete, and reliable data backup is very important. CAFM can indeed pose new requirements on existing enterprise backup strategies. Depending on the implemented functions and data types as well as on their physical distribution, it may become necessary to shorten intervals between consecutive data backups. Frequently needed data may need to be backed up several times per day. This may also impact the infrastructure and capacity required to make these backups possible.

At the same time, protection of the configuration of the CAFM software should not be neglected. Since very few CAFM solutions are used "out of the box," but rather are customized to meet the users' requirements, this customization (see section 12.2.6) has a distinct value and must be protected. With some applications, these parameters are stored completely in separate configuration files, whose protection is rather simple. Otherwise it might be necessary to backup data storage devices completely.

5.8 SUMMARY

Internet crime and other risks to IT have increased considerably in the last decade. This applies not only to traditional computers but also to mobile devices such as PDAs. Hence, data security is also an issue in CAFM environments and consequently a concern of the facility manager. Some of the technologies to ensure security have been considered in this chapter.

The secure support of business processes—especially the transferring mission-critical information like contract data and human resources data—is one of the essential tasks of IT.

CAFM does not only consist of the correct selection of the appropriate software. Rather, all possibilities and necessities must be considered and merged into an enterprise-wide IT strategy. This results in questions that range from software support to technical issues and must be considered alongside corporate IT strategies. In particular, many projects underestimate the costs associated with customization, integration, and maintenance of both hardware and software.

To be able to measure the necessary changes realistically, all stakeholders—including FM, IT, and corporate management staff—need to clarify their needs and processes from the outset. This concerns the aspects of both internal communication between staff members and external communication with business partners and customers. Only then is it meaningful to begin software-based mapping (process flow charts, event-driven process chains, etc.) of business processes.

6

FACILITY MANAGEMENT AND CAFM

Michael Marchionini, Dan Rusch-Fischer, Joachim Hohmann, Bill Jordan, Michael May, Peter Prischl

6.1 WHAT IS (CA)FM?

Facility management (FM) is a term that has been around for a number of years. Various definitions have been applied to it, contributing to the ambiguity that still exists over this complex subject. The International Facility Management Association (IFMA) defines FM as follows:

> Facility management is a profession that encompasses multiple disciplines to ensure functionality of the built environment by integrating people, place, process and technology.

The German Facility Management Association (GEFMA) describes FM in its guidelines as follows:

> Facility Management (FM) is a management discipline, which, through result-oriented management of facilities and services, and within the framework of planned and controlled facility processes, satisfies the basic needs of people in their workplace, supports the business core processes, and contributes to an increased profitability.
>
> This discipline allows continuous analysis and optimization of cost-relevant processes, improves facilities, and delivers benefit to the company's internal services that are not part of its core business.

The complexity of the topic, the breadth of application, and the potential of this multibillion-dollar market all become immediately apparent from the definition above. Accomplishments within FM constitute a substantial portion of the gross national product of industrialized countries. Focusing on the building life cycle as a whole requires not only a broad range of knowhow from multiple disciplines, but also a highly efficient information management and related powerful IT tools for its monitoring and control.

One such tool is Computer Aided Facility Management (CAFM) software. CAFM focuses on the information management of an organization's real estate portfolio. A typical requirement of CAFM in an enterprise environment is to interface with existing IT systems for the purpose of sharing common information.

The introduction of a CAFM system in an enterprise must be well organized as a complex project from conception through implementation, and it should be consistently managed throughout the process (see chapter 13).

While frequently used interchangeably, there are fundamental differences between the terms CAFM software and CAFM system. A CAFM system is a complete solution for the support of FM, adapted to the specific needs of an enterprise. CAFM systems can consist of CAFM software, the combination of domain-specific software, and/or other standard software tools. If necessary, CAFM software needs to interoperate with commercial enterprise software and building automation systems via appropriate interfaces. Figure 6.1 clarifies the complexity of a CAFM system.

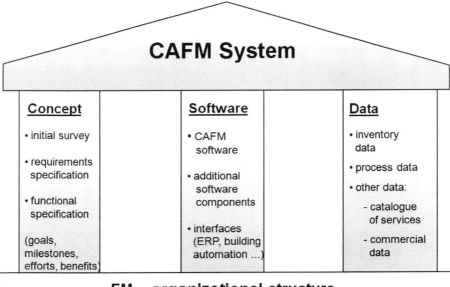

Fig. 6.1: A CAFM system needs a stable base

CAFM *software* programs support the specific processes of FM and the parties directly or indirectly associated with FM. As a minimum, the following *FM processes* and/or functionalities are considered to be core requirements of a CAFM software program:

- Space management

- Move management

- Occupancy management

- On-demand and preventative maintenance management

- Property and lease (portfolio) management

- Asset management

In addition, the following processes and/or functionalities are considered desirable aspects of a CAFM software program:

- Project management

- Contract management

- Room scheduling/hoteling

- Fleet management

- Key and access control management

- Cleaning services

- Energy systems and environmental management

- Document management

(These CAFM topics are discussed in more detail in chapter 11.)

A distinguishing and indisputable characteristic of CAFM software is its ability to seamlessly integrate and associate graphical drawing data with tabular database data. The visual representation of spatial data and its modification/alteration is a necessary feature of CAFM software. The ability to dynamically query simultaneously across both graphical and tabular information is essential.

In addition to multifunctional CAFM software, there are numerous software packages on the market that focus on a single aspect of FM. Examples of these are Computerized Maintenance Management Software (CMMS), cable management software, and event management software. Due to their focus on a single aspect of FM, many of these software programs do not meet the requirements of a comprehensive CAFM software solution.

Below are references to extensive *guidelines* GEFMA has prepared about CAFM. These guidelines are intended to provide support and direction for the potential user in design and implementation of individual, object, and portfolio specific CAFM systems:

- GEFMA 400   Computer-Aided Facility Management CAFM— Definitions, Capabilities, and Characteristics

- GEFMA 410   Interfaces for IT-Integration of CAFM Software

- GEFMA 420   Deployment of a CAFM System

- GEFMA 430   Database and Data Management in CAFM systems

- GEFMA 440   Procurement of CAFM Software

- GEFMA 444   Certification of CAFM Software

- GEFMA 450   Building Automation in FM

- GEFMA 460   Economic Benefits of CAFM

6.2 WHY CAFM?

The answer to the question "Why CAFM?" is as individual as each potential user, and it is determined by the specific requirements of each organization. All requirements, including potential future capabilities, should be identified during the conceptual design phase of a CAFM implementation process (see chapter 13). The use of an experienced, independent, and reputable CAFM specialist to conduct a comprehensive needs analysis may be of great value at this point.

However, if a potential CAFM user decides to perform a needs analysis, it needs to provide a critical, unbiased assessment of the actual processes and goals of the respective organization. This assessment will uncover goals, challenges, additional requirements, and potential issues. It also will provide vision, clarity, and a high level of motivation for the long-term project's success.

Typical issues and/or questions uncovered during a CAFM assessment include the following:

- Information (drawings and data) documenting the buildings and their assets (occupants, furniture, technical equipment, etc.) exists in electronic format but is inconsistent and incomplete or, in some cases, available only in paper format. This results regularly in high additional expenditures for data acquisition or update.

- Nonexistent space and utilization standards.

- Baseline information for items such as electrical and water consumption are not available in electronic format.

- Lack of data detailing losses in supply networks (e.g., water, heating).

- Unacceptable response times in emergency situations.

- Pursuit of maintenance cycles and warrantee periods require substantial expenditure.

- Problems in determining infrastructure costs at the building and/or cost-center level.

- Requirements for comparing one's own costs to existing industry benchmarks.

- Budget planning for maintenance and assessments of expenditures and risk.

- Problems with inaccurate data during the quantitative analysis and assessment of infrastructural costs (e.g., maintenance, cleaning).

- Code compliance.

- Adherence to existing industry standards and determination of which standards to use (e.g., BOMA vs. IFMA for space definition/polylining)

The complexity of addressing issues becomes immediately apparent from this incomplete list. Almost all FM-related aspects of an enterprise are affected, with different relevance and priorities for each individual workplace.

A key responsibility of the project team is to find and determine the answers to "Why CAFM?" successfully for each group. The answers from each group must

- Coincide with the increasing requirements of the core business of FM

- Conform to the ever-changing requirements within the profession of the operator and/or manager, and ultimately the FM organization, resulting from it

This means that in addition to the establishment of priorities and an awareness of the constantly rising costs in the management of real estate, one must pay attention to the question of "Why CAFM?" from the various points of view of the financial sponsor and/or owner, the facility manager, and all other stakeholders. The primary benefits of CAFM include the following:

- Efficient, simple, and accurate completion of operational sequences, like data entry, reporting, and data analysis

- Supported FM processes with controls that conform to industry-accepted standards

- Guarantee of a high level of information, that is, a supply of consolidated information (assessments) as a decision basis for senior management, for example, with incident evaluation

- High cost/performance transparency and potential cost savings in areas such as cleaning contracts and energy consumption

- Capacity to perform extensive analysis of current and historically detailed information on costs associated with ongoing and preventative maintenance of buildings and facilities

- Increase in value of the built infrastructure through purposeful modernization

- Determination of property improvements that positively increase the productivity of white and blue collar workers

- Real-time reporting on queries about the building and asset investment

- Support of management decisions (by current and understandable information)

- Support of advertising and public relations activities (e.g., site development) by current and consistent FM data

- Precise valuation of fixed assets

- Accurate cost allocation and accounting

- Optimization of space utilization (master planning and optimization, allocation scheme, and efficient churn management)

- Accurate cost allocations

- Precise construction and bid documents and specs

- Reduction in lead times and costs associated with preventive and on-demand work orders

- Higher availability and quality of the real estate portfolio

6.3 FM VS. CAFM?

What is missing from FM cannot easily be replaced by CAFM. It must be clearly noted that the purchase and implementation of CAFM software in itself, along with the initial data gathering and population, will result in significant costs with no immediate return on investment. In other words, the success of CAFM relies on a stable FM organization with well-established and documented business processes. Whether these are defined within the FM organization's policies or are established at a higher level of the organization's standard procedures document is insignificant.

What is important is that these processes are well defined and serve as a basis for defining appropriate workflows for use in CAFM. With clear goals resulting from this approach, CAFM users can much more easily understand the requirements and goals necessary. When supported in this way, CAFM becomes an integral component of the success of the FM strategy.

A building's utilization phase will always be the focus of FM's core business, though FM considers the complete life cycle. As a result, there is a need to offer optimal building performance. This circumstance defines the type and range of the necessary process supported by CAFM. This includes the required functionality and the inventory data that must be collected and maintained as well as the information and communication technologies that can be used. Consequently, we note that CAFM has become an enabling technology for successful facility management.

6.4 HISTORICAL DEVELOPMENT

6.4.1 THE 1960S AND 1970S—MAINFRAME, MINICOMPUTERS, AND MODEST BEGINNINGS

Computer Aided Facility Management developed in parallel with facility management and developed within the advances of information technology. In the sixties and seventies, the discipline facility management was not yet defined. The FM that did exist at that time resided in some major U.S. corporations. Some of these corporations used large mainframe computers with rudimentary databases and CAD diagrams. Databases consisted of individual, standalone databases created by internal programmers, whereas some commercial CAD systems were already in place. All of these solutions were primitive, ad-hoc solutions: architecture sketch plans and room lists. There was no commercially available CAFM software.

The next generation of computers, so called minicomputers, brought about a quantum leap in computing with affordability and efficiency as well as versatility in the 1970s. A major application area of minicomputers was Computer Aided Design (CAD). Although a typical CAD implementation still cost more than 100,000 dollars, CAD started to become an accepted standard within the architectural industry.

Except for an increase in the use of CAD plans within FM, minicomputers played no special role in the development of CAFM during this time.

6.4.2 THE 1980S—THE PERSONAL COMPUTER: THE CRUCIAL INNOVATION

Nineteen-eighty was the year that the term *facility management* was created, though the first FM approaches existed earlier. There were also early developments in information technology. Already in the 1970s, amateur inventors had developed the microcomputer.

In 1982 IBM rolled out its first personal computer and its abbreviation, PC, soon became the universally accepted acronym for the entire classification of computers that serve an individual; this remains the case today. IBM played an important role in the large-scale deployment of its PCs within large corporations. IBM developed the PC from the beginning as an open, personal computer system. It was based on Intel processors, and its other hardware components were expandable and changeable. The operating system MS-DOS from Microsoft was also expandable and capable of running application software of a nearly unlimited number of software developers. Soon to follow behind the IBM PCs were the clone PCs, developed by multiple manufacturers, which drove down the initial costs of computers significantly.

Significant MS-DOS software programs developed at the time that impacted FM were AutoCAD, which quickly became the predominant CAD software on PCs and continues to enjoy that position to this day, and Dbase, the leading database management system at that time.

6.4.3 THE 1990S—MICROSOFT AS THE DOMINANT IT-PLATFORM

In the 1990s Microsoft created the Windows platform off its MS-DOS operating system Windows, and it quickly became—and continues to be—the dominant operating system. The success of Microsoft Windows consists particularly in the fact that it offers a universal deployment and development environment for software to perform in cooperation with most other software and hardware. Step by step, Microsoft triumphed over nearly all other collective software options, despite those other software developers being the original pioneers (e.g., Microsoft Office replacing WordPerfect and Lotus123 as the standards). Microsoft's operating system, network, server, and Internet software succeeded in this long run of dominance with persistent, market-driven practices.

Certainly, there are survivors such as Apple as well as the LINUX operating system, which is a repackaging of the extremely skillfully marketed UNIX operating system that was successful for many years.

So how did CAFM software get developed? Although there were some interesting CAFM developments based on UNIX and MS-DOS, it was the Microsoft Windows operating system that became the preferred platform for the development of CAFM. In fact, the development and propagation of CAFM directly correlates to the development and propagation of Windows.

Most of the significant CAFM products and tools that exist today use the Microsoft Windows operating system. This applies to standalone as well as network, client/server, and web-based systems. The 1990s were crucial for the distribution and acceptance of CAFM technology. Initially, the development was strongly impacted by the CAD market. Later, however, a trend developed toward database-dependent CAFM software, which was developed in modules and was increasingly flexible.

6.4.4 CAFM "GENERATIONS"

Sometimes we read about "generations" of CAFM. Depending on marketing aggressiveness of some CAFM developers, their software packages are in the second, third, or even seventh generation. While this information can be helpful in providing insight into how many times the software has had a new release, it really serves no purpose in comparing the current versions of different CAFM software. The generation or release number of the software does not serve as an indicator of the tangible utilization and comparison of the technical capabilities of the respective software.

6.4.5 THE TWENTY-FIRST CENTURY—THE WEB CHANGES EVERYTHING

In the midst of the hype of the "New Economy," migration to the web has been a trend and an absolute challenge for the CAFM industry. In the 1990s, CAFM software packages were often a mixture of modules that the software producer had already marketed for other targeted applications, like CAD, maintenance software, and other "add-on components." Today it sometimes appears that a software provider develops any web-enabled component for its CAFM software just to be able to say, "We are also on the Internet!"

It is a positive development that some CAFM software providers have done a complete redesign and rewrite of their software to a web-based (three-tier) platform, but it is important to note that the software providers have made different choices in the programming language they use. As an example, some providers have chosen to use Sun's Java, while others have decided to use Microsoft's .Net framework.

Facing the challenge will not only require reasonably priced CAFM software packages, but also fundamental support of the FM discipline. Experiences with using software packages, such as CAD or word processing, only serve as a minimal point of reference. Experience with integrated enterprise software such as Enterprise Resource Planning (ERP) or Workflow Management may be better suited for use as a guideline for vendors, users, and consultants.

6.5 STRUCTURE OF THE FM MARKET

6.5.1 FM AND CAFM MARKET

Providing a description and a structuring of the actual FM market for both the United States and internationally is not easy because of the dissociation of other markets (e.g., project development, office furniture, utilities supply). However, it should be noted that the FM provider market currently is divided worldwide into the categories of large (international) generalists and small (regional) specialists.

Since the FM service providers seldom have a preference for any CAFM software ("We use the system that the customer needs") or have developed their own proprietary CAFM system, we cannot draw any conclusions between FM service provider market and that of the CAFM providers. Nevertheless, a structuring attempt is to be undertaken below, at least for the German CAFM market. A look at how there is a very different market structure internationally can be found in chapter 15.

6.5.2 HISTORICAL STRUCTURE OF THE (GERMAN) CAFM MARKET

In Germany, the first CAFM software was developed in the late 1980s by extending AEC (Architecture, Engineering, and Construction) CAD systems with non-graphic attributes that were stored in a separate database. Some of these solutions used purely proprietary CAFM software, while others integrated with existing, standard CAD software (e.g., AutoCAD).

The concept of database-oriented CAFM system developed, influenced by the U.S. CAFM market and at about the same time in Germany. The building data is stored in a structured database, and the graphical interface is through a simple diagram system (e.g., Visio) or a standard CAD system (e.g., AutoCAD, MicroStation). Some software providers visualize their graphical information directly from the database. Real-time visualization from the database will become the generally accepted standard, so that the artificial separation between alphanumeric and graphic data will vanish.

Most recently, smaller, innovative software providers introduced web-based integrated CAFM systems into the market. However, none of these have gained widespread acceptance. Also, recently, some of the leading software vendors have achieved the transformation from their original software to web-based solutions.

An interesting recent development in the German CAFM market is an infiltration into the market by ERP and CAD global market leaders like SAP and Autodesk with FM-oriented extensions of their standard systems.

6.5.3 VENDOR STRUCTURE OF THE (GERMAN) CAFM MARKET

The CAFM market in Germany reached an annual volume of approximately 100 million dollars in 2009, according to careful estimations of the GEFMA CAFM working group in early 2010. This includes the market for software licenses and software-referred services such as installation and maintenance. The associated market for CAFM referred consulting services falls in the range of approximately 40 million dollars, which is divided fairly equally between the software providers' own consulting departments (e.g., Conject, Loy & Hutz) and software-independent consulting firms (e.g., IBM Global Services and BearingPoint). The relevant annual market reviews conducted and published by GEFMA identifies approximately fifty providers of CAFM software in Germany. On a worldwide basis, one can expect that today there are more than one hundred CAFM providers in the marketplace.

The ten largest CAFM providers in Germany represent approximately 80 percent of the local market volume. We can conclude from this that the remaining market of CAFM providers in Germany consists of very small companies. Some of the bigger German CAFM software providers are selectively expanding into international markets (primarily in Eastern Europe and the Gulf region). In general, only global providers like Archibus and Planon achieve the size of medium-size software companies and have considerable installation numbers in Europe. The same can be said of the North American market, where the vast majority of CAFM software providers acts locally with the major difference that the market comprises only about ten vendors.

The projection for market growth for CAFM in Germany varies between 5 percent and 50 percent per year. This becomes even more amazing when you consider that different market surveys conducted in Germany in 2009 concluded that there were hardly three thousand installed CAFM systems as defined in the comprehensive sense of GEFMA guideline 400 (NN 2007b). The market leader in the United States claimed an install base of at least ten times the size of the entire European install base at that time. In Germany, as in the United States, a considerable number of CAFM companies have either folded or disappeared through mergers and acquisitions by competitors, and as new CAFM software companies are constantly popping up in the market.

The prediction of a market shakeout that would result in around five survivors has been around for several years but has not come true, nor does there appear to be any indication that it will occur in the near future. In fact, the local German market leaders have lost some of their market share without a clear-cut shift of their market share to other providers. CAFM software providers can be broken down into the following segments for the German language (Austria, Germany, Switzerland) market (see also May et al. 2007):

- Established local CAFM providers (mostly CAD drawing-oriented)

- Small, innovative niche offerings (mostly web-oriented)

- Internationally successful CAFM providers, which penetrate the German market (mostly IWMS-oriented),

- Software world market leaders from adjacent market segments (ERP, CAD) (mostly integration-oriented)

Predicting what developments will occur in the future that will affect the structure of the CAFM market is a difficult endeavor. What seems most likely is that there will be an increase of integration with other large systems, usually with ERP systems (in Germany, primarily SAP), which utilize an industry-standard database (Oracle or MS-SQL). In addition, small, low-priced, and web-based solutions that can be easily deployed and are targeted toward small and medium enterprises will become generally acceptable. Only the more IWMS-geared (Integrated Workplace Management Systems), truly international providers with state-of-the-art software architectures and user interfaces will gain significant market shares.

6.6 CAFM DEVELOPMENTS AND TRENDS

The development of CAFM as an application software consisting of a database, processes, algorithms, and graphics always follows the substantial progress made in these respective computer science subdisciplines (see section 6.7).

Beyond that, there are already attempts to compile CAFM software by employing methods of artificial intelligence and a higher degree of process orientation that is more intuitive and user-friendly. For example, it is conceivable that instead of several operating steps for the reservation of a conference room, a user can use natural speech to inform the CAFM system to, for example, locate a conference room that can hold twenty people, equipped with a projector and screen, for a specific date and time.

The system could then respond with the availability of the conference rooms that meet the requestor's parameters, suggest possible alternatives and additional options (such as network connection, seating configuration or teleconferencing), and provide references to additional services like catering or IT. Such systems are currently under development and are expected to be commercially available in this decade.

Internet technology is likewise integrated as standard in CAFM software (see chapter 11). This has the advantage of easier usability and almost unrestricted availability, including wireless network connectivity. All of the leading CAFM products currently available in the United States already exhibit such characteristics, which go well beyond a simple web-based drawing viewer.

Considering the integration of CAFM into other system environments, we expect an increase in standardized and release-independent interfaces and system distributable workflows (procedures). Thus, service-oriented architectures (SOA) will play an increased role, and reporting possibilities will clearly improve.

The higher integration of ERP systems with standard graphic systems will result in a redundancy-free database for all FM-relevant data, that can be distributed physically or virtually.

In each case, advanced software development will move CAFM systems away from the specialist corner and into widely used web portals that will allow FM services providers to increase their customer base by offering CAFM as SaaS (software as a service) or as part of a cloud computing solution.

6.7 CAFM—A COMPUTER SCIENCE DISCIPLINE?

In exploring this question, we recall both definitions of the term *CAFM* provided earlier:

- CAFM as a type of software: a category of application programs and/or software applications

- CAFM in the literal and broader sense—general computer-based assistance for FM

Let's begin with the first category: CAFM software usually contains elements and algorithms of vector graphics and relational or object-oriented databases in accordance with GEFMA guideline 400 (NN 2007b). The inherent tasks and solutions are neither unique nor very FM-specific. The creation of such software relies less on specific algorithms and more on their FM-specific framework. This is, however, an application-oriented problem definition, which does not justify an independent computer-science discipline.

If CAFM in the second sense is actually holistically implied, then system integration becomes the central practical function. Furthermore, this is only to a small degree FM-specific and once again revolves around application-software design knowledge. Additionally, if use of the Internet continues to be the trend in FM, those stated arguments become all more valid.

So should computer science be concerned with the field of FM as an activity? Facility management will not have its own exclusive discipline within computer science, because it would be difficult to justify due to a lack of concrete specifics. It is instead anticipated that it will develop in a way similar to GIS (Geographic Information Systems) in the realm of geoinformatics.

From an academic perspective in computer science, CAFM is suitable as a discipline within the applied computer science curriculum (May 1999). It is there that it fits best, especially considering that the purpose of "the aid of computers in facility management" resides within the name (CAFM). But also in traditional FM curricula, the role of IT topics within FM must be enforced in order to bring FM into a position to steer the process of CAFM implementation successfully.

6.8 SUMMARY

Successful FM today is heavily influenced by "tailored" CAFM. The tangible needs in each case of FM are determined by the function of the core business and by the size as well as complexity of the facilities. This results in unique requirements that influence both the FM organization and the related IT support using CAFM implementations. The purchase of CAFM software, however, does not by itself guarantee success. An effective CAFM system is characterized by the following:

- Suitable conceptual design with, among other things, setting the goal and considering the cost/benefit

- Suitable CAFM software for the process support needed

- Inventory documentation with the required level of detail

In addition, a suitable FM organization structure, in which the daily work with CAFM is integrated, must be developed. Evaluating the current CAFM market, we note this:

- In 2009 approximately fifty CAFM software providers in Germany shared an estimated market size of around 100 million dollars.

- Structuring the market based on contents/focus or technology is a difficult endeavor.

- Very few providers with international focus become as large as medium-size.

The fact that future CAFM software will increasingly be defined by the integration of web technologies as well as a purposeful integration with existing enterprise software such as ERP systems, greatly informs the crucial requirements for the developers of CAFM software. In addition to advances in technology (e.g., web portals, mobile solutions, RFIDs), legislation and regulation (e.g., carbon footprint reports, building certification) will have a major impact on future CAFM developments. The success of accomplishing these complex requirements will probably lead to a shakeout of the global CAFM market.

7

APPLICATIONS

Alwin Schauer, Gary Kropp, Alexander Maier

7.1 GENERAL

The potential use of information technology applications in FM involves nearly all facility functions. It is important to distinguish between using standalone tools for individual tasks and using a comprehensive FM software solution. This chapter focuses on comprehensive applications in which the solution, as part of an integrated system, is important.

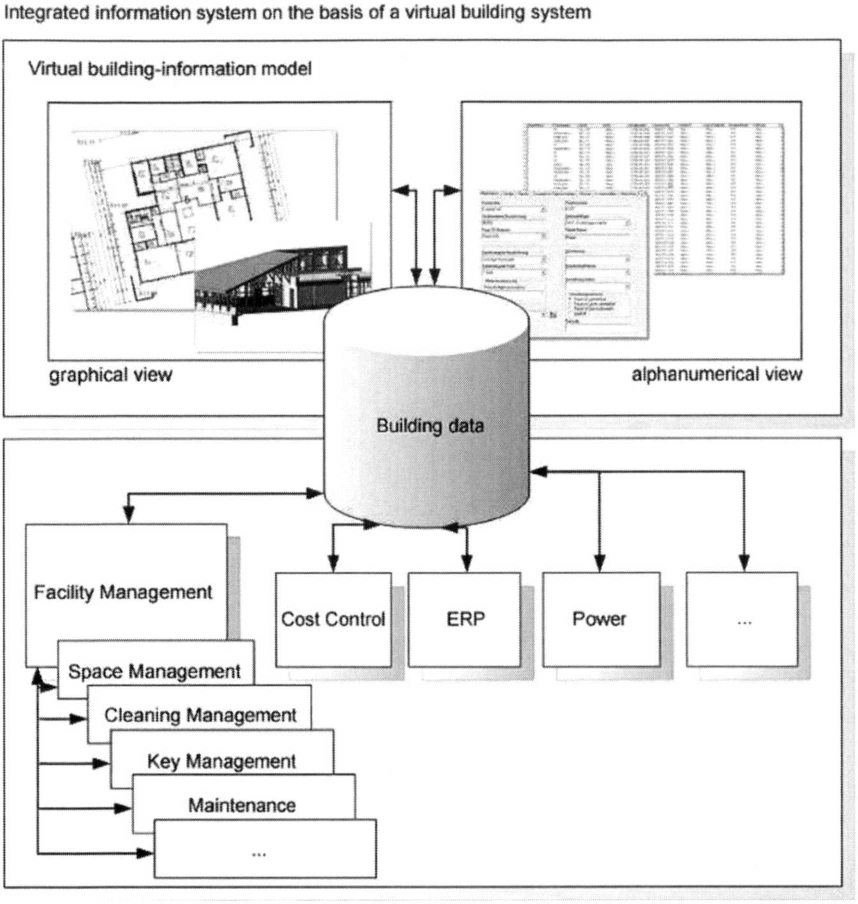

Integrated information system on the basis of a virtual building system

Fig. 7.1: Integrated system based on a virtual building model

An integrated FM system places the building data at its core (see figure 7.1). With the use of the "virtual building," information is entered in a structured format into a central database. The building data can then be viewed in multiple formats (i.e., graphic or alphanumeric).

7.2 FACILITY INVENTORY DOCUMENTATION

The IT Business Processes and Procedures (IT-BPP) supporting the work processes in FM require that comprehensive and timely information is available on the entire facility, including accurate data for the following:

- Land

- Buildings

- Plants

- Equipment

- Service contracts (both internal and external)

This data can be varied to include some of the following data categories:

- Graphical and alphanumerical building components data

- Facility process data

- Financial data

- Facility performance data (for benchmarking purposes)

- Facility condition data

- Energy and utility consumption data

The first four categories of data directly above are relatively static. They tend to remain constant over a long period. However, the last two types of data are very dynamic if they are made available "real time" or collected on a timely basis. Real-time data acquisition is especially important when an FM solution includes applications integrated with high availability plants and buildings, and the data needs to be analyzed on a daily basis.

Facility management inventory data is generally available through various documents, spreadsheets, tables, CAD files, scanned images, and graphics. If this data is managed through FM software applications or modules; it allows users quick, structured access without them knowing the exact location of the data on the corporate network.

The use of flexible search criteria includes

- The hierarchy or levels (e.g., floors) of a building

- User-definable attributes (e.g., for assignment to crafts and/or trades)

- Predefined data characteristics (such as "created by," "date created," etc.)

These should be mandated for any CAFM software. For ongoing updating and maintenance of the FM-related documentation, it is also helpful for it to be integrated with a document management system (DMS).

Facility inventory documentation is the basis for all supporting modules of a CAFM system. This is vital when defining the data structures as well as in the definition of the criteria regarding quantity (volume) and quality (quality assurance) of data collection. To gain the maximum efficiency of the FM application, the data completeness, level of detail, and accuracy are crucial during the implementation of the system.

When surveying and documenting buildings, there are additional sources of data (e.g., manufacturer info or other industry standards), depending on the building type and age (i.e., new or existing building), that can be used to supplement facilities where nominal, incomplete, or inaccurate documentation is available for the FM system.

Since facility inventory and condition information acquisition is a substantial part of the costs to implement an FM system, it makes sense to use the appropriate method of data acquisition. Often several data items are collected that will, in practice, not be used. This has the consequence that the data may be structured differently and/or be redundant.

The four primary methods for collecting inventory data (see chapter 10) of existing properties and buildings are the following:

1.   Drawing-oriented CAD acquisition

2.   Model-oriented CAD acquisition

3.   Alphanumerical data collection

4.   Semiautomatic data collection

Drawing-oriented CAD acquisitions. Utilizing a drawing-oriented CAD-collection inventory method means that the real estate data and building data is managed and displayed as a 2-D drawing. For any given drawing representation—whether site plan, floor plan, view or section cut—there is a separate drawing file. Individual floor plans can be used to create polylines with attributes attached to the drawing objects (see figure 7.2), which form the basis for graphic and alphanumerical analysis (such as space-related information).

Fig. 7.2: Drawing-oriented CAD acquisition utilized for space management

Examples of drawing-oriented CAD collection methods include the following:

- Calculations of land area and appraisals (on ft² or m² basis)

- Building-area analysis with occupancy or space information

- Updating of drawing components to "objects" with attributes

- Infrastructure of the property (mechanical, electrical, telecom/data)

- Detailed documentation of the property, buildings, rooms

- Furniture and equipment inventory information

Model-oriented CAD acquisition. Utilizing CAD-oriented model collection means that the real estate and buildings are represented as parametric, object-oriented 3-D models (see figure 7.3). With increasing levels of complexity and changes during the life-cycle stages of the facility, such as planning, construction, occupancy, and ownership, these models are permanently being enriched.

A 3-D model consists of a single physical file containing each facility and is used to create representations—whether site plan, floor plan, view, or cut—as reports from the 3-D model. It contains "components" such as walls, ceilings, windows, and doors. Working in direct association with a database, the relevant planning, building, and user information in an integrated digital environment is always up-to-date.

New to this methodology is the development and use of object-oriented building information models (BIM), which are created initially by the design team and maintained throughout the rest of the building life cycle, including construction and occupancy by the respective process owners.

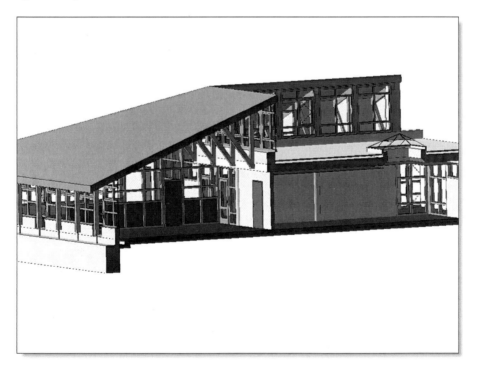

Fig. 7.3: Model-oriented CAD inventory utilized for volume and mass analysis

Examples of the model-oriented CAD collection method include the following:

- Documentation of the property, buildings, rooms

- Volume analysis of spatial information

- Detailed component evaluation (e.g., part lists—windows, doors, etc.)

- Basics for parts—volume and mass evaluations

- Simulations for energy, noise, fixtures/furnishings

- Basis for life-cycle data model

- High value-added due to building information for CAFM

Alphanumerical data collection. Alphanumerical data collection is based on use of existing databases in which data for the property and building information are separately maintained. In addition to defining the hierarchy of a property, the organizational structures for buildings, parts, floors, rooms, components (walls, windows, ceilings, etc.) and equipment are also developed and included.

The data field structure is so defined that unique data fields can be created. This is beneficial in that during the collection of the data and the condition of the components (or facilities), the critical dimensions for construction and operating criteria or tolerances can be collected and maintained.

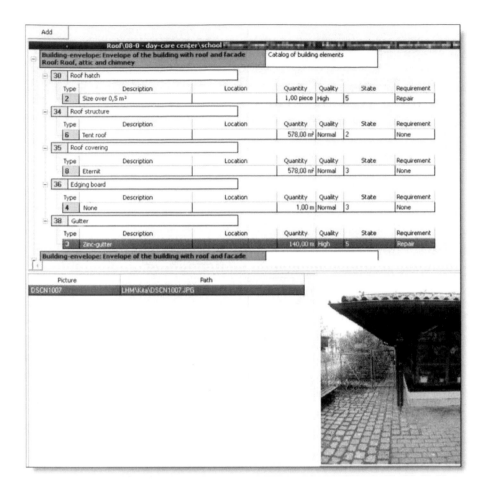

Fig. 7.4: Alphanumerical inventory data collection example: Building condition assessments for building maintenance and determination of corrective measures

Examples of alphanumerical data collection include the following:

- Existing facility standards for space/use/occupancy classifications

- Condition assessments of real estate and facilities

- Identification of the maintenance backlog

- Definition of corrective measures for maintenance of the facilities

- Detailed valuations of building and property

Semiautomatic data collection. Semiautomatic data collection processes consist of combining mobile tools, such as PDAs, laptops, or tablet PCs, with barcode or RFID technology (see chapter 4).

The data maintenance of the components, equipment, or parts inventory is handled in a centralized database. Only the component properties are collected via onsite barcodes (see figure 7.5) or RFID chips. Thus, site codes and the current location of the object are inserted directly into the database via the facility's network. The advantage of this method is that both asset managers and FMs gain immediate access to this information, and the maintenance of inventory data can begin.

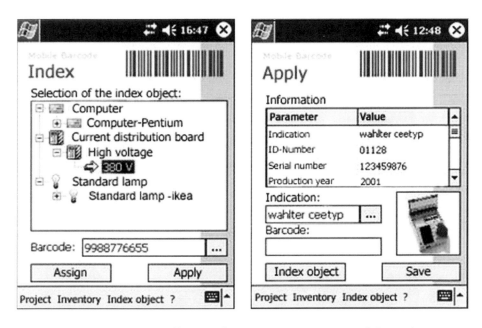

Fig. 7.5: Inventory collection of equipment via PDA with bar codes or RFID technology

Examples of automated data collection are

■ Basic data collection for physical inventory management

■ Basic data collection for mechanical, plant, and technology equipment inventory

■ Locations of components, equipment, and objects

- Fast, predefined recording of operational data

- Other high-level details of object and plant information

7.3 SPACE MANAGEMENT

Space management takes on special importance because it affects the technical infrastructure, services, and commercial management aspects of the facility. The main objectives of space management are

- Optimizing the building construction to increase the usable space

- Better space utilization by economic occupancy of space

- Ergonomic and functional design of the workplace

Since the majority of FM processes need space, space management occupies a key role in CAFM. On the basis of graphical and alphanumerical space data—including space allocation, occupancies, and equipment—can be analyzed, planned, and both graphically and alpha documented.

The support of space management processes through CAFM includes the following tasks:

- Space structure analysis

- Space occupancy analysis (related to space, time, and volume)

- Space allocation planning (size, geometry, position)

- Space use analysis (occupancy and utilization rate)

- Space utilization optimization (e.g., alternatives, assessment)

- Internal accounting of space costs (e.g., extra costs)

- Rental space management (tenants, lease agreements, charges for leased space)

- Use of specific real estate/facility standards (floor space per office or job classification)

Inventory documentation (see section 7.2) forms the basis for space management; thus the functionality for real estate management in CAFM includes the following:

- The collection and storage of data objects along with object descriptive data:

  - Basic information (such as location, real estate, building, floor, room, zone) collectively with their dependencies and assignments (such as real estate on the site, floor area)

  - Predefined attributes to basic data, such as for art objects and land use

  - Additional user-oriented attributes and criteria (such as office furniture, IT equipment, roles, rooms or space zones)

- Allocation of area calculations to data fields from other modules of the CAFM software:

  - Assignment of employees (as users of work areas) to spaces, space zones or job classifications

  - Assignment of organizational units to spaces, space zones, or job classifications

  - Assignment of costs to spaces or zones (if not to an assigned staff or assigned organizational units)

  - Assignment of inventory, spaces, zones or equipment, and services to areas (such as HVAC, cleaning, and security requirements)

- User analysis of the data in the form of graphical and alphanumerical screen displays and formatted reports (see figure 7.6)

The considerations covered in this chapter for rooms and room zones are also valid for external spaces, such as green areas, roads, sidewalks, or parking spaces.

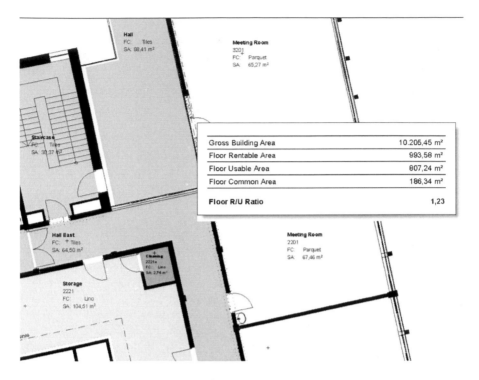

Gross Building Area	10.205,45 m²
Floor Rentable Area	993,58 m²
Floor Usable Area	807,24 m²
Floor Common Area	186,34 m²
Floor R/U Ratio	**1,23**

Fig. 7.6: Graphical and alphanumerical reports in space management

7.4 CONTRACT MANAGEMENT

In FM, there are numerous types of contracts to manage.

- Rental and lease contracts

- Project-related contracts (such as for construction and renovation activities)

- Service-related contracts (such as for cleaning or maintenance services)

- Management contracts (such as housing management and construction management contracts)

- Insurance contracts

- Warranty contracts

- Energy supply contracts

Contract management is composed of the following:

- Contracts planning

- Contracts design

- Contracts negotiation

- Contracts implementation

- Contracts monitoring and control

Contract management, within FM, can be organized around core business process activities. For contracts with long lead times and dates, timely action is important for continuity of business operations. Contract information also can be accessed via the database by contract managers for objective evaluations of the data as a basis for decision making.

In CAFM, key contract data is important and includes the following:

- Contract performance requirements

- Contract duration

- Contract termination date and renewal options

- Addresses of contract parties

- Location of the contract property/equipment

- Division of the contract responsibilities

If the contract is available in digital format, contract managers can also have direct access to the actual contract document through the CAFM software.

Also, the relation of contract data to the basis data held in the CAFM system should be possible, such as a room to the related lease contract or the maintenance agreement to mechanical equipment.

7.5 CLEANING MANAGEMENT

The definition of IT-supported cleaning management depends primarily on the function of the building. Complex requirements can be monitored with the help of a cleaning management application in certain industries, including health, specialized services, or other heavily regulated industries. In addition, in more conventional environments, the use of a cleaning management application can contribute to user satisfaction and cost control.

Cleaning management includes the following:

- Planning (i.e., the development of cleaning standards, specifications, and contracts with service providers)

- Monitoring

- Quality control of the cleaning procedures

With an accurate description of the existing quantities and quality-of-service levels combined with consistent quality monitoring with appropriate documentation, it is possible to have a regular, high-quality cleaning of the facility. Under cleaning and care services fall, among other things,

- Exterior glass cleaning

- Maintenance and plant cleaning

- Specialty cleaning

- Outdoor facilities, parking, and street cleaning

- Ice/snow removal services

- Landscape and plant care

Using occupancy data (see section 7.6) and linking occupancy and occupancy-related service levels belonging to the areas objects, actual cleaning results in terms of quality and quantity can be documented.

After accurately recording the occupancy data, the cleaning procedures are used to do the following:

- Define the daily cleaning services

- Define the specialized cleaning services

- Record a fair and accurate accounting of the cleaning activities

- Adjust the cleaning procedures to meet business requirements

- Implement quality-control procedures

A continuous evaluation of the cleaning data according to user-specific requirements should also be possible.

Cleaning management applications contain primarily static information. When mapping complex and dynamically changing environments it makes sense that the building data is linked to dynamic operational data, such as attendance of employees or work orders, in order to collect data on the cleaning activities and to be able to adapt to changing requirements.

7.6 MOVE MANAGEMENT

With the addition of inventory data (see section 7.2), the critical components for the use of FM applications to track internal and external moves are available.

Additionally, for external moves, the collection of the new premises as "spaces" with technology connections (i.e., data and telecom) is essential. A move plan can be produced graphically on a CAD editor as well as by moving objects or groups of objects (such as with an associated inventory) in the structured database. In either case, automatic adjustment based on alternate scenarios is possible. Furthermore, modern CAFM software has the ability to present multiple planning alternatives in parallel. Thus CAFM can contribute to the decision-making process and their optimization during moves. With the use of graphics, including 3-D representations, acceptance by affected employees and decision makers who are concerned by move can increase substantially.

Collection of the move data in a CAFM system is a prerequisite for documenting the current space inventory. Development of a move plan includes the following tasks:

■ Identification of available open space

■ Use of installation and move standards

The move itself is made up of the preparation phase and the implementation of changes phase regarding the following:

■ Affected inventory items

■ Job classifications for employees

■ Affected organizational units (i.e., organizational divisions) at each location

For the move execution, the following information is necessary:

■ Stickers to mark the destination of the moved inventory

■ Updated layouts and facility plans (including new spaces and after-move conditions of existing spaces)

■ Instructions for move vendor/contractors

■ Instructions and/or schedules for the construction of the technology infrastructure (e.g., electrical and communication connection requirements)

■ Instructions for door signage

■ Instructions for keying (see section 7.9)

A consistent barcode marking of the inventory is helpful for internal move management planning. As a result, items that are to be transferred, added, or disposed of, or that are lost can easily be included into the planning in lieu of dealing with problems created by unmanaged internal changes.

CAFM software requires an interactive synchronization with the existing data tables against the data captured by the bar-code readers. These tables (containing the current assigned room, inventory tag, etc.) are typically captured by a personal digital assistant (PDA) equipped with a bar-code reader used to scan the code number and space of the marked objects in the existing spaces.

7.7 ENERGY MANAGEMENT

In energy management applications, all energy consumption values are collected along with other measurement data (such as weather data) and analyzed. Automated data collection, either directly or remotely, captures data into the energy management application. Managed data includes all possible sources, including sensors (temperature, humidity, etc.). The cycles and patterns for each type of counter should be freely defined.

Energy management today is usually divided into two areas:

- Energy management (review and evaluation of energy consumption in real time)

- Energy planning (energy planning of buildings and calculating future consumption)

In the field of energy management, the following information is important:

- Coverage of all existing meters

- Meter readings

- Area calculations to facilitate allocation (charge-back) of energy consumption

- Weather data for weather normalization adjustments

- Rules-based energy consumption policies for events management

In addition to being used in the production of electricity, heat and water are used during special manufacturing processes. The objective is for maximum transparency in regard to consumption and costs. This is confirmed by a manual collection or by automated detection recordings.

The frequency for the collection of energy consumption data is highly dependent on the type of reporting desired. Manual data collection over short intervals is very expensive. Using direct-read capabilities of meters, an up-to-the-minute reading can take place very effectively without special instrumentation.

Mobile devices such as PDAs can be utilized for quick, efficient, paperless data collection for multiple meter readings. With the use of PDAs, consumption data readings (see figure 7.7) are possible without performing additional manual data entry.

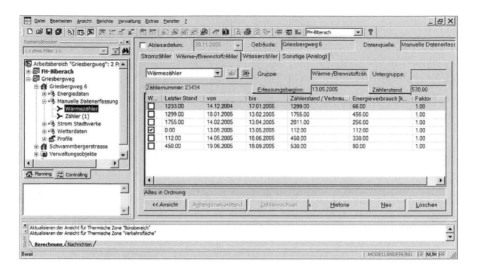

Fig. 7.7: Manual collection of counter readings

Regular analysis related to the reduction of energy consumption with the objective of obtaining timely detection of irregularities is important. The areas referenced within CAFM software and the associated assignments to users or user groups are used as the basis for data ratio calculations and benchmarking.

7.8 MAINTENANCE MANAGEMENT

Efficient management of buildings, equipment, and maintenance activities require the use of a maintenance management application. With modern IT tools, highly detailed reporting for the work processes is displayed. There are basically two types of system concepts on the market:

- Standalone CMMS systems

- Integrated maintenance modules found in CAFM or enterprise level financial software (such as ERP solutions)

Computerized Maintenance Management Systems (CMMS) are utilized in all types of facilities, from industrial plants and manufacturing to aviation, health care, educational, and corporate office facilities.

Specialized modules for maintenance management within CAFM software are relatively rare because the requirements for a maintenance solution and CAFM software often differ. In the best case, both systems are integrated and maintained so the objects for both the CAFM building structure as well as a classical plant structure can be allocated.

A key component in this kind of process management software is accessibility to employees through mobile devices, kiosks, or web portals. Only then can it be assured that maintenance employees and their maintenance activities are properly recorded on a timely basis.

Maintenance management applications include procedures for developing the following:

- Preventive maintenance programs

- Planned maintenance activities

- Management of unplanned maintenance work orders

The focus of the application is on documenting equipment failures, maintenance activities, and contract/warranty management, which can then be integrated to a CAFM system with the related objects containing facility inventory documentation.

The following business processes must be supported:

- Failure reporting by equipment object and facility location

- Inventory of equipment, including billing assignments

- Organizing maintenance personnel, tools and supplies, work lists, and tasks definitions

- Tracking of planned maintenance tasks and their assignment to individuals or contractors accessible through a simple user interface

The following master data is required in the software:

- Facilities or plants where maintenance is to be performed

- Standard maintenance task lists

- Standardized task times

- Personnel and key contract data from contractors or suppliers

- Maintenance plans

- Contract documents

- Logistics and supply areas for materials and tools

Each employee records his or her daily tasks on a screen (see figure 7.8) along with the current status of the work order.

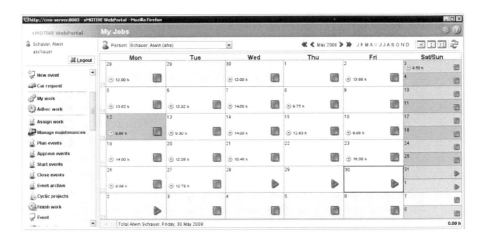

Fig. 7.8: Calendar view of maintenance work activity

Optionally, one can also perform the tasks of planning of resources required to support the maintenance procedures. These include the human resources and planning inventory requirements for spare parts and tools. A significant optimization potential exists, due to the coordination of planned activities and available resources within the same system.

The process of reporting or recording work requests/incidents can include the requirement to collect the contact telephone number of the person reporting the request on a screen in the work-order application. It is then possible to view work-order status (rejected, requested, work in progress, work completed) directly, without additional inquiries (see figure 7.9). Optionally, urgent messages can be automatically routed via email or SMS to the responsible party.

In larger buildings or technically complex facilities, a direct connection to the building automation system makes sense. As a result, based on related events (e.g., a failure or reaching predefined operating hours or consumption values); maintenance orders are automatically triggered and routed.

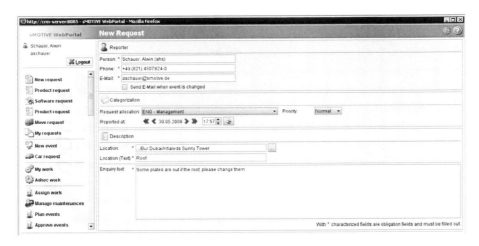

Fig. 7.9: Fault reporting on the Intranet

7.9 SECURITY AND ACCESS CONTROL MANAGEMENT

Security and access control solutions in FM are extremely important applications, particularly in the case of keying lists (i.e., who has a key) and access privileges (i.e., who can go where). Such solutions should automatically generate key issue procedures and key return procedures.

The exact documentation regarding security in a facility is a prerequisite to ensuring a high degree of certainty and clarity of actions. A combination of the information from the key for the lock and the door accessed by the user of the space ensures transparency in monitoring the entry system. Besides tabular reporting capabilities, the system should provide appropriate integrated graphics. Also, hierarchical floor plans can be created (see figure 7.10).

The following information should be provided in the security and access control solution:

- Assignment of locks to locking systems

- Lock with cylinder type and model number for the manufacturer, and pin position according latest plans

- Persons to which the key that has been assigned

- Key with opening number, quantity, and permanent location

- Key class or key hierarchy levels

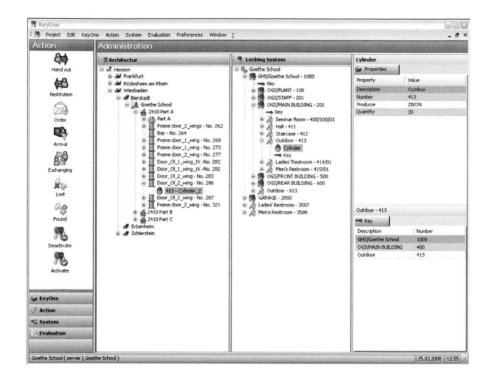

Fig. 7.10: Key data example

Database links for this information are required for the following:

- Rooms or doors

- Persons, tenants, and contractors as key holders

Similarly, graphics such as the mapping of door groups in plans should be provided.

Security and access control software can manage analog electronic locking systems. It is important for the management of electronic locking systems and the access control solution to be connected to a redundant data management source to prevent reprogramming of the plant immediately by the CAFM system being monitored.

7.10 PROPERTY MANAGEMENT—LEASES AND RENTALS

In management of external and internal leases/rentals, the use of a CAFM application solution is especially useful in supporting organizational activities, similar to contract management (see section 7.4). This includes providing relevant lease data for compilation of lease summaries as well as for the management of existing lease/rental agreements.

The required leased/rental areas can be extracted from the real estate portfolio management application (see section 7.3). This application includes information on location, type of rental space, and features. The size of the leased/rental space is available in the property management application from a lease/rental perspective as an area characteristic or data field. Such data need not necessarily coincide with those established by the real estate management agreement, as they have been agreed upon in the lease contracts. In addition to the alphanumerical data, it is also beneficial to have graphical data, such as floor plans with room stamps and the location of the areas in the building, along with a visual representation of the overall object and the interiors.

In a lease/rental tracking module of a CAFM application, additional lcase agreement data is available:

- General tenant information

- Duration of the contract, notification periods, options

- Allocation of rentable spaces, open and common/public spaces

- Building access information

- Recording of the contract history

- Contract document in digital form

The above items include information about tenant and landlord responsibilities, maintenance of the leased area, special equipment requirements, special provisions for the landlord or tenant, and information on additional costs (see section 7.11).

7.11 OPERATIONAL COST MANAGEMENT

Operational cost management includes the documentation and analysis of all relevant FM cost elements. By agreeing that a referenced space in CAFM (e.g., an office on the ground floor has no costs for elevators) is the basis for a fair market rate for users or tenants, the base charges or base rates to be approved may be changed at any time by the FM user. In addition to analyzing standard operating costs, such as

- detailed annual or monthly operating costs per user or tenant,

- building settlements showing understandable distributions, and

- the annual ledger for an entire property,

different searches of all types are possible, within the framework of cost clarifications, such as creating an examination of unbalanced liabilities or the initiation of appropriate measures for the management objectives.

The integration of energy management and maintenance applications in the same system increases the accuracy and clarity of the calculation basis.

7.12 FINANCIAL MANAGEMENT

Financial management controls are functional management tools that focus on business decision and control processes by developing targeted information and supporting processes. Financial management controlling in this respect is far beyond simply "controlling" the performance improvement of the enterprise. It includes targeted economic dominance, guidance, control, and regulation of processes within a company, and thus has a leadership-support function.

To meet the needs from the perspective of financial management requirements, modern financial systems have both quantitative and qualitative indicator statements. These essential processes must be developed by the company in charge of the management of buildings and properties. Theyocus on targeted-performance comparisons through the continuous analysis of progress in all key controls performance.

The general objectives for financial management of real estate include the following:

- Low capital commitment and low real estate costs

- High availability and quality of the use of the property

The requirements for controlling FM processes vary greatly (e.g., a real estate company controlling the core business of a company as a secondary process, especially as the core functions of the goal-oriented process).

However, even with facility management as the core business of the company, the tools of financial controlling are much deeper into the entrepreneurial process.

The requirements for controlling real estate vary also according to the ratio of company-owned property. For the real estate investor, the yield and value of the property is in the forefront. The property is used exclusively for the development of financial resources and is usually leased out. For the property owner, his property is for the realization of its core business use, and he or she is most interested in the cost-effective delivery of the property terms over the remaining useful life, whereas for the tenant of rented property, only the current cost and quality demands for expected use of the property are important.

The different views of the property therefore imply different objectives and requirements of the tools of real estate controlling. This requires the property manager for a company's real estate to have a sophisticated accounting capability as the necessary controls emerge. Regardless of the use of the property, the planning, information, and controlling function of managing property to control the real estate portfolio remains.

A basic requirement that can be fulfilled by controlling these functions is a detailed recording of all the property and the use of real estate. The basis for this is usually a company accounting system with real estate management-oriented cost accounting functionality. On this basis, data on the plant structure, energy consumption data, and equipment costs are derived. It is also necessary to collect more data, such as the quantitative values of cost accounting with qualitative information about the buildings and equipment. These include the remaining useful life of construction, plant, and technology equipment, along with the maintenance and inspection cycles.

Finally, financial statements deliver on the following aspects:

- The implementation of the company's strategic objectives in terms of the resources required

- The properties affected by the cost structures and development costs

- The provisions for the settlement of the core business necessary-use qualities

In general, in addition to internal company comparisons, benchmarking has already been valuable in many sectors. It involves the comparison of the company's performance with others, possibly with the best-performing companies of their own industry sector, or with foreign companies. The aim of benchmarking real estate is to identify competitive disadvantages and measures to eliminate them. Key performance indicators (KPIs) of a single property over a period of time can also be considered (see figure 7.11) as well as of several buildings where KPI figures are compared with each other.

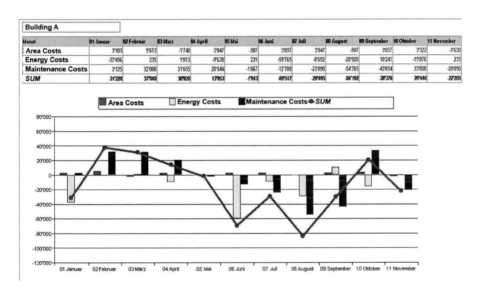

Fig. 7.11: Benchmarking as a controlling tool

From the benchmarks, the optimization potential is apparent, which ultimately leads to development of an effective and efficient management of real estate.

Benchmarking is based on analyzing the data of control indicators. Currently, quantitative indicators of cost and financial improvements are at the center of the comparison. In the future, qualitative indicators will gain more importance, though their collection and objective evaluation is much more complex. The key figures of real estate financial controlling include figures for the buildings or facility annualized costs.

Today's CAFM systems are usually referred to as control indicator systems, but they usually do not meet all the above requirements. Above all, there are always interface problems with the applications under different software systems when trying to establish full realization of using software systems for dynamic data analysis.

Included among the specialized software solutions in this area are Data Warehouse systems (see chapter 11). These consist of different data tables in a comprehensive system integrated to produce the necessary management performance indicators. The data comes from commercial IT systems (ERP), customer relationship management systems (CRM), and other administrative systems. CAFM systems are utilized to deliver this important data. It is necessary that the CAFM software uses standard interfaces for data access or that standardized databases are built specifically for this purpose.

CAFM systems are often designed as operational work processes in a business way. These work processes are usually in the lower layers of the hierarchy. To achieve a vertical penetration of this hierarchy, the data is provided with various filters and processed. This type of information processing is called "data mining."

Such business warehouse systems, or MIS (Management Information Systems), are in a position to provide predefined management performance indicators called "executive dashboards" at the touch of a button. By defining a certain ratio as an early warning system, when it exceeds a threshold value, the control system is automatically made available to produce a counteraction immediately.

7.13 OTHER APPLICATIONS

Outlined in the preceding sections were important FM applications and the resulting functional requirements for FM software solutions. In addition to these major challenges, there are a variety of other specialized FM process applications, such as events management, food service management, and fleet management, which can be integrated with CAFM systems. Increasingly used by CAFM systems are visitor management applications with integration to electronic locking systems and conference-room applications with integration to property management and operating-cost management applications. Moreover, well-known features from maintenance helpdesk applications are often used for general service-desk applications to generate requests for office supplies, catering, technical equipment, etc. New applications for integrated systems arise from technological developments such as in mobile systems. For example, office furniture is currently manufactured with imbedded RFID chips (see section 7.7), which work in conjunction with a CAFM system so at any location the users can track inventory for its actual location, and current configurations of doors and exits can be used for viewing emergency escape routes.

Another emerging FM solution consists of the integration of a CAFM system with a professional portfolio management application for managing large inventories of real estate. Here, in addition to maintaining the current inventory documentation (see section 7.2), FM control functions (see section 7.12) have a special importance.

7.14 SUMMARY

All FM application implementations should be subject to full analysis of the costs and the benefits, including those not fully identified above. A comprehensive analysis of the anticipated expenditures for the implementation and their respective cost drivers makes sense in these areas (see chapter 8).

If the top priority is to support FM applications, the detailed processes can then be derived (see chapter 9). The selected FM application software can then be gradually implemented in the areas where the highest potential for benefit exists. The previously referred-to conditions required for the integration of company or building relevant application fields should be identified from the start by selecting an appropriate IT strategy and CAFM application in the framework of the implementation strategy (see chapter 13).

8

ECONOMIC BENEFITS OF A CAFM IMPLEMENTATION

*Peter Prischl, Joachim Hohmann, Stefan Koch, Michael Quadt,
Ted Ritter*

8.1 IS CAFM USEFUL?

8.1.1 PRINCIPAL CONSIDERATIONS

Through a study on successful CAFM projects, GEFMA's CAFM Working Group hoped to identify many candidates that are benefiting from a CAFM implementation (case studies, see appendixes 1-6). There are potential users who question the use and the benefit of CAFM systems, and CAFM dominance at FM exhibitions and conferences is sometimes criticized. Some successful facility managers maintain that they survive with little or no CAFM. All these points beg the question whether Computer Aided Facility Management is worthwhile. Of late, this has led CAFM through a new range of studies, in the IT world and elsewhere, which give more definitive answers.

We know that management frequently analyzes the financial results of CAFM projects more stringently than other IT applications and that prospective CAFM customers frequently encounter questions regarding technology's provable benefits. The reasons for this are various.

- FM and thus CAFM are not part of the core business of many organizations.

- In many countries, CAFM is still not recognized as a distinct software application category, in contrast to ERP, CAD, CRM (Customer Relationship Management), etc.

- The need for CAFM frequently arises at lower levels of organizational hierarchies.

- What the FM responsibilities are (which, in itself, is a valid reason for IT support)? It is difficult to establish holistic concepts in a decentralized system.

- Data for the operation of a CAFM system are often missing or hard to locate in an organization, and the responsibility for the data is unclear.

- When calculating cost, the costs associated with real estate are dispersed across many different cost centers.

On the other hand, we can infer from successful CAFM implementations that no other IT application leads as quickly, as sustainably, and with as little risk to *return on investment (ROI)* (and is, therefore, as profitable) as a well-managed CAFM implementation (Hohmann 2003b). Below, two examples illustrate successful and unsuccessful CAFM projects. Furthermore, they show how applying the ROI model of GEFMA's CAFM Working Group will lead to action options for one's own CAFM implementation (Hohmann 2002 and 2003a).

8.1.2 A TYPICAL UNSUCCESSFUL CAFM PROJECT

The operating company of a large international airport discovers facility management as a holistic management concept for its complex and technically demanding facilities. For the implementation of FM processes, it would like to use a comprehensive and uniform CAFM system. For many years, some processes have already been covered by an established SAP R/3 system; however, this system has so far found no great acceptance with its users. So now each department—maintenance, leasing, infrastructure management and IT—separately initiates CAFM projects and selects CAFM providers to suit its departmental CAFM goals. The combined projected budgets greatly exceed the limits set by top management, which now stops all individual projects and hires a consulting company with industry and integration experience, which analyzes the existing and planned processes in a short study and suggests developing an integrated CAFM concept and a number of suitable providers to choose from.

In the meantime, however, the individual departments have assigned their own advisers to develop separate department solutions, and one has already developed its own software with another airport operator. As a result, the departments reject the holistic solution suggested by top management's consultancy. Consequently, management ignores the project, the budgets are consumed by consulting assignments, new real estate capabilities of the airport go without IT support, and there are interdepartmental disputes over the project.

Now several successful departments begin to introduce small, specialized systems for real estate and facility management functions funded by their own budgets. The IT department finds out that it already has SAP RE (Classic) licensed and, with its resources, introduces this system within a year for the leasing function. However, this system is based on an older SAP version, which soon will need to be replaced (at additional cost). Afterward, another consulting company is assigned to integrate the heterogeneous systems, and the cycle begins again. As a result, after the project has run for approximately five years, the airport has neither a functioning CAFM system nor the structured data necessary to operate such a system. Instead, the cost of a thoughtfully planned CAFM implementation has been spent several times over. The anticipated value added from CAFM never materializes, and several million dollars have been needlessly spent.

The typical reasons for a failure of CAFM implementations can be inferred from this scenario:

- Unclear or nonexistent objectives

- Budget and performance requirements are not aligned

- ■ Top management provides no policy guidelines and no support
- ■ Project is unstructured and overly ambitious

8.1.3 A SUCCESS STORY

A county's building department is responsible for real estate management, new construction and modernization, redevelopment, and operations of approx. Eighty schools and ten administration buildings as well as special real estate properties are in its portfolio. For several years, CAD and tendering software have been successfully implemented. Like everything else in the public domain, the building department must perform existing tasks with fewer personnel, and there is an increased need for detailed and up-to-date real estate information since the introduction of new accounting standards. The need for administrative efficiency leads to the decision to establish the building department as a separate entity.

As these events unfold, the department's leadership recognizes that suitable intelligent tools will be necessary to fulfill future requirements and decides to procure and implement a CAFM system. After a cost estimate, the building department has the appropriations committee approve the CAFM project in the upcoming fiscal year's budget.

A project manager from the department is appointed, and she forms a project team with other colleagues affected by the changes. They research CAFM systems at relevant seminars and exhibitions, and quickly realize that the market is extremely unclear and that the department will probably need to expend a large part of the available budget for data acquisition. After public lobbying by a local CAFM provider, the project team engages an independent CAFM consulting company, which proceeds to a large extent according to the method described in chapter 12. Thus a first step is a market poll for both CAFM and CAD data acquisition providers.

Concurrently the internal FM processes are analyzed and are aligned with the future demands. The workers council, the IT security officer, the IT department, and the controlling department are involved as the requirements are being specified. This requirements profile is used for separate and limited tenders for the CAFM software and the CAD data acquisition. Three bidders make it to each of the two shortlists and are invited to present their products and services with the focus on how they fulfill the requirement profiles.

In accordance with public tender regulations, the vendor selection and contract proposal are submitted to and approved by the responsible political committees. Then the contracted vendors begins working with the project team to implement the requirements. It is extremely helpful that all three parties constantly coordinate their work during all project phases.

In a first trial phase, only one part of the property portfolio is put into the system and only a few selected departmental staff are trained to use the CAFM system. The project team consists of three employees of the building department, two employees of the system supplier, two employees of the CAD data collectors, and the external adviser. After successful final tests of the pilot project, the full rollout is performed with the following application modules:

Technical building management

- Maintenance

- Warranty tracking

- Project management

- HVAC object management

- Document management

- Utilities management

Infrastructural building management

- Space management

- Exterior installations

- Cleaning management

- Graphical object management

Commercial building management

- Job order management

- Cost planning (budget)

- Contract management

- Address administration

The addition of the help and service desks is moved to a third project phase during the next fiscal year.

The overall project wraps up approximately six weeks before the planned deadline within budget. The county administrator can hand the CAFM system over for operation when the building department starts operations as a separate entity. The anticipated savings begin to show in the accounts.

In summary, we can describe the success factors for this project as follows:

- Management set clear goals and milestones to track progress

- Improvement potentials for the CAFM implementation were concretely defined

- Methodical and step-by-step approach supported by an independent external consulting company

- Holistic approach, including data acquisition

- Involvement of all affected persons/departments and functions

- Realistic expectations and project planning

- Reasonable personnel, technical, and financial resources

- Project implementation was seen as a department responsibility involving both suppliers and consultants

8.2 ROI DIMENSIONS

The original ROI approach of GEFMA's CAFM Working Group dealt only with its functional dimension, which is described in section 8.2.3. The practical application of the ROI model has shown that this does not always guarantee economic success. Rather, further "hard" and "soft" factors must be taken into account. These are arranged in further ROI dimensions, creating an altogether three-dimensional ROI model with drivers in each dimension. The three dimensions are as follows:

- Organizational dimension

- Functional dimension

- Power dimension

8.2.1 ROI ORGANIZATIONAL DIMENSION

In the organizational dimension, ROI drivers that form the conditions for CAFM deployment are described:

- *Budget:* Without a certain financial appropriation, even a small CAFM project can hardly succeed. In most cases, the financial framework ranges from approximately 50,000 to 500,000 dollars. This includes the costs of software licenses, implementation support, data migration, training, and consulting. Lower-priced offers frequently fail to meet the desired project aims or result in additional financial charges or project delays.

- *People:* To implement and operate CAFM systems, internal personnel resources must be dedicated. Taking into account the project extent and the size of the respective organization, a minimum of two employees are needed for the introduction phase and 0.5 employees for the operating phase.

- *Expertise:* If the FM and IT departments form a common CAFM project team and if both have extensive expertise in FM processes and IT application systems, CAFM projects can be mastered with internal means. Otherwise it is necessary to seek supplementary expertise through external consulting.

- *Time:* CAFM implementation projects need a similar time frame as other software applications. Typically the timelines range from three to twelve months, depending on the project extent and the milestones marking the project phases. Frequently, the data CAFM requires is missing, which means that additional time for data acquisition is needed.

- *Organization:* The professional organization and the hierarchical integration of a CAFM project crucially contribute to a project's success and is a ROI driver, independent of the power dimension described in the section 8.2.3. Here the CAFM user should pay attention to the provider's methodically developed procedure and organization model, which have been developed according to internationally accepted project management models such as PRINCE2 (NN 2006c).

8.2.2 ROI DRIVER MODEL

8.2.2.1 RETURN ON INVESTMENT

The use of IT in facility management is usually connected with IT investments and must be considered in a quantitative cost-benefit analysis. Projects fail again and again due to the question of the *economic benefit* of a CAFM implementation. To make the use of IT-supported facility management calculable, one must go beyond the pure determination of cost saving. Cost saving is one of several FM goals, but it is not the sole aim. This is also shown by the development and use of modern management concepts like the Balanced Scorecard (Kaplan and Norton 1997), which do not consider cost aspects.

Thus, only a comprehensive analysis of the relationships between an investment and its financial result is meaningful. To measure cost-effectiveness, suitable measured variables are needed, like return on investment (ROI, also called *profitability*; Olfert 2001).

In the following sections, a new profitability model (ROI model) is presented with which the relevant ROI drivers as well as the resulting *priorities for the system introduction* can be determined.

ROI was first introduced by DuPont and later codified in Germany into the KPI system of ZVEI (Central Association of the Electrical Industry) (Wöhe 2002). In its simplest form, ROI can be explained as follows:

$$ROI = \frac{\text{Return}}{\text{Investment}} =$$

$$= \frac{\text{Quantified monetary benefit}}{\text{Investment (= one - time cost) to achieve these benefits}} =$$

$$= \frac{\text{Difference between revenne and cost before and after the investment}}{\text{Investment}}$$

ROI is thus a relative value, expressed as a percentage, for a certain period (typically one year), whereby its constancy is (for the sake of simplicity) assumed over several periods. Therefore, ROI is classified as a *static method* of economic calculation.

8.2.2.2 ECONOMIC VALUE ADDED

When investor expectations are to be factored in, ROI is insufficient as an exclusive deciding factor. The Economic Value Added (EVA), which the American management consulting company Stern Stewart & Co. has developed and popularized (Stewart 1991; Stern 2001) tries to consider *shareholder value*. The profit of a business unit is set in relation to capital costs—both equity and liabilities. Only if profit exceeds the weighted capital costs, an added value is created for the shareholders:

$$EVA = Earnings - (Capital \times Weighted\ Capital\ Costs)$$

The outside capital costs are determined easily and purely through computation without additional assumptions. However, when calculating *equity capital costs*, shareholder expectations for the specific enterprise become a factor. Factors that can be quantified indirectly, such as the comparison to similar enterprises, the comparison with the enterprise itself over the course of time, or the expectations created by the enterprise itself (e.g., on the occasion of an IPO), play a role.

Our ROI model for CAFM uses the EVA as a relative, enterprise-dependent yardstick. The model must be individually adapted to the respective enterprise. Here we introduce a *relative EVA*:

$$EVA = \frac{ROI}{Weighted\ Capital\ Costs}$$

Thus, the relative EVA is also a relative value for a certain period, expressed as a multiple, again simplifying assuming its constancy over several periods.

- A relative EVA of 1 means that the ROI of the CAFM investment concerned is equal to the weighted capital costs of the enterprise. So this EVA *meets* shareholder expectations.

- A relative EVA of >1 *exceeds* shareholder expectations.

- A relative EVA of >0 and <1 delivers an ROI, but does not meet shareholder expectations anymore.

This viewpoint causes the decision makers to put money into investments that exceed past expectations of the shareholders, which are expressed (or should be expressed) in the share price, and so increase shareholder value. This disciplined financial model and analysis also benefits CAFM.

Businesses not publicly listed and public institutions can still use the following analyses. For these, instead of the EVA, other well-known metrics can be used (Olfert 2001).

8.2.2.3 ROI DRIVERS

In the ROI model, drivers are differentiated by the speed with which their effects take hold (one month to five years) and by their contribution to the Economic Value Added (EVA) of a business. The horizontal center line in figure. 8.1 corresponds to an EVA of 1 and the lower delimitation an EVA of 0. The highest ROI is set at an EVA of 3.

The drivers possess different *potential* respective volumes. The potential reflects the monetary value in reference to the enterprise and/or project. In Figure 8.1, the potential is represented with three separate circles.

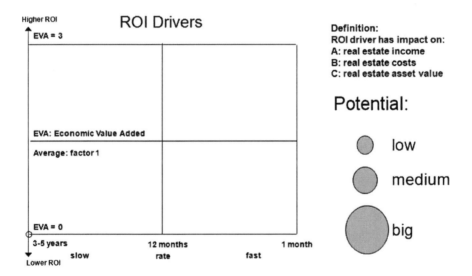

Fig. 8.1: Diagram illustrating ROI drivers

These relationships can be described with an example: vacancy management. By investing an additional 30,000 dollars in a CAFM system, three vacant rooms were identified and subsequently let. As a result, the owner receives a rent income of 15,000 dollars per year. The profitability of the investment, thus the ROI, amounts to 50 percent (in one year). The ROI is high, while the volume (potential) with only 15,000 dollars is small.

ROI drivers can principally be divided into two groups:

- ROI drivers that represent and affect typical FM processes such as contract management, maintenance management, portfolio management, and vacancy management

- ROI drivers that represent process-independent economic potential, such as transparency, standardization, and the contribution to the Corporate Identity (CI)

Preconditions for the classification and evaluation of ROI drivers are a structured database and a suitable IT tool. The database comprises all relevant graphic data (e.g., CAD data and pictures) and alphanumeric data (e.g., facility data or personnel data).

Altogether, seventeen *drivers* were identified by the GEFMA's CAFM Working Group. These are described below in greater detail:

1. Maintenance

   - Damage-induced repair

   - Status-induced maintenance (e.g., if determined values are exceeded)

   - Routine maintenance (e.g., four times a year)

   - Guarantee management

2. Cleaning

   - Cleaning categories

   - Building cleaning, window, exterior, floors, furniture

   - Site and grounds

3. Space utilization

   - Occupancy rate (the number of persons, etc., per surface area)

   - Occupancy intensity (temporal, duration, and frequency)

   - Proportion of traffic area and auxiliary area to directly usable office area

4. Vacancy

   ■ Vacancy ratios related to certain building types and locations, within defined periods (internal and external leasing)

5. Contribution to the Corporate Identity (CI)

   ■ Promotion of the corporate identity

6. Standardization

   ■ Processes (e.g., trouble ticket systems, maintenance, visitor service, space reservation, move management)

   ■ Procurement of products (e.g., furniture, services, material, technical equipment)

   ■ Master data (e.g., building structure, building/space identification system, designation of equipment)

   ■ Contractual relations with partners

7. Transparency

   ■ Concerning real estate resources (space, use, condition, availability)

   ■ Costs

   ■ Contracts (maintenance, leasing, periods)

   ■ Metrics/key ratios/benchmarking

   ■ Visualization

8. Move

   ■ Move planning (graphically, variants)

   ■ Move execution (agency, execution, accounting)

9. Integration (e.g., IT, organizations)

   ■ Process chains are recognized as such

   ■ Processes are substantially accelerated

- Processes can be performed across department borders
- Improved quality
- Improved mutual understanding
- Partner administration
- Promotes IT integration, dismantles expensive interfaces

10. Service Desk

- Centrally accessible for all
- Media independence (telephone, email, intranet)
- Standardized processes

11. Safety and access management

- Technical master data
- Central control possible
- Entrance log

12. Contract management

- Contract administration (renting, leasing, services)
- Rent adjustments (turnover rents, index rents)
- Correspondence
- Standardized service packages (Service Level Agreements)

13. Procurement and outsourcing

- Purchase-order request
- Order
- Incoming goods
- Purchase invoice
- Accounting

14. Tenant/user/service charges

- Account management, debtors, accounts payable

- Energy (electricity, water, sewage)

- Taxes, fees

- Prepayments

15. Sales Support

- Prospective tenant management

- Proposal management

- Customer administration

- Promotion and campaign management

- Evaluations

16. Energy and environmental management

- Integration with building automation (on management level, not on process level)

- Counter management

17. Portfolio management/real estate valuation

- Clustering

- Key ration compilation (e.g., total return)

- Scoring

- Economic analysis

- Risk and sensitivity analysis

The drivers are now entered into the diagram from figure 8.1. Circles representing drivers with a high and/or fast ROI will be located toward the top right quadrant (see figure 8.2).

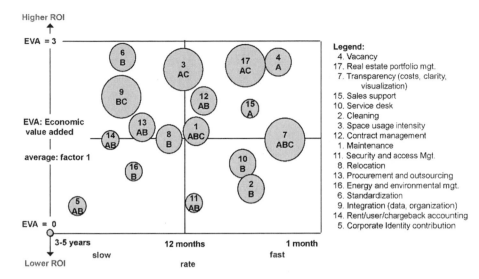

Fig. 8.2: ROI drivers ranked by high ROI and speed of impact

The drivers can be divided, as previously mentioned, into processes and process-independent factors (see figure 8.3). The majority of the processes will be described in detail in chapter 9.

	ROI Driver	FM Processes	Cost Drivers
4	Vacancy	X	
17	Real Estate Portfolio Management	X	
7	Transparency		X
15	Sales Support	X	
10	Servicedesk	X	
2	Cleaning	X	
3	Occupancy / Space Utilization		X
12	Contract Management	X	
1	Maintenance	X	
8	Relocation/Move Management	X	
11	Security	X	
6	Standardization		X
13	Procurement and Sourcing	X	
16	Utilities Management	X	
9	Integration		X
14	Lease Admiministration	X	
5	CI Contribution		X

Fig. 8.3: ROI drivers ordered from highest to lowest according to the expected monetary volume and speed of impact

To prioritize CAFM support of individual processes and factors, it is helpful to classify ROI drivers according to their relevance for a concrete company (see figure 8.3).

It must be pointed out that the weight and relevance of ROI drivers will be different for each company. In some cases, certain drivers will be entirely irrelevant, or new drivers should be introduced. Furthermore, drivers must be examined individually to determine their importance for a specific FM organization. Time plays a significant role in the ROI interpretation. We will call the length of time that is necessary to recoup allocated funds with interest the *ROI period*. Individual ROI drivers can differ by the ROI speed (longer or shorter ROI period), but as a rule the drivers with high ROI speeds are more promising.

The drivers "Vacancy" and "Real Estate Portfolio Management" make up the top group in the majority of situations. The use of IT tools for these processes leads to the highest ROI. IT tools can quickly identify vacancy and data related to certain building types and locations. A real estate portfolio management system enables instant structuring and analysis of investment criteria, valuations, risk management, and risk transformation.

The drivers "Contract Management", "Transparency", "Space Utilization" and "Sales Support" also represent considerable ROI potential. While contract management and sales support are typical FM processes, the other three drivers represent "process-independent ROI potential.". The transparency of real estate resources, including surfaces and uses as well as availability, directly affects user, owner, and operator decisions. The ROI driver "Space Utilization" refers to the number of persons per area unit, to the use intensity (e.g., conference rooms) regarding duration and frequency, or to proportion different space types to each other.

However, the drivers "Standardization" and "Integration" have a high EVA with a somewhat slower conversion speed. Both do not represent a process. Rather, they generally relate to synergizing and standardizing processes, such as the procurement of products, contractual relations to affiliates, or the standardization of master data. Similarly, IT implementation recognizes that integration links processes and substantially accelerates them. Integration also means that processes are performed seamlessly across department borders.

"Move management", "Maintenance", "Procurement and outsourcing," "Lease administration (Tenant/User/Service Charge Accounting)" and "Utilities management" are drivers with ROI periods of one to three years and an EVA of around 1. "Move planning and execution," the supervision of "maintenance" as well as contract management are efficiently accomplished with IT tools. However—and this applies only to positive drivers in the middle area—one should expect more expenditures before these drivers yield profits for the enterprise.

From the perspective of a CAFM team, "Security" and "CI Contribution" represent ROI drivers with little economic potential. Entrance handling is relevant in every business, but contributes only slightly to the ROI. This is also the case for the "Contribution to Corporate Image" driver. Computer-Aided Facility Management benefits a business and its "Corporate Identity" in general, however, the ROI is modest.

8.2.3 THE ROI POWER DIMENSION

Apart from technical and factual reasons and approaches, political feasibility and likelihood of success certainly play a significant role. Can technically well-justified and budgeted projects actually be executed as planned? Which power structures within the organization must be considered?

Power issues can advance or impede the realization of projects:

- Expansion versus reduction of responsibility related to

    - Organizational unit(s) as a whole
    - Management
    - Workforce

- Management versus workers' council/union

- Finance versus technology

- External contractors versus internal personnel

- So-called "holy cows"

    - Difficult to alter responsibilities
    - Difficult to alter processes

- Outside influences
  - Consultants
  - Suppliers
- Extent of management involvement and its concrete interests
- Supporters versus opponents of certain solutions
- Persuasive powers of the persons involved
- Willingness of the persons involved to take risks

When evaluating new potential areas of IT application, all these considerations are of great importance. Power dynamic adds a third dimension to the two-dimensional ROI driver paradigm.

In addition, technical and material results must be critically evaluated regarding their likelihood of success. After such an evaluation, priorities will often change.

8.3 ASSESSMENT OF THE ROI DIMENSION

8.3.1 GENERAL CLASSIFICATION

The classification of the ROI drivers in the ROI diagram in figure 8.1 is conceivable after several approaches.

First, users would arbitrarily arrange the drivers according to their own discretion. This is logical in principle and in practice for a given businesses. Advantages are the small expenditure of time and energy and the clear reflection of the participant's preferences and expectations. The disadvantage is the high probability of error: at this point, the user is too invested to be impartial. The inclusion of an expert, such as an experienced consultant, can greatly increase accuracy.

8.3.1.1 ASSESSMENT AFTER ORGANIZATIONAL DIMENSION

The assessment of the ROI drivers according to the organizational dimension is of both quantitative and strategic nature. According to the basic factual conditions for the CAFM implementation, the classification of ROI drivers is influenced as follows:

- *Budget:* Budget volume can affect the number of the effective drivers and the speed of effect.

- *Workforce:* The availability of employees affects both the speed of effect and the number of drivers that can be considered, and, in particular, the exhaustion of their ROI potential.

- *Expertise :*Existing expertise influences the type of ROI drivers and their speed of effect.

- *Time frame :* This assessment is similar to that of the budget.

- *Organization:* The organization has similar influence on the speed of effect, as well as on the qualitative exhaustion of potential ROI drivers.

However, the crucial point to take from the classification of the organizational dimension is the feasibility of the fulfillment of the minimum requirements of the above-mentioned conditions. In other words: classification according to functional and power dimensions makes sense only if a positive organizational dimension is given.

8.3.1.2 ASSIGNMENT ACCORDING TO FUNCTIONAL DIMENSION

An assignment of the ROI drivers to the ROI diagram, made on the basis of functional criteria, needs to fulfill one of the two following criteria:

- The classification is the result of quantitative analyses, either with monetary or physical quantities.

- The classification is the result of a coordinated interpersonal evaluation—that is, all relevant persons achieve a fully discussed consensus.

In practice, it is difficult to fulfill either criterion. A calculation of physical quantities will be difficult. For a monetary analysis, refer to section 8.3.2.

Also, the interpersonal consensus on such a complex subject must remain theory. However, the authors have successfully tested a similar practicable inception—the Delphi method (see section 8.3.3).

8.3.1.3 ASSIGNMENT ACCORDING TO POWER DIMENSION

The *SWOT* analysis (Strengths, Weaknesses, Opportunities, and Threats, NN 2006a) is a tool of strategic management. In this simple and flexible method, both internal strengths and weaknesses, and external opportunities and threats that affect the scope of the business functions are considered. Using the combined strengths/weakness and opportunities/threats analyses, one can deduce a holistic strategy for the further adjustment of the firm's structures and the development of the business processes. The results are represented in table 8.1 (based on NN 2006a).

The influencing factors described in section 8.2.3 can be organized and evaluated in this format. For each, the ROI driver would be identified through SWOT analysis.

Table 8.1: Overview of the SWOT analysis

SWOT Analysis		Internal Analysis	
		Strengths	**Weaknesses**
E x t e r n a l	**Opportunities**	*S-O strategies:* Pursue new possibilities, which suit the strengths of the business.	*W-O strategies:* Eliminate weaknesses, in order to use new possibilities.
A n a l y s i s	**Threats**	*S-T strategies:* Strengths that can be used to defeat threats.	*W-T strategies:* Develop defenses to prevent existing weaknesses from becoming the targets of threats.

8.3.2 QUANTITATIVE EVALUATION

An accurate evaluation of each driver in its firm-specific development with its ROI would be to make its effect on speed and its absolute result volume or potential using quantitative economic analysis (Olfert 2001). This is possible in principle but extremely complex (Scharer 2002). As the work of Scharer demonstrates, extremely extensive knowhow and time are needed for the employment of practical quantitative analyses. Consequently GEFMA's CAFM Working Group has released a specific guideline on (quantitative) economic benefits of CAFM NN 2010; GEFMA 460).

8.3.3 DELPHI METHOD

The Delphi method is defined as a tightly structured, iterative query of persons and groups within and outside the enterprise involved in CAFM with feedback of the intermediate results. The procedure can be outlined in simple terms:

- The ROI model is explained to all participants.

- Each person arranges the drivers in the model for himself.

- The results of all participants are presented in visual form.

- The participants ask each other how they arrived at that classification, explain their reasons, and then analyze those reasons. The objective is to ask questions, not to argue one's own position.

- Each person then has the opportunity to revise his or her original assessment.

- The next iteration begins.

This procedure can also occur between groups and take on very different forms. It is important that experts are involved but without dominating the group. This method of *iterative expert questioning* is generally known as the Delphi method in the social sciences.

The authors of the model are aware that they have not applied the Delphi method with scientific rigor. About one hundred CAFM experts were involved in the development of the ROI model using the Delphi method. But we do not claim a strict scientific application of methods. We try, however, to initiate scientific work to further validate the ROI driver model.

8.4 IMPLEMENTATION IN PRACTICE

8.4.1 GENERAL APPROACH

As described before, we look at the ROI of CAFM in the following facets or dimensions:

- ROI organizational dimension

- ROI functional dimension

- ROI power dimension

We will now deal with the implementation of the model for the *functional dimension*. We focus on the power dimension in section 8.3.1.3 and describe how the SWOT method is applied. With the organizational dimension, we refer the reader to proven methods of investment planning and budgeting.

8.4.2 APPROACH—ROI FUNCTIONAL DIMENSION

After describing the general idea and the boundary conditions of the ROI view in the previous sections, the question arises now how this model can be made concretely applicable and usable for a user.

The respective user of the ROI method must first answer these questions:

- Are there other important ROI drivers for my circumstances besides those already described?

- Do I associate other potentials to these new or existing drivers?

- How do I value the Economic Value Added (EVA) for the respective drivers in my specific case?

These set elements must now be individually adjusted. Before we pursue this, we consider possible factors of influence. Naturally, these relate to the real estate itself, how the property is used, and on what business areas the business is focused. We would like to focus on and orient ourselves to the business types listed below:

- Commercial

- Corporate

- Residential

- Public service

- Service providers

We assume that within each category very similar conditions prevail. Highly specialized spaces, such as hospitals or airports, are considered separately.

When considering these respective business categories, it is helpful to examine

- Which significant FM processes must be performed for it, and

- Where the weaknesses lie in the current facility management.

In answering the former, one will determine the concrete ROI drivers. Answering the latter will help determine both the potential and the EVA. Follow each step below when doing this:

- *Identify the FM processes:* Determine the essential business processes in the FM area (see chapter 9). Determine and define all FM weaknesses.

- *Determine the concrete application of ROI drivers:* The ROI driver is derived by answering the two previously mentioned questions. The ROI drivers suggested here provide some guidance (see section 8.2). An ROI driver can be both a process, such as maintenance management, and another factor, such as transparency—that is, it adds to ROI drivers beyond the processes. When submitting a solution proposal, organizational obligations are to be omitted at first.

- *Determine the potential of ROI drivers:* Try to determine the potential of individual drivers on the basis of concrete numbers. The controlling function is to furnish the numbers (e.g., for income and costs from leasing and renting or cleaning costs). With these data, the potential of concrete ROI drivers can be specified.

- *Determine the ROI period (speed of effect):* For each driver, determine how quickly it becomes effective. Vacancy management will become effective relatively quickly (high speed of effect). It takes much longer to apply general standardization to entire existing buildings.

- *Estimate EVA:* Estimate the relative Economic Value Added for each individual driver.

- *Place the drivers in the diagram.*

It is important to point out that no one person or department should make these definitions. A small team of employees selected from the different areas of FM and supported by an experienced consultant should decide together.

8.4.3 TWO EXAMPLES

8.4.3.1 CORPORATE BUSINESSES

We want to describe the approach using two examples from the business categories Corporate and Commercial.

First, we identify processes relevant to the respective business category. The relevant, corporate FM operations are shown in figure 8.4. We determine now (in italics) the ROI drivers relevant for corporates:

1. *Maintenance*

2. *Cleaning*

3. *Space utilization*

4. External leasing (vacancy)

5. *Internal leasing (vacancy)*

6. *Contribution to CI*

7. *Standardization*

8. *Transparency (costs, clarity, visualization, etc.)*

9. *Move Management*

10. *Integration (of data processing, of organizations, etc.)*

11. Service desk

12. *Safety and key/lock management*

13. *Contract management*

14. *Procurement and outsourcing*

15. Tenant/user/building charges accounting

16. Marketing: faster, more correctly, more attractively

17. Utilities management

18. Real estate portfolio management

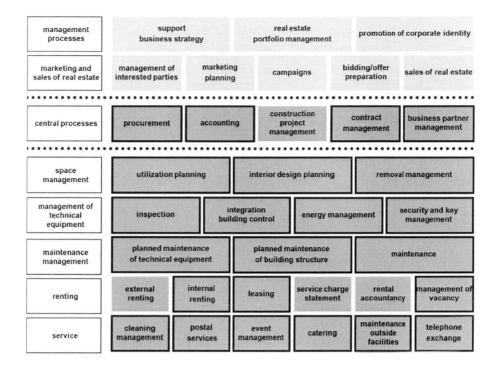

Fig. 8.4: The relevant FM processes of the Corporate business category

In this example, vacancy and lease management is divided again into internal and external, since this entails two different processes. Thus the number of drivers compared to section 8.2.2.3 increases from 17 to 18.

Below, a possible concrete evaluation of a corporation is performed. Some concrete accompanying assumptions could be:

- External leasing is of lesser importance (quantity)

- Churn rate is limited to 20 to 40 percent per year

- Existing buildings have no significant deferred maintenance

The classification of the twelve relevant drivers results in the ROI diagram in figure 8.5.

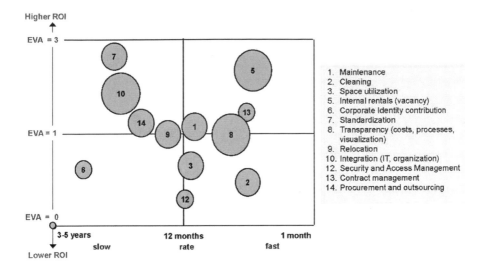

1. Maintenance
2. Cleaning
3. Space utilization
5. Internal rentals (vacancy)
6. Corporate Identity contribution
7. Standardization
8. Transparency (costs, processes, visualization)
9. Relocation
10. Integration (IT, organization)
12. Security and Access Management
13. Contract management
14. Procurement and outsourcing

Fig. 8.5: Relevant ROI drivers of a specific corporate

8.4.3.2 COMMERCIAL BUSINESSES

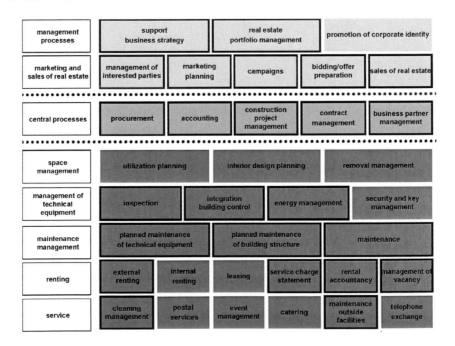

Fig. 8.6: Relevant FM processes for the Commercial business category

In figure 8.6 the FM processes relevant to a Commercial are shown in the framed boxes.

From this we determine the relevant (in italics) ROI drivers:

1. *Maintenance*

2. *Cleaning*

3. *Space utilization*

4. *External leasing (Vacancy)*

5. Internal leasing (Vacancy)

6. Contribution to CI

7. *Standardization*

8. *Transparency (costs, clarity, visualization, etc.)*

9. Move Management

10. *Integration (of data processing, of organizations, etc.)*

11. Service desk

12. Safety and key/lock management

13. *Contract management*

14. *Procurement and outsourcing*

15. *Tenant/user/building charges accounting*

16. *Marketing: faster, more correctly, more attractively*

17. *Utilities management*

18. *Real estate portfolio management*

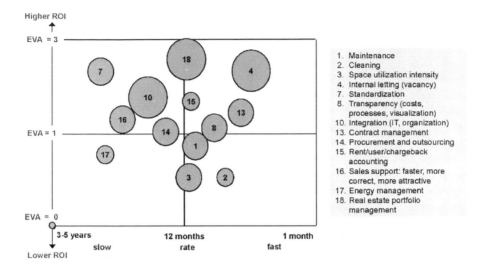

Fig. 8.7: Relevant ROI drivers of a specific Commercial

This is what a concrete evaluation of a Commercial could look like. Definitive conditions could include the following:

■ Renting of lesser priority (quantity)

■ Maintenance and cleaning services are directly furnished by the Commercial

■ No substantial deferred maintenance at existing buildings

The thirteen relevant drivers are classified into the ROI diagram shown in figure 8.7.

8.4.4 CONSEQUENCES OF "ROI DRIVER RANKING" ON FURTHER MEASURES

The available results help to continue the approach. Since there is usually a variety of FM processes in the enterprise, it is valid to separate the wheat from the chaff and concentrate on the really important processes: those that guarantee the desired economic success. Looking back at our two examples, a priority list of ROI drivers would be

- Corporate

  - Vacancy management (internal leasing)
  - Contract management
  - Transparency

- Commercial

  - Vacancy management (external leasing)
  - Contract management
  - Portfolio management

After conducting a SWOT analysis for each driver (see section 8.3.1.3), the priorities can be finally specified.

Then a project can be planned and budgeted. Thereafter the process analysis can begin.

8.5 PRACTICAL EXAMPLE OF ECONOMIC ANALYSIS

8.5.1 A CAFM CASE EXAMINED

The model for determining the cost-effectiveness of CAFM includes seventeen ROI drivers that have been identified as factors that influence profitability. The economic analysis presented in this section applies these ROI drivers to a CAFM system used in everyday life. The following questions were at the center of this investigation:

- Does the CAFM system have the functions required to analyze the ROI drivers?

- Will the results of the analysis offer clear possibilities to increase the profitability of the real estate managed by the system?

- Does the investment in CAFM pay for itself through the expected increased savings and/or yields?

Such an economic analysis of a CAFM implementation presupposes that the system has been in use for several years, has an established database, and has an owner who agrees. The authors found a real estate management unit for the Treptow-Koepenick district administration in Berlin that met these conditions.

As one of the twelve districts in Berlin, it has eighteen office buildings with approximately 800,000 gross square feet and approximately fifty properties with approximately 380,000 gross square feet (youth facilities, senior centers, libraries, music schools, cultural attractions), in total approximately six hundred properties registered in their asset accounting. In 2006, the real estate portfolio expanded by eighty additional schools and libraries. In 1999 CAFM software was procured and a CAFM system was developed over the last years.

In 2005, the district analyzed its CAFM implementation, five years after the system's introduction. The seventeen ROI drivers were combined into nine thematic groups. The available structures and functions of the system were used to extract the necessary data for the ROI driver analysis. The data represented in the figure 8.8 is partially intentionally changed.

8.5.2 TRANSPARENCY AND STANDARDIZATION OF THE OVERALL DATA

The ROI drivers, transparency, and standardization of the overall data were examined as the first ROI group. The analysis yielded the following conclusion concerning the demand for a single database for all properties:

- Navigation is arranged hierarchically and operates intuitively, using both a structural navigation tree and a linked graphic guide.

- The real estate properties, lots, buildings, floors, areas, parking bays, and other resources are uniformly presented (see figure 8.8).

- Detailed information, like room book records, is available for all objects in the system.

- The database is easily expandable, without requiring programming knowledge or an IT expert.

- Any number of attributes can be assigned to an object; only those attributes filled with values are visible for the user.

- The system's access rights administration permits a user specific representation of the data down to attribute level.

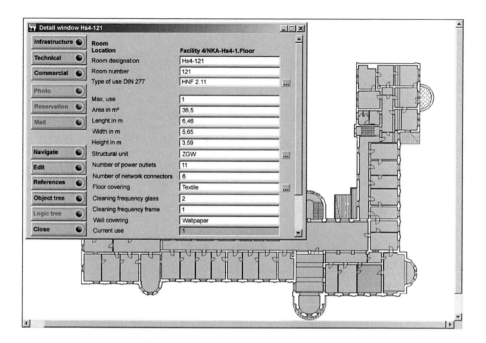

Fig. 8.8: Analysis of transparency and standardization of the overall data

The CAFM system has a bidirectional linkage of alphanumeric with graphic data, which allows one to work with the entries in both alphanumeric and graphic format.

Reports can be customized by the user. This allows queries and overviews of the data in the system, such as key figures for space types and for types of usage or cost centers.

In summary, the analysis results reveal that the CAFM system can supply the necessary functions for transparency and standardization of the overall data. This would never be possible with data in conventional files. This proves a new quality of real estate information but cannot be enumerated directly in monetary benefits.

8.5.3 ANALYSIS OF ALLOCATION, SPACE USAGE, AND VACANCY

The analysis of space usage combines three ROI drivers: allocation, efficiency and vacancy. The system allows analyzing space usage per capita (see figure 8.9).

A search across locations for persons as well as room and telephone numbers is supported.

Tabular and graphic overviews of the space allocation are available. By defining a standard occupancy, an under- and/or over-occupancy can be shown. Vacant workplaces and rooms can be reported.

For the planning and administration of space allocation, a reservation functionality is available (see figure 8.9). This supports allocation overviews as well as the onetime and cyclical reservation of rooms and equipment.

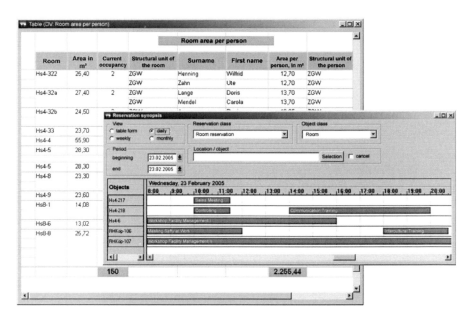

Fig. 8.9: Analysis of allocation-relevant system use

In summary, the analysis shows that the CAFM system has the necessary functions for the determination of allocation, efficiency, and vacancy.

The system user receives meaningful information about the allocation of his real estate. This understanding can be used for space optimization. Due to the heterogeneous nature of their properties, the district could not convert their data into a continuous optimization of space use. This was particularly true for older buildings, in which a high portion of auxiliary space and the fixed walls between the offices caused a lower density of use than found in new buildings.

8.5.4 MOVE PLANNING, SIMULATION, AND EXECUTION

The CAFM system can provide a range of support when considering the ROI driver "Move Planning." This begins with inputting the move simulation and developing as many move variations as desired. The process of move planning, also invariants, can be based on graphs or on tables. The results can be stored and printed for each planning stage. Move planning does not influence the existing data until the move is executed (see figure 8.10).

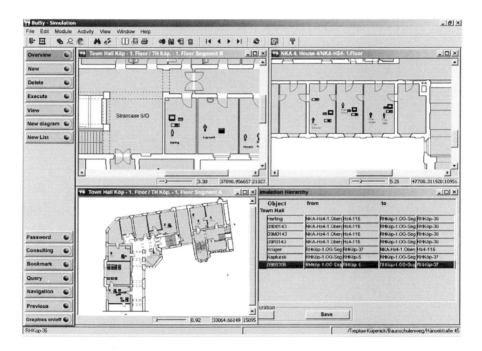

Fig. 8.10: Analysis of move planning-relevant system use

The move planning variant can be used to detail individual steps and can be supplemented with dates as well as with ancillary activities (e.g., necessary renovations, technical adjustments or installations).

During the execution of a move, the CAFM system supports and steers the necessary processes. This includes generating process-specific documents. Simultaneously the database is updated.

The current CAFM system supports these ROI relevant functions for move planning. The easy planning of contingencies, generation of planning documents for meetings, as well as planning and follow-up with dates and costs are substantial advantages over move planning with scissors and paper.

8.5.5 SECURITY AND KEY/LOCK MANAGEMENT

Here the CAFM system primarily supports storage and representation of master data. These include the locking plan, in which the locks and keys of multilevel lock systems are shown. A locking plan gives an overview of the access authorizations available (see figure 8.11).

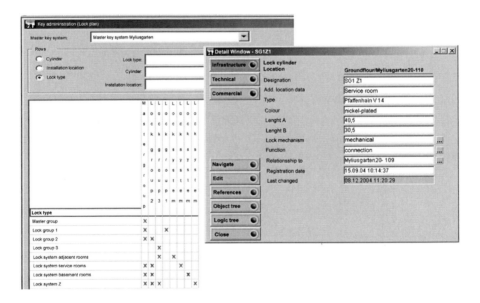

Fig. 8.11: Analysis of security-relevant system use

The key management has a booking system, with which one can evaluate the following:

- Overviews of persons and assigned keys

- Key issuance

- Tracking of time limits for issued keys

- Tracking of lost and recovered keys

- Key return

- Key handling documents

Access logging, which had been identified as an ROI driver, is possible in the CAFM system. The workers' council, however, has not agreed to this so far.

8.5.6 CLEANING MANAGEMENT

The analysis of cleaning management examines the aspects of cleaning the floor, glass surfaces, and the exterior. This details the cleaning requirements such as surface, cleaning type, or cleaning frequency, so that tender specification and contract documents can be generated from the system.

The administrative data breaks down the cleaning contracts into the cost for each kind of cleaning as well as a linkage to the cleaned objects and the contracting parties, and this can be linked with the contract documents, allowing direct access.

Those CAFM system functionalities allow graphic visualization according to the cleaning criteria contained in the data model. So graphic reports can be generated directly for the cleaning personnel, which greatly improves their understanding of the tasks at hand (see figure 8.12).

For winter services, the winter services surfaces and facilities, such as bus stops, and the contracting parties are stored in the system. The linkage to the contracts allows one to view the relevant contract data directly and fast.

One of the great cost-saving aspects of the cleaning management functions is found when providing tender documents. Both the costs of preparing these documents and the cleaning costs themselves have been reduced.

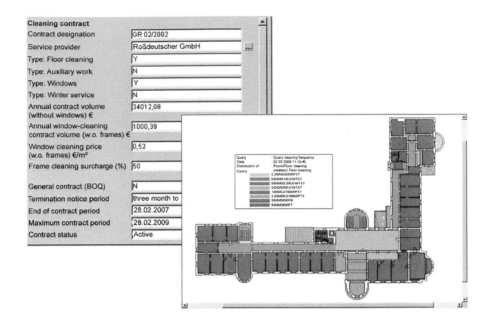

Fig. 8.12: Analysis of cleaning-relevant system use

8.5.7 MAINTENANCE AND INSPECTION OF TECHNICAL INVENTORY

For the building construction office, the existing CAFM data model was expanded in 2005 to the technical inventory. The maintenance module makes it possible to plan and document subject-related and condition-referred maintenance and inspections.

A stored service contract specifies and details maintenance tasks (see figure 8.13). These tasks and maintenance plans form the basis for the administration as well as the execution of a maintenance schedule. The CAFM system contains all data for the management of these processes.

With condition-based maintenance, the individual object conditions are captured and placed into relevant categories (e.g., pollution impact) (see figure 8.13).

The implementation of the CAFM system gives the district building construction office the ability to do systematic scheduling and to monitor standard services. The CAFM system automatically schedules the next required procedure according to the correct interval after conclusion of a maintenance contract. This transparency and support facilitates work in ways that were not possible in the past.

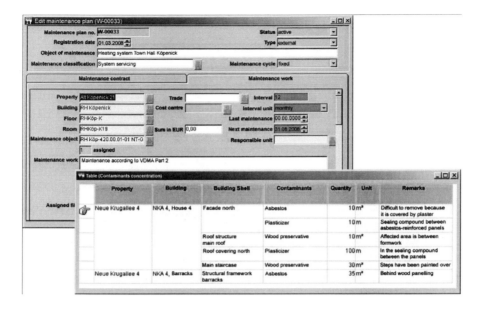

Fig. 8.13: Analysis of maintenance-relevant system use

8.5.8 FAILURE-BASED MAINTENANCE AND HELPDESK

The CAFM system can help entities such as the Treptow-Koepenick district office for building administration handle typical failures and repairs in all areas of real estate and facility management, including IT physical equipment. The following steps support the management of damage-related repair (see figure 8.14):

1. Employee issues fault report

2. Service desk evaluates problem

3. Internal or external maintenance assigned

4. Execution of repair

5. Feedback, cost registration, and completion of the fault correction

At any time, one can compare the existing budget with the actual costs.

The CAFM system will provide alphanumeric and graphic reports on maintenance according to different criteria (type, period, frequency, cause or costs) (see figure 8.14). The responsible persons can provide accordingly for co-workers and their respective needs.

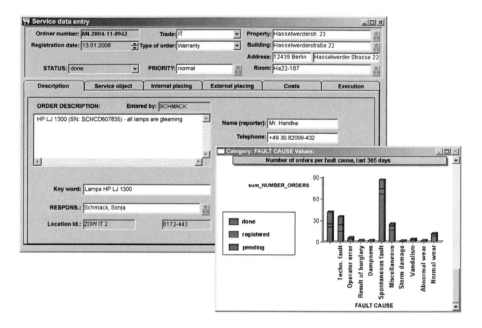

Fig. 8.14: Analysis of breakdown-related maintenance system use

A service desk's systematic collection of data, internal or external assignment of the repair, and monitoring of conditions leads to uniform maintenance procedures. The management of dates and procedures makes maintenance substantially more reliable and thorough. The system support of these coordinated tasks clearly increases the number of maintenance procedures handled by the respective service departments.

8.5.9 BUILDING SERVICE CHARGES FOR TENANTS AND USERS

The CAFM system analyzed includes building service charges (ancillary cost) accounting. These accounts provide for each tenant's annual service charges based on consumption and costs (see figure 8.15).

Cost information is defined and structured by infrastructure cost objects, cost centers, and cost categories. Utility consumption and costs are entered into the system.

The building service chargeback calculation is performed based on lease contract provisions and allocation indicators defined in the system. Various evaluations make it possible to represent consumption and cost for each property in a highly comprehensible form.

| Ancillary costs account | | | | 02.03.2008 | | District office Treptow-Kö |

| Period from: 01.01.2007 till 31.12.2007 | | | | page 1 of 2 | | Service unit central mainten |

Account designation: Hänselstr. 45, Psychotherapy_KZ013000051819
Tenant: Hänselstr. 45, Psychotherapy
Address: 12437 Berlin, Hänselstr. 45,
Rented object: Hänselstr. 45

Type of cost	Total costs incurred during billing period in EUR	Type of allocation	Allocation surcharge	Share of anicillary cost in EUR	Advance payments mode in EUR	
II.BV Property tax	3585,78	per m²		472,12	4.740,04	
Remark:						
II.BV Cleaning building	2648,39	Fixed percentage	0,2088	552,98	0,00	
Remark:						
II.BV Cleaning / technical	222,9	per m²		29,35	0,00	
Remark:						
II.BV Heating/hot water sup		directly		1506,21	0,00	
Remark:						
II.BV Waste disposal	2034,71	per m²		267,90	0,00	
Remark:						
II.BV Snow disposal	254,88	per m²		33,56	0,00	
Remark:						

Fig. 8.15: Analysis of ancillary cost-relevant system use

This functionality reduces the work involved to the entry of consumption and cost data. The CAFM system clearly makes this increased efficiency possible. Improved quality and transparency increases customer satisfaction and reduces invoicing disputes.

8.5.10 REAL ESTATE VALUATION / PORTFOLIO MANAGEMENT

To compare the building stock objectively, the objects must be evaluated according to set criteria. The systematic collection of data can assist in the strategic planning of the building maintenance as well as the development of the overall portfolio (see figure 8.16).

The CAFM system analyzed allows one to evaluate the buildings of the Treptow-Koepenick district according to specified valuation standards and to evaluate the criteria systematically in order to plan appropriate measures and to estimate time and budget planning.

In this way, one develops a thorough understanding of the properties' capabilities, and this creates a basis for strategic decisions. For budget planning, one can efficiently identify aspects that retain or add value to properties and adjust real estate planning to meet needs and future uses.

One can evaluate the information distilled from this relationship according to the necessary criteria (e.g., by object, condition, measure, functional security, building element, or time period).

Property	Building	Designation	Current condition	Rating	Current condition date	Functional safety
Neue Krugallee 4	NKA 4, Barrack	Roof in barrack NKA	dirty	3	26.01.2008	100 percent
		Foor in barrack NKA		4	17.01.2008	40 percent
	NKA 4, House 4	Roof covering Town Hall	Holes in floor covering			

Planned action	Planned for (year)	Trade	Expected costs in EUR
Repainting	2009	Painter	600
Repair floor covering	2008	Flooring specialist	1200
Replace loose roof tiles	2008	Roofing specialist	500
Fix affected areas	2008	Joiner	780
Basic cleaning	2007	Building cleaner	1300
Cleaning facade	2007	Building cleaner	400
Remove graffities	2007	Building cleaner	350
Screw down loose edge strips	2006	Janitor	150
			5.280

Fig. 8.16: Analysis of valuation-relevant system use

8.5.11 RESULTS OF COST-BENEFIT ANALYSIS

The CAFM system implemented in the office of the Treptow-Koepenick district of Berlin contains most functions necessary to evaluate the ROI drivers.

Key figures derived from the ROI drivers result in a clear representation of the cost-benefit status of the properties. It is thus possible to assess and compare the economic dimensions of different objects. The CAFM system goes beyond static data, supports alternative views of real estate development, and can be used as a management tool.

CAFM systems not only lend themselves to supporting new functions, but they also transform existing processes and analyses. It is difficult to assess the ways the CAFM system affects the organization's ability to improve its operations. The economic advantages are not always quantifiable monetarily.

Finally, it can be affirmed that implementing the CAFM system clearly contributes to the standardization of data and processes, and thus, for all involved in these processes, it clearly facilitates the completion of management tasks.

8.6 SUMMARY

The question of economic effectiveness of CAFM systems is valid and can be answered with the methods described in this chapter. The same standards as with other IT investments should be applied.

As a rule, the preparation of an IT Business Case (Brugger 2005) is required today. This includes determination and analysis of the costs, recognition and quantification of the benefits, and proof of the realization of savings. A modern IT Business Case frequently requires the methods described in this chapter, such as NPV (Net Present Value), IRR (Internal Rate of Return), or MIRR (Modified Internal Rate of Return) in addition to static methods such as ROI (see also NN 2010).

Since these concepts are not CAFM-specific, they are not explained in this book. Nevertheless, an IT Business Case for a CAFM investment will most often bring above-average results if the implementation strategies described in chapters 12 and 13 are employed.

9

FM BUSINESS PROCESSES AND THEIR IT IMPLEMENTATION

Kevin Janus

9.1 WHAT IS A PROCESS?

A process is a series of actions, changes, or functions bringing about a result. It is the method by which an objective is achieved. When you think about it, everything runs via a process. Take, for example, something as simple as baking cookies. The reason it is simple is because it is a clearly documented, well thought out process or actually a series of subprocesses that allow for the desired result.

To complete this task, certain steps and conditions must be met. First you must identify the needed ingredients in the required amounts. Then the oven must be preheated to the correct temperature. The ingredients must be mixed in the proper order. Then the dough must be baked for the proper amount of time. If all goes well, you have a delicious result. Those of us who have tried to bake cookies know the importance of following the recipe (process) to get the desired result.

9.2 FACILITY MANAGEMENT PROCESS

Facility management is made up a hundreds of processes and sub-processes. They can be as simple as changing a light bulb to as complicated as annual budgeting. Some typical FM processes include the following:

- Preventative maintenance

- On-demand maintenance

- Lease management

- Move management

- Renovations

- Budgeting

- CAD work

Although facility processes vary by type of organization, for the purposes of our discussion we will speak in some general terms. When analyzing facilities processes, you must first look at the overall organizational goals and then evaluate if the facility processes support them. Once you have determined that the processes do indeed support organizational goals, you need to look at the existing resources and their alignment to accomplishing the process. This information is useful for understanding the relationships among the resources, the departmental organization and structure, and the process flow of facility tasks. A department's organization should be aligned with the primary processes and primary workflows of each group.

You should then look at the organization by identifying the primary processes, the workflow for each process, the level of effort for each workflow item, the task flow for each workflow item, and the information flow for each task. Each of these steps is described below.

9.3 PRIMARY PROCESSES

The primary processes are organized into two areas: one for each of the departmental groups and one for processes that all groups participate in (departmental processes).

The primary processes are organized according to departmental groupings. They are then analyzed by developing work, task, and information flows.

Discrepancies between the primary process diagram and the organization chart may indicate inefficiencies in the management of the tasks.

9.3.1 PRIMARY PROCESS FOR ONE GROUP

A primary process represents a complete task or an area of responsibility. Typically, a single person is responsible for an entire process and that process may contain one or more tasks. A task should not be split between two processes.

Each group should then be analyzed separately and then analyzed as a subset of the whole department. The primary processes for the equipment team are as follows:

- Manage existing equipment

- Manage existing vendor

- Service escalation.

- Evaluate new technologies and equipment

- Liaise with commercial sales

- Manage facilities rollouts and special projects

9.3.2 WORKFLOW FOR ONE GROUP

The workflow for each of the primary processes is generated by defining the major tasks required to accomplish the primary process. Each of the workflow items (see figure 9.1) defines a complete set of tasks and may or may not indicate a change in resources—personnel, systems, or both.

They may delineate contractual obligations such as an outsourced function. They can also denote a boundary for information exchange and

separate the areas of responsibility; as in the case when two or more people are responsible for accomplishing the same goal.

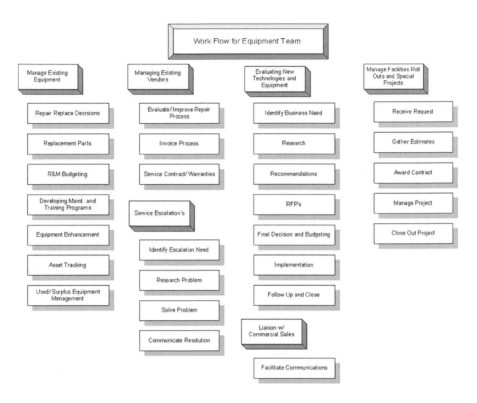

Fig. 9.1: Workflow diagram example for one departmental group

9.4 TASK FLOW FOR ONE PROCESS

The task flow describes in detail the steps for completion of a workflow
task. While it does not usually describe every minor task, it does describe
all decision points and delineates the systems and information required
to accomplish each step.

Each step defines a single operation that is defined as a decision, a
process, an action, or an exchange of information. The task-flow diagram
indicates a change in ownership within the group, within a department,
and/or between departments.

The task-flow diagram (see figure 9.2) has distinct starting and ending indicators for all processes. It indicates all exchanges of information. The task-flow diagram is used to define the information flow and the resource requirements.

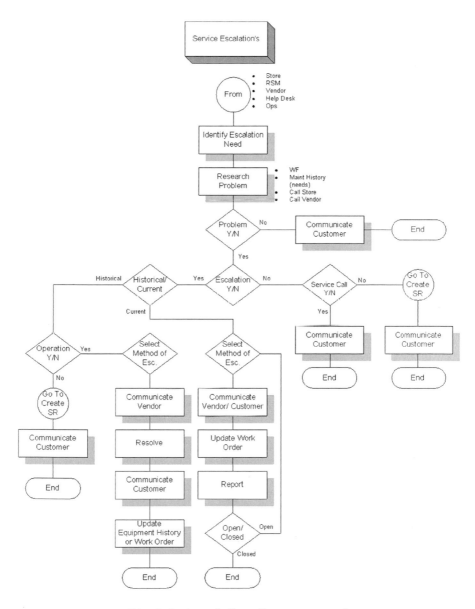

Fig. 9.2: A task-flow diagram example

9.5 INFORMATION FLOW FOR ONE PROCESS

The information-flow diagram (see figure 9.3) indicates all systems, points of information exchange, the format of the information, and references to sample documents.

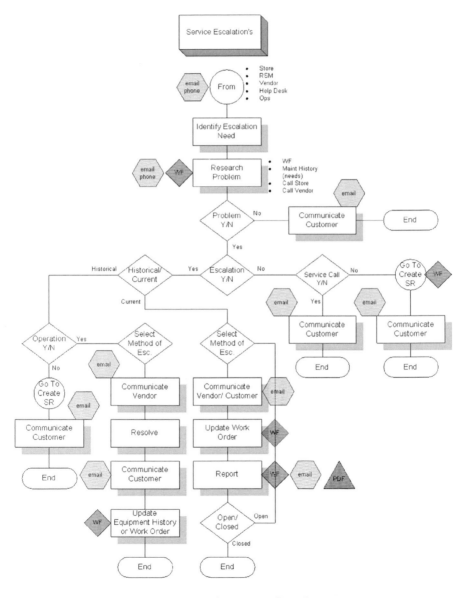

Fig. 9.3: An information-flow diagram

This diagram is used to analyze the existing systems and the efficiencies of information exchange. It also highlights potential bottlenecks from within groups, between groups, and between departments.

9.6. PERFORM THE ANALYSIS

The analysis balances organizational resources (organizational chart), the technical resources (information flow), the processes (work and task flows), the level of effort, and new technology, with the business objectives to define new processes.

This analysis produces two specifications:

- Identify business processes
- Identify required tools

The specifications for the processes and tools are developed with the inherent capability to produce key performance indicators (KPIs), simply by using the tools (system) to perform the tasks described in the processes. These KPI metrics are defined by applying process-improvement techniques like Measure-Analyze-Improve-Control, or Six Sigma (Pyzdek and Keller 2009).

The key to the integration of FM processes is to make sure the processes are sound and only then to look for ways that the automation can improve the execution of the optimized processes. If not, you have efficient, but poor processes that negate the value of automation. This is something that must be closely monitored to make sure you do not become enamored with automation. The key is to support sound, validated processes (Tsai 2003).

9.7 SUMMARY

Facility processes that are properly aligned to the overall organizational goals will, if supported properly with staff and proper task management, make for a more successful FM department. Once clearly understood, processes can then be considered and analyzed to determine if automation will improve the efficiency of task and process completion.

10

DATA TRANSFER AND DATA EXCHANGE FOR CAFM

Marko Opić, Stefan Koch, Eberhard Laepple, Alexander Maier, Michael May

10.1 THE IMPORTANCE OF THE DATABASE FOR A CAFM SYSTEM

Facility management depends on reliable information to successfully operate. *Information management* provides the supply of this information in the correct content, sufficient extent and detail, necessary format, and at the right time and place. The needed information for FM predominantly serves conception and planning, support of decision-making processes, problem solving, task completion, and controlling.

The fundamental task of CAFM software is the assumption, administration, and evaluation of all data, which is necessary during the entire building life cycle of a facility, in order to support and direct FM processes efficiently (NN 2007b). A structured, current, and consistent database is thus a precondition for any facility management program. Since a digital database becomes the basis of a useful CAFM system, without data, there can be no CAFM.

If there is no data, incomplete data, or outdated data, the failure of a CAFM system implementation is inevitable. The collection of FM data is one of the largest challenges during the implementation of a CAFM system. There are a number of different techniques and aids, whose employment must be examined and planned. In particular, one must evaluate the digital data already available (e.g., space and inventory lists in spreadsheet format, floor plans in CAD, etc.) and whether this information is current and can be transferred into the CAFM system. Depending on the availability of current and accurate data, the costs of the data integration and collection can often exceed the cost of CAFM software itself. Underestimation or lack of awareness of this expenditure frequently leads to the failure of a CAFM implementation project.

Apart from the pure *collection* of the data, the data *integration* into a CAFM system and/or the access to this data directly from a CAFM system needs to be examined. The primary goal of CAFM is to use the data without further adaptation expenditures. This requires suitable interfaces and rules concerning data structuring. A smooth data transfer is one of the critical selection criteria toward the system choice.

10.2 DATA FORMAT AND DATA STRUCTURING

As previously stated, an accurate inventory survey is a mandatory condition for the structure and successful operation of a CAFM system. A CAFM's main functions include data transfer, maintenance, and reporting of FM-related information, which supports FM processes and decision making.

CAFM systems differ in the way they format the available data. The different views of the facilities in figure 10.1 show the variety of necessary data.

The GEFMA guideline 400 (NN 2007b) differentiates between the following FM data:

- Inventory data

- Process data

  - Order data
  - Condition data
  - Consumption data

- Other data, such as

  - Service listings
  - Commercial data

Inventory data describes a facility's properties and technical components. This includes alphanumeric and graphic data. Inventory data is relevant for space allocation and management or building cleaning. Moves, Add, Change (MAC) require frequent adjustments of this inventory data.

Order data results from the completion of orders for FM (e.g., maintenance, moves, and reservations) and serves as a basis for the planning, execution, tracking, and billing of all activities and achievements resulting from it. Order dates are usually kept for historic tracking.

Condition data describes the present condition (status) of buildings or plants. This includes binary data such as operating conditions as well as messages and warning signals. Status data is dynamic and is relevant for building management and monitoring.

Consumption data shows consumption such as energy or water during a given period. Collection of this data takes place through manual or automatic meter readings by means of building automation or logging systems.

Alphanumeric and graphic data require a closer look. Although both are digital data, the generation of both data types differs fundamentally. Figure 10.2 illustrates a possible classification of the FM data formats based on Richter (2000).

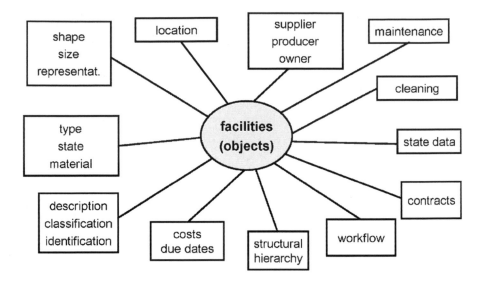

Fig. 10.1: Different views of the facilities

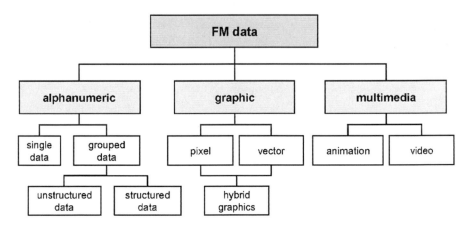

Fig. 10.2: Different FM data types

Alphanumeric single data addresses names, characteristics, values, or attributes. Such data appears in text documents such as letters, contracts, structured data document lists, formatted ASCII files, tables, or catalogs.

Pixel data is the result of digital photography or any data resulting from scanning existing analog documents and plans. They are represented by a matrix of pixels (picture elements) in which each pixel is described by its x/y-position and by its color value. Examples include a scanned floor plan or a photo of a technical plant.

A substantially more compact kind of graphic representation is *vector data* in which graphic elements are mathematically described. A line is described, for example, by its start and its end point. Vector data are produced by CAD or vectorizing software, among other techniques. For the graphic representation, additional data is necessary for line type, width, and color. Similar representations are used for visualizing both 2-D drawings and 3-D models.

Hybrid graphics result if both graphic data types are overlaid. For example, a scanned floor plan could be overlaid by a polyline in vector format. Today, all CAD systems have the ability to process hybrid graphics.

Finally, computer-generated *animations* or video films can appear as FM data. For example, this can be a walk-through of a building, a simulation of a construction process, or an operating instruction for the maintenance of a technical component.

To present FM data, the evaluation of different systems must be structured in an appropriate way. *Layers* are still the most common form for the structuring of CAD drawings and models. The layer technique permits complex drafts to divide into parts whose design information can be overlaid, hidden, frozen, or turned on and off as required. Graphic elements, which are assigned to the same layer information, can be represented together on a single layer. Also, layers can be assigned uniform drawing style attributes. Through the combination and overlay of different layers, particular views of a CAD model are generated and examined. For the furniture and occupant plan, for example, the walls, areas, furniture, and occupants can be visible (see figure 10.3), while the remaining layers are turned off and appear invisible. In addition, layers are important for assigning access rights on selected components of the plan to CAFM user groups.

This technology is also used to distribute work among different persons (e.g., architects, engineers, FMs) and for data exchange between different systems. For example, only parts of a model can be exchanged by means of selected layers. Likewise, the layer technique is used when using hybrid graphics.

trade/craft   layer/foil

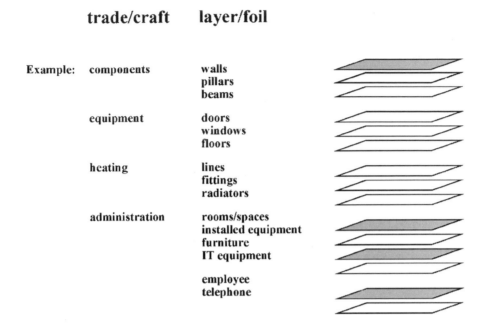

Example: components   walls
                          pillars
                          beams

           equipment   doors
                          windows
                          floors

           heating   lines
                          fittings
                          radiators

           administration rooms/spaces
                          installed equipment
                          furniture
                          IT equipment

                          employee
                          telephone

Fig. 10.3: Structuring of CAD drawings by means of layers

This however has nothing to do with a necessary (hierarchical) modeling of a building. Almost all architectural CAD systems already support this object-oriented modeling and the related exchange formats, such as the Industry Foundation Classes (IFC) based on construction components and their properties (see section 10.6).

Besides the visual data, the alphanumeric FM data also requires a meaningful structure. This data structuring is practically forced by the use of database systems to store and process the data. Structured data is defined here as volume of data with systematic subdivisions (categories) and linkages (Zehnder 1998).

During the considerations of data, different levels are to be differentiated. First there are facts in the material world—for example, "Mr. Miller moves into Office 211." Mr. Miller and Office 211 are components of the physical world. On the second level, the information level, certain questions get clarified regarding the material world. To do so, this must be described and modeled by data, for which terms and content are used, such as words, numbers, or also pictures. These considerations are still completely independent of any hardware and software system.

The lowest level is dedicated to considerations close to these systems. They relate to hard-drive storage and their technical characteristics, such as memory densities and configurations. The next level is the physical data organization. Here sequential and inverted files as well as table organizations are regarded. With the employment of a database system, this task is addressed automatically.

In the center is the logical level, where computer science and user application meet. At this level, the facts of reality (e.g., person or space) are described so that they are understandable for the user and precise enough for subsequent information processing. The result of this design is the *data schema*, which is a structured description of the volume of data. Hereby the structure of the database is specified.

The facility manager, who is tasked with the implementation of a new CAFM system, should be able to set up a *conceptual data schema* and thus a description of the database independent of the actual used database system and any related tools. In most cases this will result in a relational data model, for which various notations were established. The most well-known model is the Entity Relationship Model (ERM).

The ERM assumes that the "world" to be modeled consists of definable individual instances of items, people, terms, etc., and that between these entities, relationships exist. These entities and relationships have certain characteristics (attributes).

The modeling and/or structuring proceeds as follows (see section 3.3):

- Selection of all characteristics/attributes to be recorded in the database

- Definition of the entities

- Definition of the relationships

- Definition of the hierarchy and multiplicity of relationships

Thus every concrete entity is clearly characterized by the values of all of its attributes. Similarly each concrete relationship is defined by the related entities and relations attributes involved.

Frequently not all attributes are needed to specify an entity unambiguously. The combinations of the necessary attributes are called *keys*. The keys are likewise a part of the data schema.

The integration of *alphanumeric data*, already present in machine-readable form, is usually not critical. Examples include building data that is already captured in a database or spreadsheet program. Data exchange with the CAFM system in this case takes place either off-line (e.g., ASCII) or through an online interface (e.g., SQL, ODBC, JDBC).

Alphanumeric data that exists only on paper must typically be newly captured to be used in a CAFM system. In selected cases, the use of an optical character recognition (OCR) system can be utilized. However, this depends on the quality of the source documents.

The larger challenge lies in the collection of *graphic data*. For new buildings, these graphic documents, generated by the architect or planner, often already exist in digital format (see section 10.3.5). In this case, the building can be modeled according to appropriate guidelines and structures. However, clear structures, such as *CAD standards*, are not always established or adhered to. In this case, significant adaptation expenditures are required.

The real problem arises with existing buildings in which free modeling of the building structure is not possible. Using the isometric digital facility survey (see section 10.3), the digital building model can be aligned with the actual building to a certain degree of detail and accuracy. Only then can facility management supply the desired correct results. The extent to which existing plans (e.g., hard paper copy, transparency, microfilm, etc.) can be used depends both on the condition of these documents and on their integrity and accuracy.

10.3 DATA TRANSFER FOR CAFM

CAFM data can be divided into alphanumeric and graphic information. While graphic data is usually present in the form of technical and building plans or models in CAD, alphanumeric data comes from different IT systems and is often in the form of paper documentations. A third category is external documents of any kind, which provide further description of buildings and plants. This includes contracts, operating instructions, and data sheets, which must be stored in the CAFM system in connection with the related objects. In some instances, these documents contain information that needs to be administered actively by the system, such as guarantee/warranty periods.

10.3.1 LEVEL OF DETAIL AND ASSOCIATED COSTS

In the case of a CAFM implementation, the data transfer often represents the largest cost portion constituting up to 75 percent of the costs of the overall project. Figure 10.4 shows a representative evaluation, based on different-sized facilities and the following assumptions (May and Müller 2002):

- Data mix of one-third of current inventory plans (paper), one-third of control measured inventory plans, and one-third of newly measured inventory plans

- CAD drawings in 2-D of the type FM plan (as-builts at construction documentation level at a scale of 1:100)

- Collection of room data for each space with ten attributes

- Software: Base software, standard number of modules, CAD interface

- Hardware: 50 percent of the hardware costs are assumed since existing computers are also used

This list does not consider costs that usually occur prior to the CAFM implementation (e.g., for the reorganization or the project management) or ongoing operating costs of the CAFM software (e.g., software and data maintenance costs)

The amount of the actual costs for data transfer is determined by different factors. Apart from the volume of data to be captured, the size and number of the facilities (see figure 10.5) and the condition of the original data available has a substantial influence on the total costs. A further driver of cost is the desired level of detail of the data. Contrary to the first two commonly constant factors, the level of detail of data is specified by the requirements to the later CAFM use and can be controlled to some extent. With an increased level of detail, potentially more information can be drawn from the CAFM system, but the cost for data transfer and maintenance will also increase.

It is important therefore to first identify the information, whose representation and processing are deemed appropriate for the new software. For each requirement posed, the use resulting from it must be compared with the necessary *expenditure to maintain* the underlying data. In principle, each system is able to realize any level of detail of data.

However, whoever has erring faith in "the more, the better" will suddenly face a dataset whose maintenance cost stands in glaring contrast to the originally expected efficiency. The system considers the additional data when processing the alphanumeric and diagrams, which can affect the performance of application. "Little is more" should be the principle of the data transfer, especially since a subsequent extension and detailing of object information usually presents no problems. A stable database can be created by concentration on relevant operational information, which can be deepened in resuming phases of the project.

No data should be collected and maintained that is not used regularly in a report by the FM organization.

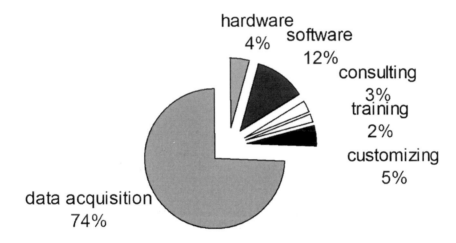

Sample project with 10 workplaces and 500.000 m² gross floor area

Fig. 10.4: High share of the cost of data transfer in a CAFM project

Rough Calculation
(costs in Euro, averaged from 3 software providers)

area in sqm (GBA)	number of workstations	hardware (€)	software (€)	consulting (€)
50.000	2	6.000	20.000	5.000
500.000	10	30.000	80.000	20.000

training (€)	customizing (€)	measurement, CAD drawings (€)	equipment data (€)	total (€)
4.000	8.000	50.000	20.000	**113.000**
12.000	32.000	400.000	100.000	**674.000**

Fig. 10.5: Sample cost allocation in a CAFM implementation

10.3.2 COLLECTION OF FLOOR PLANS

The quality of the facility management data before the implementation of CAFM is very similar for both private enterprises and public entities. A multiplicity of different data pools that contain no structured organization usually exist, and therefore no sufficient overview can prevail. The information potential of archived documentation cannot be underestimated, even if the data are not completely up-to-date.

To convert the mix of paper and digital documentation of different quality and topicality in as economical a way as possible to current and accurate inventory data, the four-phase model in figure 10.6 has achieved satisfactory results (Müller 2003).

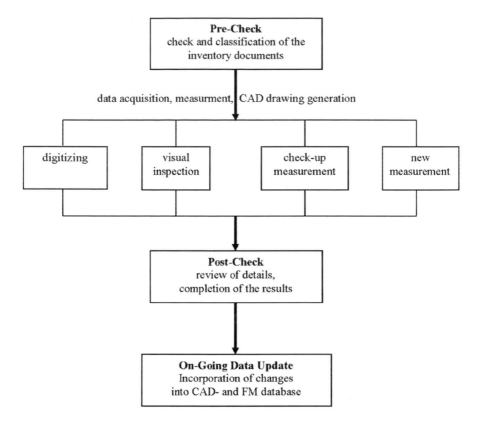

Fig. 10.6: Procedure during the collection of building floor plans

10.3.2.1 PRECHECK

As the first phase, the precheck is an extraordinarily important basis for an economical data transfer. In cooperation with owner representatives and with knowledgeable about the building or users, the service provider collecting the information examines and classifies the existing paper plans. Table 10.1 shows the possible result of a precheck.

Table 10.1: Exemplary result of a precheck

Object	Gross Square Feet	Documents	Measure
Building 1	135,500	Floor plans good and up-to-date	Digitization of inventory plans without walk-through
Building 2	489,000	Floor plans sufficient, not completely up-to-date, some building conversions	Building walk-through (inspection) with control measurements
Building 3	161,300	No current floor plans available	New area measurements with normal accuracy required
Building...	...	...	...

The precheck phase can take up to two days for an object that is about 1 million gross square feet.

10.3.2.2 DATA TRANSFER AND CAD PROCESSING

One method for obtaining current CAD plans is the *digitization of* existing paper plans. Different procedures can be employed, which are described briefly in the following.

During the conversion of paper inventory plans into CAD files, building plans are completely redrawn in CAD by draftsmen on the basis of the dimensioning. This very extensive procedure is necessary whenever the physical quality of the available inventory documentation does not permit photocopying.

If the paper drawings are in better condition, the *hybrid* method can be applied. The paper plan is scanned and then scaled. The graphic file developed is loaded as background image in the CAD program. Based on these images, the CAD draftsman retraces the drawing on a new layer. Space polylines can be created in this fashion, for example. CAD files generated in such a way usually cannot replace the originals; however, they are sufficient and usable for FM applications.

Depending on the quality and date of the available inventory plans, an additional building walk-through might be necessary in which missing or doubtful measurements can be verified with the help of a modern *total station*. After a visual check, recognized changes are surveyed, document-ed manually in the inventory plans, and transferred later into the CAD file. A control measurement might be recommendable during which, first, the gross building areas are measured by determining the correct outer borders of a building by a total station and then all other measures are verified by use of handheld lasers (Müller 2003).

To provide FM-appropriate evaluations, the documented spaces must be supplemented with further attributes within the CAD system. This would be the use of areas according to a specific space measurement stan-dard (NN 2008a). The allocation of space attributes is made by *space poly-lines*, thus closed continuous lines, which are drawn around each space. In 3-D building models, space polyhedrals are used instead. Depending on the selected CAD software, information can be assigned to a space (e.g., block attributes in AutoCAD or space properties in ArchiCAD). Some of the space measurement standards and/or guidelines that are in use for space categorization are as follows:

- BOMA, IFMA (NN 2008a)

- OSCRE

- DIN 277 (NN 2005a)

10.3.2.3 POST-CHECK

In a third phase, the post-check, questions and problems arising from the second phase are clarified and include the following:

- Examination of the provided plans in coordination with the client

- Integration of missing data (e.g., room numbers or types of use)

- Integration of space polylines that could not be reconciled during the measurement locally

- Clarification of other questions

10.3.2.4 DATA MAINTENANCE DURING OPERATION

The fourth phase is continuous data maintenance. While during initial CAFM implementations immense expenditures are applied to capture and generate accurate inventory documentation, if the data is not maintained, it becomes outdated within a short time. Figure 10.7 gives an example of the high dynamics to which building information and drawings are subject (Milbach 2002). Within the first ten months after successful inventory documentation, 1.9 percent of the BGA (Building Gross Area) geometrical changes took place, which generated high demands on the data maintenance. For current information maintenance, at least two full-time positions are necessary in this example (about 120,000 dollars per year):

A structured organization of data maintenance secures the investments for data transfer. The largest challenge has proven to be the definition of *responsibilities for the data maintenance*. Particularly in large distributed organizations, a variety of units have to be coordinated to generate, modify, and use data. Some service providers within the realm of the data transfer now offer data maintenance for CAFM as a full-fledged service.

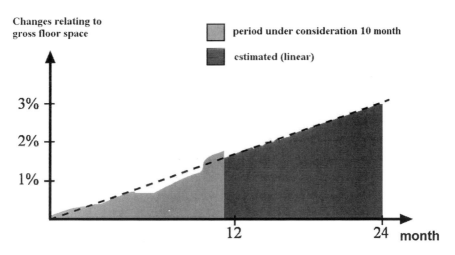

schematic diagram
consideration 2001 - 2002: 147 buildings between 25 and 70.000 square meters gross floor space
period under consideration 10 month

Fig. 10.7: Rising expenditure for maintaining building data

10.3.3 COLLECTION OF ROOM AND EQUIPMENT DATA

It is advisable to first provide a *building data model* in which the building-referred data is represented conceptually in a unified format. The structure of the objects and object data should correspond, if possible, to the structural conditions of the building and the technical equipment it contains. In addition, individual objects should be represented in relation to their location to the building and its units. Particularly within the range of technical equipment, a suitable building-wide code, which covers the entire volume of data, proves indispensable. The extent of such a *code system* (Essig 2002) is frequently underestimated. This system makes it possible to provide a clear identification of an object within its hierarchical object structure (equipment/unit identification) and also indicates where an object is located (location code). Figure 10.8 and 10.9 clarify this connection. Both codes in combination provide the unique identification of an entity within the facility.

This part of the data transfer relies on database or database-like systems to be able to automate the transfer of the data into the CAFM software. In tables (e.g., by means of Excel), captured data can be easily and quickly imported into a CAFM software, which is not possible with manual data input. During the study of the existing IT environment, very different *data sources* are found, which can serve for the provision of information. If these sources are not linked through interfaces to the CAFM software, they can be disconnected after implementation of the system (see section 10.3).

If these data sources need to be converted into a usable data format, integrated export functions of the appropriate software can be used in many cases. The experience of more than one hundred data transfer projects proved that there is no project in which the same data is captured, even though the tasks are the same.

The following premises remain fundamental:

- Only capture the data needed to fulfill certain FM tasks.

- No reserve or additional data should be captured.

Therefore, the data to be acquired or captured and to the level of detail needs to be defined on a case-by-case basis.

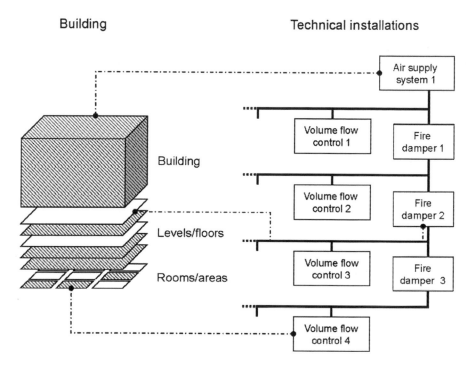

Fig. 10.8: Structure of the technical building equipment related to the building structure

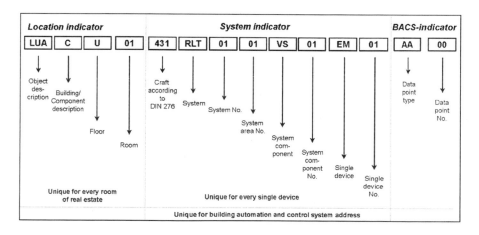

Fig. 10.9: Example of an object identification code

10.3.4 COLLECTION OF EXTERNAL DOCUMENTS

Besides the fundamental building data, the *inventory documentation* plays a vital role during initial data capture. If the CAFM software should be able to administer references to external drawings, contracts, operating instructions, or the like, then this data must be available during implementation of the system. To make this as fast and efficient as possible, the integration of external files needs to be structured following a uniform system.

For example, it is meaningful to name technical documents related to work instructions after the associated technical piece of equipment. The user of the CAFM software can establish automated procedures and linkages of the particular entity with the appropriate documents. Data that the CAFM system actively administers, such as contract data and expiration periods, are captured just like alphanumeric data and are assigned to the appropriate objects.

10.3.5 NEW FACILITY PLANNING IN ACCORDANCE WITH FM

While data capture for CAFM represents an enormous organizational and financial expenditure for existing buildings, substantial cost savings can be achieved during planning of new buildings. In particular, at the beginning of a new building project, decisions can be made for an economic and future-oriented use of the facility. The objectives for the whole building life cycle can be set during the conception and planning phase, and appropriate requirements for a CAFM system can be derived. During this crucial phase, the requirements of the facilities' operation should be considered and reflected in the building and its equipment design. However, the basic conditions for the future use of a facility rarely receive the necessary attention, though the starting situation after planning is favorable, because up-to-date and well-documented data is available at this point.

It is a matter of organization to obtain data immediately and input it into the CAFM system at the end of planning for a building project. As figure 10.10 shows, the planning process and the data transfer should run in parallel; however, the following preconditions must be fulfilled:

■ *Requirement specification for the documentation obligations of all project participants:* In the requirement specification, the rules are uniformly fixed for the production of the inventory documentation for all project participants. It serves as a mandatory guideline for all kinds of documentation, from the structured CAD design over the plant notation through to the file structure of the documents.

■ *Suitable IT tool for the collection of all required data:* Such a tool must allow the structured file storage of all project-specific data, including alphanumeric inventory data, CAD data, and others—preferably on one project server. Here the deployment of replication databases (see figure 10.11) proved favorable because it offers the possibility of a data input separated according to trades and allows examination by architects, planners, and the executing companies.

■ *Legally binding commitment of all project participants to the CAFM compliant data transfer in accordance with the requirement specification:* To bind all project participants to the correct documentation in accordance with the requirement specifications, the appropriate requirements must be integrated in the contract. The project participants must recognize how crucial complete documentation is for the later utilization phase of a building.

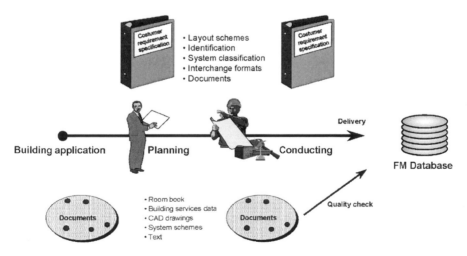

Fig. 10.10: Planning process with parallel data capture and transfer

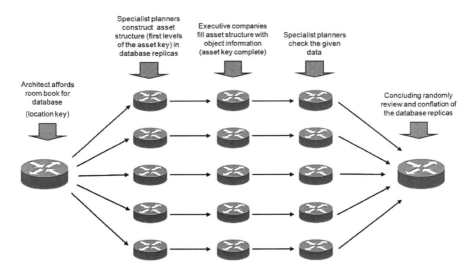

Specialist planners construct asset structure (first levels of the asset key) in database replicas

Executive companies fill asset structure with object information (asset key complete)

Specialist planners check the given data

Architect affords room book for database

(location key)

Concluding randomly review and conflation of the database replicas

Fig. 10.11: Approach during the data transfer by means of replication database

10.4 DATA PREPARATION FOR THE IMPORT INTO CAFM SYSTEMS

10.4.1 CAD AS-BUILTS

Regarding the import of the building plans, common CAFM software supports the DWG/DXF format, although there are significant differences with this function. Within the context of BIM, the advanced IFC formats, which also transfer logical relationships (building model), is increasingly used. The most important questions concerning the efficiency are summarized below:

- Are CAD files and the CAFM database coupled online?

- Does the CAD file need to be imported if changes are made, and/ or does an update function exist?

- Can data be written back from the CAFM database into the CAD file if changes to the space data occur (e.g., type of use or space number)?

Since CAFM software is currently in an advancement stage, no documentation of the status quo is contained in this chapter. We recommend that paying attention during the selection of a CAFM software to the points above and querying it with the software vendors. The selection also depends on the individual requirements of the future users of a CAFM system.

10.4.2 ROOM AND EQUIPMENT DATA

There are two fundamental variants for the storage of the room and equipment data prior to their import into the CAFM system:

1. *Collection in CAD*

   With this procedure, the captured equipment data are attributes to the space polyline in the CAD system. The space polyline receives the same clear identification (unique ID) as the area in the CAFM database. With the import, the CAFM system can assign the geometric data to the appropriate data record. As an alternative approach, complex buildings can be collected and/or transferred with a single file through integration into a building model (e.g., in the IFC format).

   Advantage/disadvantage: There is a single file per building component, in which both the geometry data and the room and equipment data is stored. For large facilities with a small data collection depth for the room and equipment data, this is a proven advantage. The main disadvantage is that the procedure is applicable only for collections with few attributes per area with a limit of about ten attributes.

2. *Collection in a separate table*

   With this procedure, the floor plans and room and equipment data is stored in separate files—CAD and database files. The room and equipment data receive the same space key ID as the space in the CAD file.

   Advantage/disadvantage: This procedure permits a more comfortable input and administration of the data in the database (e.g., Excel, Access) and is suitable for a larger number of attributes.

10.5 QUALITY ASSURANCE AND DATA PREPARATION OF ALPHANUMERIC DATA

10.5.1 GENERAL APPROACH

After the data transfer process is completed, the captured object data is available as mass data in a structured, raw form. Before this data can be imported into a CAFM system, the quality of the available mass data must be addressed. Knowledge of the data quality is an indispensable condition to measure the reliability and integrity of this data for all subsequent steps.

For all FM processes that include a monetary evaluation, data accuracy is an indispensable condition. A comprehensible quality assurance of the captured data can be achieved only if all project participants reach agreement during the data transfer process that

- A quality standard for captured data is introduced, and

- All captured data is checked against this quality standard.

The procedure represented above has proven satisfactorily during large data transfers. The following procedure has also been proven successful:

- Definition of the transfer attributes derived from the requirements of the operator

- Determination of the check mechanics from the required structures and definitions

- Data capture locally by a service company and/or own staff

- Automated control of the data on the basis of check mechanisms

- Necessary correction of the data, including renewed control

- Transfer of the checked data into a structured format, independent of the system

- Necessary transfer of the structured data into the format of the target system

After execution of these steps, it is guaranteed that the data acquired during the collection is reliable with a clearly defined quality standard. In the following sections, some of the details of this approach are outlined.

10.5.2 DEFINITION OF THE REQUIREMENTS

The requirements of a CAFM user determine the width and the depth of necessary data collections. It is a goal of the building owner or operator to generate bills of quantities from the captured data, which form the basis for subsequent placement and completion of orders. On the basis of these requirements, a data model (see figure 10.12) is sketched, including the structures and developments necessary for the planned application.

Trigger object class (structural element)

The table below describes the specific columns of the import file t_structuralelement.txt when used for the class "Trigger object (structural element)"

Column	Attribute	Explanation	Data Type
name	Identification	**Mandatory field**	**Identification** Trigger object
k01	Type of signal	**Mandatory field**	**Catalog** - Fire alarm - Motion detector - Pushbutton detector - Glass-breakage sensor - Glazing - Conveyor detector - Leak detector - Photoelectric barrier - Magnetic contact - Fusible Solder - Flow sensor
k02	Type	**Optional**	**Catalog** - Optical - Thermal - Ionization
k03	Registration number	**Optional**	**Free text** (string)
k04	Trigger control	**Optional**	**Catalog** - Only centrally - Only individually - Centrally and individually

Fig. 10.12: Data model and quality standard for the data transfer

Based on this data model, a data import specification is created that forms the basis for the entire data transfer process. This specification is coordinated with all parties involved. Likewise, based on the data model, a quality assurance software is established to examine the acquired data for its adherence to the specification.

10.5.3 COLLECTION OF DATA ON SITE

The planning and coordination of data transfer is completed by a service company in close coordination with the real estate operator and its customers. The sequence of the data transfer depends on the priorities of the client with consideration of the service provider's capabilities. Usually the acquisition of data is conducted by the staff of the service provider. Staff members of the client are available during the collection process to clarify questions and discrepancies. If required, staff of the operator and/ or its customers can acquire parts of the data in self-direction. In this case, the collection tool used is provided to the appropriate staff at their disposal.

Depending on the volume of data, the collection can take place in different ways. For example, it is possible that the data transfer is through customized Excel tables, DWG/DXF files, or by means of customized collection software.

10.5.4 AUTOMATED CHECK OF DATA

For a check of the data, an *online portal* is provided. The data packets can be loaded, and the data check can be executed (see figure 10.13). The captured data is checked for accuracy, according to the import specification. Here plausibility checks take place as well as data groupings and completing of the data. Any arising error messages and warnings are registered in an issue tracking table and then presented via the online portal to the data collection service provider and the building operator.

The necessary data correction checks are processed until agreement with the specification is reached. Next the acquired data is transferred into a system-independent structured format. The data is then reformatted to fit the selected CAFM system based on the requirements of the operator, or it can be transferred directly. This allows a large number of systems to be supported, and therefore the selection of the system has no influence on the data transfer process.

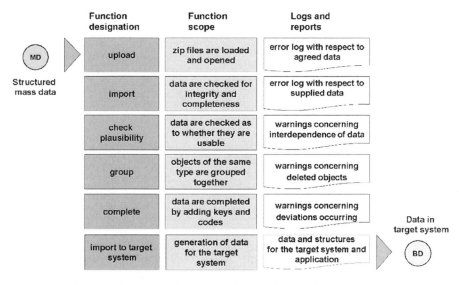

Fig. 10.13: IT-supported examination and processing of captured data

10.5.5 SOFTWARE SOLUTION FOR THE AUTOMATED QUALITY ASSURANCE

The automated quality check between the IT solution for the data transfer and the CAFM system (see figure 10.14) is realized by the data check software.

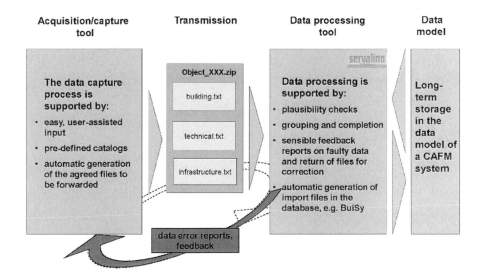

Fig. 10.14: Software solution for the automated checking of the data

In this way, all necessary information related to the real estate is available in a CAFM system in adherence to a predefined quality standard.

10.6 DATA EXCHANGE IN CAFM

10.6.1 GENERAL

CAFM software has traditionally had multiple interfaces to other IT applications within and outside the organization. Therefore, the question of data exchange is of central importance during both the implementation and the operation of CAFM. A variety of data exchange formats must therefore be considered.

Of core importance are the structured tables of the central database of a CAFM software, which include information about the building structure of the administered facility (building model) as well as classical documents with alphanumeric and graphic contents.

10.6.2 APPROACH DURING THE IMPLEMENTATION PHASE

Since the value of data is essentially determined by its topicality, only the information that is needed for the current operation of the CAFM system should be included. The conversion of ten-year-old planning documents for the illustration of the current building makes little or no sense. In this case, it is preferred to newly document and capture the information directly in the format used by the CAFM software. Data that is constantly exchanged (e.g., occupants data) should by connected through automated interfaces.

During a onetime procedure, the data is captured and/or imported in the CAFM system, and in the future it will be updated within this system. Items in this category include space lists, equipment catalogs, inventory lists, maintenance information, and various other documents related to the facilities. A list of all programs used so far in the field of FM including the pertinent data is helpful. On the basis of this list, one decides which data should be disregarded, recaptured, imported once, or connected via an interface in the operating phase. For the onetime import, the techniques described in sections 10.6.4 to 10.6.6 are used. The permanent exchange via interfaces is treated in the following section, whereby the establishment of the interface is associated with the first import during the implementation phase.

10.6.3 APPROACH DURING THE OPERATING PHASE

During the operating phase, data is needed from the outside constantly, where the exchange remains a onetime procedure. This is executed just like the implementation phase. However, regular exchange of information of the same kind should be supported by established interfaces. Before the setup of the interfaces, a list of all data necessary is generated (as in table 10.2) for processes to be supported by the CAFM system and that are currently processed in different IT systems.

Table 10.2: Examples of data available before setting up an interface

Data to be captured	Example 1	Example 2
Description	Cost centers	Drawings
Data type	Table	DXF
System type	ERP	CAD
System	SAP	ArchiCAD
Data maintained in CAFM=1, External system =2, Both=3	2	3
Alignment interval	Monthly	On demand
Priority	Very high	Medium

Now beginning with the highest priority, the appropriate interfaces are established. The applicable techniques for the different data types are described in sections 10.6.4 to 10.6.6.

Redundancies of data exchanged between different systems can hardly be avoided, but there are a few rules for the avoidance of conflicts. The most important rule is that information in the system that the data is not maintained in is read-only accessible. This guarantees that the most current information is based on the last alignment with the determining system. If data is maintained in two systems, only one system at a time should have the change rights of the data. Below are two examples:

■ The costs of maintenance operations are captured regularly in the CAFM system but are evaluated monthly in SAP. The solution here would be a monthly data export of the cost table to SAP with simultaneous denial of access to the data records in the CAFM system to prevent data input before the last actualization date. This alignment can be automated via a batch interface.

■ The floor plans in the DXF format are updated by the architect or engineer and in the FM department. The solution here is that in each case only partial information is exported and/or imported, for which the respective planner is responsible. Thus the architect uses the walls; the MEP engineer updates the plumbing information; and the FM department the furniture. The use of so-called reference technology in CAD editors and/or special DXF filters takes advantage of the different layers.

10.6.4 EXCHANGE OF STRUCTURED TABLES

The focus of information exchange between different data sources is the import and export of data records (rows with several data fields) with or without relations from tables of (relational) databases and spreadsheet applications. Common database systems and/or applications of database systems are MS Access, Oracle, MS-SQL, MySQL, and SAP. The most common spreadsheet application is MS Excel. While Excel usually has no relation between the individual data records, the data records of database tables are interlinked by keys. An exception is the so-called object-oriented databases with variable data structures, which usually have exchange interfaces similar to the relational databases (see section 3.3).

In the simplest case, all data to be exchanged is part of just one table. For this, a table import/export filter is used, which works, for example, with CDF (Comma Delimited Format). The information to be exchanged, like names and telephone numbers, are written in lines separated by special symbols (e.g., comma, semicolon) into a text file and assigned to the appropriate columns of the target table. Data loss arises only if the columns in the target table do not have sufficient length (field length) to capture longer texts. In this case, the target table should be extended accordingly. With each data exchange, it should be possible to set selection filters to export only specific data records.

For the exchange of information of linked tables, their relations must be considered. Thus names and personnel numbers are stored in one table, and personnel numbers and telephone numbers in a second table.

To exchange a name with a pertinent telephone number, the linkage of both tables must be considered through the personnel number (as key). Modern database systems provide tools for the exchange of linked information, such as automated queries.

10.6.5 EXCHANGE OF DOCUMENTS

The exchange of documents is sufficiently understood from daily computer practice. The target system should have an application that can edit the used document in the respective version and format or at least can read and/or print the document. The PDF format (Adobe Systems Incorporated), which can be produced with an appropriate tool, such as Adobe Acrobat, can be read from almost any target application and/or printed with the Adobe Reader.

Each CAFM software should be able to link individual objects, such as space or inventory lists, with arbitrary documents for the purpose of reading and editing. These documents can then be exchanged via email, CD, or an ftp server.

CAD drawings are a special format of documents that are used by CAFM software without an integrated building model (see section 10.6.6). From these files, it is important to filter only the information relevant for a CAFM application. Common CAFM systems provide the respective interfaces such as filters to import graphical data into a CAFM software.

Therefore the structuring of the graphic information into layers and blocks is important. The (binary) DWG format or the basically identical DXF format (ASCII) from Autodesk fulfills this condition. In industrial manufacturing the comparable DGN format (by Bentley) is widely used. Tools for the preparation and the check of this data can simplify the work with these files substantially.

It gets complicated when information in graphical documents is linked with data fields in the CAFM database (e.g., space polylines with area measurements or attributes of a block with inventory number). Special applications exist for the DWG and the DGN format, which generate this linkage. However, usually it is not possible to exchange these linkages between CAFM systems of different manufacturers, although the IFC format offers an alternative (see section 10.6.6).

10.6.6 EXCHANGE OF STRUCTURAL BUILDING DATA

Frequently architects and building departments use architectural CAD systems (CAAD: Computer Aided Architectural Design) or BIM systems, which already contain information related to the building. The CAAD or BIM system structures generate building (information) models from objects (construction units), such as floors, rooms, walls, windows, and doors. Conventional formats such as DWG/DXF or DGN cannot depict these relations.

Therefore the prominent CAAD/BIM manufacturers, together with the building industry, joined forces in the International Alliance for Interoperability (IAI)/buildingSMART and developed the standard Industry Foundation Classes (IFC). Similar to the exchange of relational tables, this standard permits the exchange of all important alphanumeric building information, together with geometrical data. Therefore the extensive process of linking graphic objects within a multitude of design documents with the objects of the database is no longer necessary. Modern CAFM software therefore should have an IFC interface either in its graphical subsystem or directly in the database. In addition, the IFC interface allows the export of data from a CAFM system including geometry to specialized consulting engineers (e.g., for the calculation of the optimal room lighting).

10.7 SUMMARY

The collection of the building floor plans and the room and equipment data often represents the largest amount of cost during the implementation of CAFM.

For this reason it is worthwhile to understand and optimize the methods of the data acquisition and intelligently utilize existing information sources to lower the costs. Priceless knowledge is often stored in plan archives of the enterprises and authorities as well as in various other data sources.

The slogan for each data transfer should be "less is more." Before an expensive building data transfer takes place, the data that should be acquired at each level should be clearly defined. This can be achieved only if the goals pursued with the CAFM implementation are clearly defined and documented in project and process requirement specifications.

11

CAFM SYSTEMS

Stefan Koch, Nicole Lobb, Rita Görze, Michael Marchionini, Michael May, Dirk Ranglack, Geoff Williams

11.1 CAFM SOFTWARE VS. CAFM SYSTEMS

The practical experiences of past years clearly show that a CAFM system is far more than a software component or some modules or functionalities. To designate a CAFM system to one standardized software solution would often be not suitable for every FM need in all situations.

GEFMA guideline 400 (NN 2007b) shows that there is a clear distinction between a CAFM system and CAFM software. With a CAFM *system*, a complex and individually arranged software solution is understood. We can call the individual components of the system the CAFM *software ingredients*.

With these clear definitions, the CAFM user should pay particular attention to the following two points.

■ A CAFM system is as individual as its users. The employment of a CAFM system depends primarily on the focal task of the user. This can lie in a small operational planning project for a building's housekeeping or can be enterprise-wide, as in the case of large projects. One of many goals during the introduction of a CAFM system is to provide all stakeholders with optimal support for their individual tasks.

■ A CAFM system usually consists of several software components (due to the individual requirements and the evolution of the IT landscape). Thus in many cases it is not possible to implement a CAFM system with the components of only one software supplier. The challenge when building a CAFM system is often in the appropriate combination and integration of the necessary CAFM software components of different vendors.

The following example describes the connections between the CAFM system and CAFM software:

In an enterprise that provides services for a large building complex, the FM-relevant processes for the allocation of space and move management, for maintenance, and for the collection of consumption costs and additional expense accounts need to be supported. In particular, both the internal and the external suppliers need to be coordinated with the desired IT solution.

Some software components already in use should be retained. In a planning office, CAD software is used, whereas for the tenant support, a lease management tool is used.

To support the overall tasks, additional software components for space and maintenance management as well as project management are introduced. A person should oversee each of these software components. Usually this is done by an employee of the department that uses the program most intensively.

These five software components are then built up by appropriate interfaces and customizations to become the enterprise's CAFM system. For the external suppliers, the repair-relevant data and procedures in a web-based platform are also made available.

11.2 REQUIREMENTS ON CAFM SYSTEMS

11.2.1 THE PROCESS OF DEFINING REQUIREMENTS

The requirements of CAFM systems are as various as their targeted applications. Though there are individual organizational possibilities, four categories of requirements form the basis for a CAFM system planning and/or a CAFM system extension.

The four requirement categories for CAFM systems:

- Data supply

- Process flow

- Desired reporting

- Systems handling and Graphic User Interface (GUI)

These requirement categories are closely linked in two opposite directions.

In the definition phase, the system requirements should be passed on from the co-workers and merged into the FM processes. Depending on the place of work and the field of application, the requirements are first derived from the system's operating abilities. Subsequently, the required reporting abilities of the system are specified. On this basis, the requirements can be compiled to the FM processes and the FM data.

In the system implementation phase, in which the requirements are transferred into a CAFM system, the requirement categories are considered in the opposite order: The provision of a reliable data is the condition of all further steps for building the system. For this reason, the realization should begin with building the FM data. Only after the conclusion of this phase are the FM processes configured and the reporting possibilities as well as the necessary system access rights established.

For a successful establishment of the requirements of a CAFM system, it is necessary to clarify the necessary steps and interdependencies to all participants in the project (see figure 11.1).

requirement categories of a CAFM system	consideration order at requirement definition	consideration order at requirement implementation	Characteristics of the CAFM system to be defined and implemented
system handling	1	4	Creation of a user interface and access to the system by all FM participants
analyses	2	3	Supporting the creation of sound analyses and reports
process handling	3	2	Guiding the users in implementing their daily FM processes
provision of data	4	1	Provision of a reliable FM relevant database

Fig. 11.1: Structuring the requirements of CAFM systems

If these steps are not taken into consideration, poor investments and project delays could result.

A typical example of a poor procedure during the definition of the requirements of a CAFM system would be if, as the first step, the elaboration of a data model is completed and the data acquisition takes place using this model. Not coordinating the processes or reporting requirements and participants leads inevitably to some of the captured data being too detailed and some necessary data not being captured at all.

The establishment of requirements needs to be understood as an *iterative* process (see figure 11.2). On the basis of a first version of the requirements of the system users (V1 in the first quadrant) and evaluations (V1 in the second quadrant), the first requirement versions are derived concerning the processes and data supply (V1 in the third and fourth quadrant).

These first results are to be analyzed concerning efficiency, costs, and feasibility. This results in restrictions and extensions of the requirements. Hence, the second version concerning data (V2 in the fourth quadrant), processes (V2 in the third quadrant), and evaluations (V2 in the second quadrant) is derived and analyzed again. In this way an iterative approach to the system requirements (V3, V4, ... , Vn) takes place.

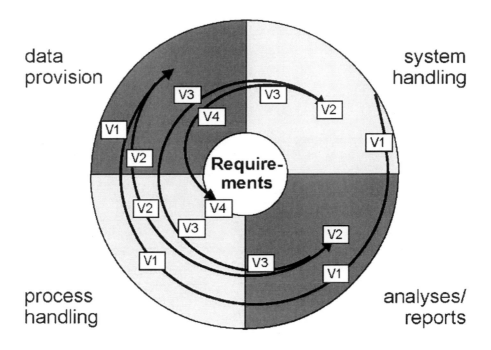

Fig. 11.2: Iterations to define CAFM system requirements

For two reasons, a partial implementation of the solution (n-th version) proves to be adequate.

On the one hand, the complexity of the real estate portfolio and also the number of FM processes significantly influence the system requirements. On the other hand, the complexity of the FM-relevant structures and processes has a significant influence on the definition of requirements. With complexity rising with each of the dependent requirements, the necessary expenditure for their conclusive and clear specification creates a stronger argument for the enterprise sustaining the cost. Therefore, the requirements can hardly be specified to a fastidious CAFM system as a justifiable expenditure before the beginning of each detail of the system implementation.

The process of the requirement definition is thus not only an iterative but, above all, a continuous task in the organization of a CAFM system.

11.2.2 USER INTERFACE REQUIREMENTS

The requirements of a CAFM system's user interface specify the access control logic and the GUI of the system for the different users. Depending on the field of application and place of work, these requirements can be very specific. For the systematic analysis of the requirements an overview of the system users, their tasks and places of work will be helpful (see table 11.1).

Table 11.1: Example requirements of handling a the CAFM system

System User	Tasks	Place of work	Requirements of the System Interface
Service unit Real Estate	Internal lease management	Office in main building, fixed workplace with PC and LAN connection	Efficient access to tenant and lease data, support for new renting, alignment with rental bookkeeping
	Cleaning management	Office in the branch office, fixed workplace with PC and LAN connection	Efficient access to data on the grounds and glass cleaning, winter services, delivery of data for tendering
Site manager	Object and tenant support locally	Onsite office with PC and DSL connection	Access to asset contract and building data, warranty and maintenance overview, insight into the handling of tenant complaints
Technical support and maintenance	Acceptance of trouble reports	Call center, no connection to the CAFM system, web portal, different browsers	Simple user interface with access to tenant data, system interface as an HTML application
External service provider	Realizing planned and unplanned work order	Own office, web portal, different browsers	Integration into job execution, system interface as an HTML application
Caretaker	External lease management	Office in the entrance area	Very simple user interface, access over mobile phone connection in the browser necessary

11.2.3 REPORTING REQUIREMENTS

The report requirements provided by the CAFM system are oriented to both the supported processes and the necessary flexibility of the reporting possibilities.

Usually the reports generated before the introduction of a CAFM system include lists, tables, overviews, and evaluations. These, for the most part, are done manually or in standard office applications such as Excel. The reports that prove to be useful should form the basis of the requirements in a CAFM system.

If reports are not already specified when setting up a CAFM system, flexible reporting possibilities is a crucial requirement. In this case, the requirements that exist are mainly to assist the user in providing unexpected reports easily on his or her own.

The reports provided are in the simplest case filters, which are applied to the characteristics flexibly selected to the FM database. For the user should not need programming knowledge to repeatedly save data for future use, essentially creating reports typical of those they often require.

Flexible provisions of overviews and lists should be available for the user by way of functions for the generation of tables. After the setup and storage of these two-dimensional matrices, these tables should be applicable to all hierarchical levels in the system. Therefore, the same analysis function can be applied, and the average room size per worker can be extracted at the scale of either a floor and or a building.

The most diverse use of the data in a CAFM system requires that reports are available not only in two dimensions but multidimensionally. This means reports can be read and evaluated on the basis of different dimensions (e.g., customer, region, building, repair processes, or time) multidimensionally. This can be done with online analytical processing tools (OLAP), which are characterized by their multidimensionality. If multidimensional data analyses (see section 11.6.2) are a high priority for a planned CAFM system, the OLAP functionalities need to be available to the reporting mechanism.

Numerous reports can be communicated by graphical means. Diagrams, sketches, and layout plans can assist in communicating the visualization requirements.

11.2.4 REQUIREMENTS ON THE PROCESS SUPPORT

Those taking part in a conversion of the FM processes expect a CAFM system that works smoothly and transparently and that is easily supported. To be able to reach these goals, the system must have workflow management capabilities that are able to model and map FM processes.

That means each a process with its different statuses and status transitions must be mapped into a process model (see figure 11.3).

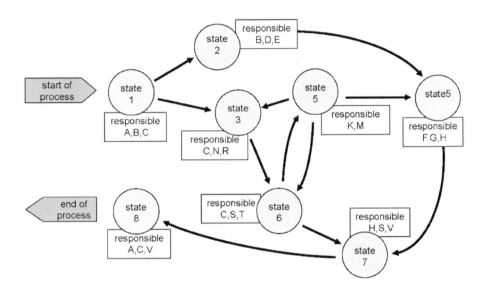

Fig. 11.3: Example of a process model with statuses and status transitions

A system user can transfer a process with a status into another status, if he or she is responsible for the process transition and given the conditions for the status transition. These competencies and conditions must also be found within the model.

In the CAFM system, it must be possible to determine individual processes through the establishment of statuses and status transitions as well as to specify responsibilities by establishing user roles and groups flexibly.

The user administration supports the assignment of roles and groups to the involved persons. Each role and group will receive an individualized view of the process as it relates to their specific involvement in that process.

11.2.5 REQUIREMENTS OF THE DATA SUPPLY

The available CAFM systems rely on data as the basis for IT support of FM processes. For this reason, a CAFM system must be able to make alphanumeric and graphical data and to make documents available.

In a CAFM system, data can be distributed on several software components. With such a distribution of data, it is necessary to determine which software component is the leading one for these data, that is, which component is responsible for data update.

For the supply of alphanumeric data, the structure and the implementation of the internal data model of the CAFM system are crucial. For the structured storage of large datasets, the integration of a database is necessary. The database should be able to illustrate the objects with their attributes, relationships between objects, catalogs, and history.

Since data models are relationally structured in most databases, they are graphically represented using entity-relationship or related diagrams (see figure 11.4).

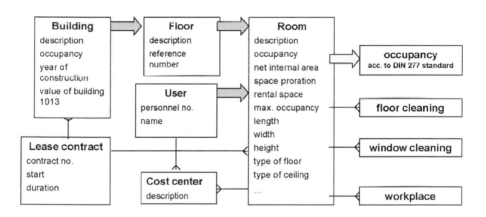

Fig. 11.4: Example of a CAFM data model

Graphic data is illustrated in CAFM systems by means of architecture and flow diagrams. To structure graphic data, layers are usually used (see chapter 10). The management of this data must be secured by a bidirectional exchange between both data types.

For the purpose of data import and export, the CAFM software must have suitable interfaces and/or an API.

11.3 SYSTEM CONCEPTS AND SYSTEM STRUCTURE

Due to the different applications of CAFM systems, there are various individual possibilities of system concepts. The CAFM system concepts available in the industry are very diversified. Figure 11.5 gives an overview of the software components that can be integrated into a CAFM system.

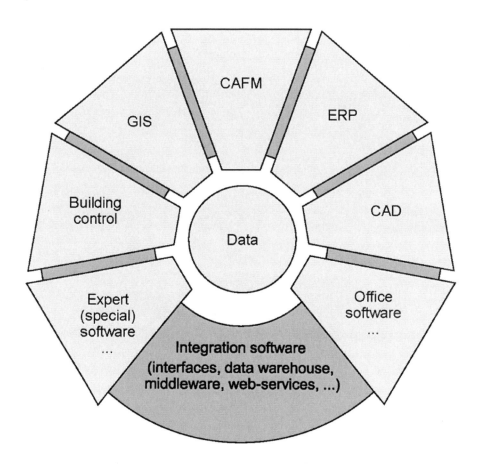

Fig. 11.5: Possible software components of a CAFM system

A CAFM system always accesses data necessary for the task and can consist of one or more software components.

Among the functional base components of a CAFM system we find CAFM, ERP, CAD, GIS, and BMS solutions. Specialized software and standard office tools are also often used as system components.

Integration of software components can be achieved using interfaces, data warehouses, or middleware software, as well as web services (see chapter 3).

In the following sections, prototypical solutions of CAFM systems integrating different software components are presented.

11.4 CAFM SYSTEM CHARACTERISTICS

11.4.1 CAFM SYSTEM BASED ON A CAFM SOFTWARE

For special, functionally aligned CAFM applications, it is possible to employ only one CAFM software (see figure 11.6). In that case, the resultant architecture is characterized by the fact that the relevant FM requirements are covered by several modules contained in the CAFM software.

When selecting a CAFM software, a prospective customer can easily receive information on the available products. Furthermore, he or she can consider the results of CAFM surveys and reviews published in the technical literature (see, e.g., NN 2011).

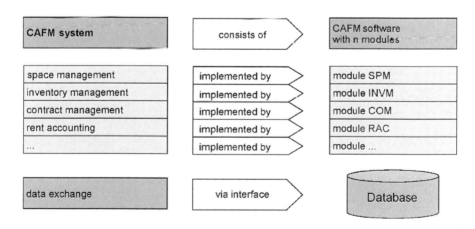

Fig. 11.6: CAFM system on basis of a CAFM software

The disadvantage of this approach is that the FM processes can be customized only as far as they are available in the selected CAFM software.

Historically there are two different architectures for CAFM software. The origin of the first lies in building architecture and CAD. The second is in building management, which usually uses alphanumeric information to a large extent (e.g., room booking).

Both approaches have their own respective values because within CAFM a central role is the ability to manage both graphic and alphanumeric data. Most systems present on the market solve this problem with their internal architectures. Basically there is on one side a graphic modeling tool (e.g., a CAD system or kernel) and on the other side databases.

The architecture that is a suitable basis for FM depends on the purpose for which it will be used. If a complex geometrical representation exists, particular graphic functions or administration of the layer structure are firm components of the functional profile, then the employment of a graphic modeling tool is favorable. However, if process data, the evaluation of processes, or large alphanumeric volumes of data are the center of attention, this can be done without extensive graphic functionality.

11.4.2 CAFM SYSTEM BASED ON SEVERAL CAFM PRODUCTS

It is also possible that a CAFM system would consist of several CAFM software products (see figure 11.7). In particular, with divisions of responsibility between different organizational units during an FM process, such constellations may be found.

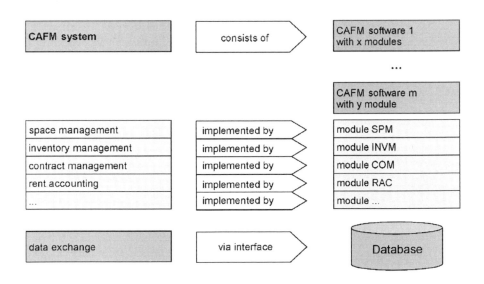

Fig. 11.7: CAFM system based on several CAFM software products

Each organizational unit uses those modules and functions of a CAFM system that best support their respective tasks. A typical example of this is the splitting of tasks into those to be planned by the purchaser and those to be executed by the contractor onsite using, perhaps, mobile devices. An integration of the different databases involved ensures the co-operation of the different CAFM software components.

11.4.3 CAFM SYSTEM BASED ON CAFM AND ERP SOFTWARE

FM processes are commercially charged like all other activities in an organization. For this reason, the integration of an ERP software into a CAFM system is frequently a substantial condition for efficient IT support (see figure 11.8).

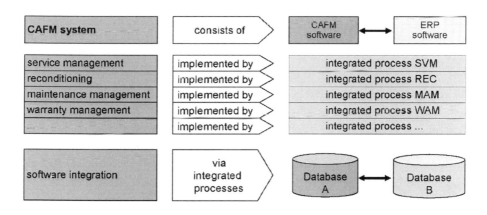

Fig. 11.8: CAFM architecture based on CAFM and ERP software

With this CAFM system approach, the FM processes are no longer realized purely by functionality but by integrated processes. To support an FM process, the interaction of both systems can be achieved by running multiple interfaces.

The ERP system can have data sovereignty concerning accounts payable and debtors, company codes, cost objectives, and cost centers during an FM process. Budgets can be made available for objects and measures, and completed operations will be invoiced.

FM services can be planned, assigned, and managed with the help of the CAFM system. Through an exchange of accounting and technical data between the CAFM and the ERP system, complete process chains are supported. CAFM and ERP systems cooperate in all their tasks, such as generating an offer, placing a work order, or controlling an order performed.

The needs for dealing with subcontractors and the numerous contracting, payment, and approval tasks need to be supported by the CAFM system. This comprises tasks like tendering, specification, and accounting. For purchase order and payment management or the management of consumption (e.g., power), the FM processes contain both technical and commercial components. Consumption costs or accounting costs of service contracts with FM subcontractors are captured and transferred to the CAFM system and to the ERP system.

To minimize the data input cost and also input errors, an interface is usually set up between the CAFM and the ERP system. Over this interface, accounting data from the CAFM system will be transferred into the ERP system for further processing. On the basis of balanced master data regarding users, business partners, commercial data, and/or operator budgets, the invoice data of completed and approved payments are seized and assigned. The payments are released and ordered, and posting records are exchanged between the systems (see figure 11.9).

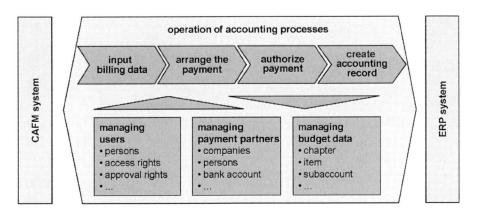

Fig. 11.9: Example of a CAFM system based on CAFM and ERP software

In the CAFM system, these datasets can lead to meaningful conclusions concerning energy and service management of a property. The correct posting of the process costs takes place in the ERP system.

11.4.4 CAFM SYSTEM BASED ON ERP AND CAD SOFTWARE

11.4.4.1 GENERAL CONSIDERATIONS

If one regards the list of processes that a CAFM software should support today and the functions that an ERP system can offer, one will find a substantial set of commonalities.

Nevertheless, an ERP system is not usually considered by FM users as software for their FM processes. The reasons for this are varied. Mainly, this is because of the lack of CAD support, which is expected with CAFM software.

Hence, many companies complement their ERP systems with CAFM software. In the past, a clear demarcation of functionalities was made:

- ERP for finances and controlling

- CAFM for the facility service processes

Some years ago, property management, facility management, and portfolio management were regarded as separate disciplines. These had different requirements for IT support and thus were covered by different software systems. In recent years, a stronger combination of these disciplines and a functional overlap of IT systems had developed. This led to the fact that, some CAFM systems have evolved by extending functionality from their roots in real estate management while ERP systems were extended by to included functionalities for facility and/or real estate management.

These functional overlaps led to the fact that with a parallel operation of ERP and CAFM software, the question of which software is used by which group of users is getting more and more complex (see figure 11.10). To achieve consistency of the processes and data when using distributed functionalities, the number and the complexity of interfaces between the program products increase (see GEFMA 410; NN 2007a).

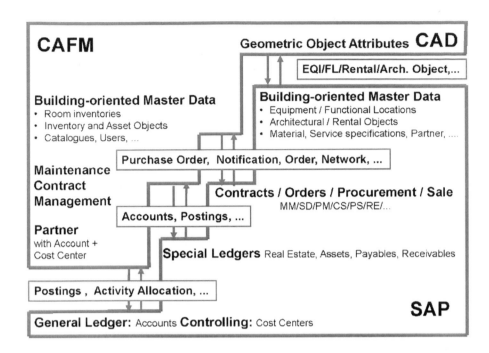

Fig. 11.10: Functional overlaps between SAP and CAFM

Therefore a question arises: to what extent can an ERP system extended by CAD be classified as a CAFM software.

11.4.4.2 CLASSIFICATION IN ACCORDANCE WITH GEFMA 400 AS A CAFM SOFTWARE

Many software products were called CAFM software some years ago, even if they could support only subranges of FM. This led to a very high number of CAFM products and to frustration among the users.

A goal of the employment of CAFM software is to support FM processes (see chapter 9). However, if all FM processes are regarded (e.g., NN 2004b), then there is hardly any software that can support all of the processes.

Therefore, to give to the user the ability to decide whether FM-related software is able to fulfill the criteria of CAFM software, guidelines have been developed. The GEFMA guideline 400 describes the requirements on CAFM software regarding substantial functionalities, the necessary technology, and the ability to be customized.

The functionalities and/or ranges of application fields of CAFM software (NN 2007b) that are particularily valueable include:

- Inventory documentation

- Space management

- Cleaning management

- Utility consumption management

- Move management

- Maintenance management

- Contract management

- Lease management

- Operating cost management

- Controlling

These were described in detail in chapter 7. A further factor for the classification of a software as CAFM software is the technology utilized. Here is a list of the main requirements:

- Software architecture (multiuser capability, multitier architectural model, Internet/intranet ability, etc.)

- Data retention (DBMS connection, object-oriented interpretation of the data, multitenancy capability, etc.)

- Visualization capabilities (clarity, CAD kernel or connection)

- Interfaces (import/export, support of standardized formats, batch or online interfaces)

Finally, the requirements on the customizability of CAFM software are formulated. Here possibilities should be available for functional as well as user-specific customization.

To judge whether a particular software is in accordance with GEFMA 400, the requirements mentioned concerning functionality, technology and customization capability must be met. If a software cannot fulfill all of these requirements, it is not CAFM software by definition; however, it could be a reasonable choice for supporting the organization's FM processes. This applies if within the ranges of FM, in which the user requires support, special functionalities or depth of integration in the user's system landscape is easily possible.

Furthermore, there is also the possibility that several software products can be integrated into a CAFM system. It should be noted, however, that the complexity of such a system needs to remains manageable and maintenance and technical support need to be ensured.

11.4.4.3 TECHNICAL POSSIBILITIES OF A CAD INTEGRATION

Interfaces between graphic systems and ERP systems can be implemented differently. Two fundamental variants are online interfaces and batch (file) interfaces (NN 2007a). If used correctly, both variants have advantages. However, only online interfaces offer the possibility of including the user interactively in information exchange between the systems. This is necessary whenever data cannot be synchronized automatically according to the rules agreed upon in the interface. In the following, an overview of the different kinds of online interfaces is given.

A view of the origin and processing of graphic data permits a division into the following kinds of interfaces:

- Graphics backend
- User interface coupling
- Web graphics

The graphics backend is the place of origin of the graphic information, that is, the CAD workplace. Changes in geometric data are likewise accomplished by CAD.

The user interface coupling offers a linkage at the level of the original user interface of the systems being used.

The web graphics distribute the graphic information to a broad group of users who can easily use the graphic for their tasks without having to possess specific CAD knowledge. The graphics can assist in navigation, selection, or information presentation, where color coding is a useful tool.

Graphics backend. Through backend integration, the connection of a CAD system with the application server of the ERP system is named. Here from of the ERP system can be transferred via an online interface into the CAD system, visualized and also modified if necessary. Over the mechanisms of the respective CAD system (e.g., block attributes or "attached" data), data records from the ERP system are linked with geometry elements. A schematic representation of this process is shown in figure 11.11.

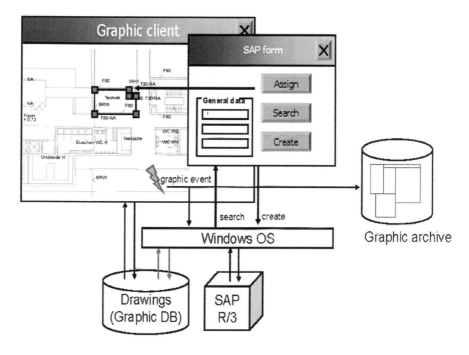

Fig. 11.11: Use of the CAD interface for the processing of ERP data

The major characteristic of this form of interface is that the CAD editor uses its familiar user interface. As a result, the ERP system interface does not interact with the CAD editor. Nevertheless, data in the ERP system can still be worked with. All objects to be transferred to the ERP system need to be uniquely identifiable and machine-readable. For this, the structuring abilities of the CAD systems are used for layers or attributes, for example.

User interface coupling. If the data of the graphic system and those of the ERP system are linked with one another, the transition between the graphical and database interface part of the system, and vice versa, is possible (see figure 11.12).

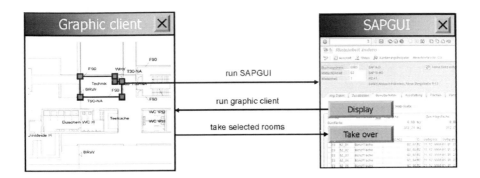

Fig. 11.12: Coupling of different user interfaces

For example, if a data record is called up in the ERP system, which at the same time possesses a graphic representation, then by pressing a button, the graphic system can be started, the corrected drawing can be loaded, and the element looked for can be highlighted. Conversely, after selection of a graphic element, the user interface of the ERP system can be started and the data record queried can be shown.

Conditions for this are the installation of both user interfaces required in the workplace, the access authorization in both systems, and the ability of the editors to serve the different user interfaces. If these conditions are present, both systems are completely functional.

Web graphics. Internet technologies and the separation of software into reusable components permit the creation of applications with a uniform interface, although functionalities are offered by different producers. For an integrated system—consisting of graphic information and processes in the ERP system—this means a graphic is made available in a browser application, which must be suitable for interaction (see figure 11.13). Based on need, this application can be integrated into the user interface of the ERP system; it can be run independently in a web browser, or the browser window can be part of the front end of a web-based (portal) solution.

The result is that the processes of the ERP system can be steered via the graphics system. The user uses the uniform interface of the integrated system, which saves on training costs and increases the acceptance of the software solution.

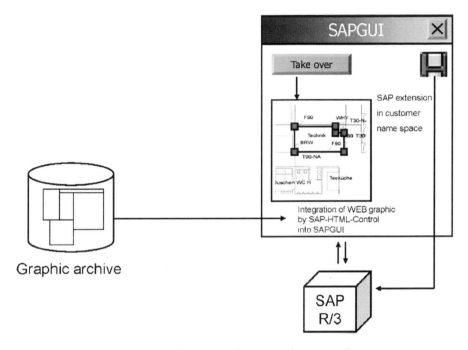

Fig. 11.13: Integration of web graphics into the GUI of an ERP System

The graphic information for such a system is usually provided and updated through backend integration. If the CAD system makes only the graphic information available, it is called a *loose coupling*. If the data of the ERP system is synchronized directly from the CAD system, this is called *close coupling*. The decision to use one rather than the other depends on which user is responsible for the synchronization.

The architecture of such a CAD integration should be developed in a manner that all kinds of coupling can be used both separately and in combination. Such an architecture is shown as an example in figure 11.14. The components that signify possible extensions are dashed.

The central element of this architecture is a web graphics server, which offers a storage medium for the historicized graphic information and also provides the Internet application by making graphic information and ERP information available in the XML format at the same time.

As an option, the archiving of the graphic data can be outsourced into a document management system (DMS). Such a web graphics server can be implemented using, for example, Microsoft Internet Information Services (IIS) or by means of the web application server of the ERP system.

In the case of SAP by remote function calls (RFCs), BAPIs (Business Application Programming Interface) and/or RFC components are called. If the SAP system takes over the role of the leading system and calls the CAD system as service, communication is made via RFC.

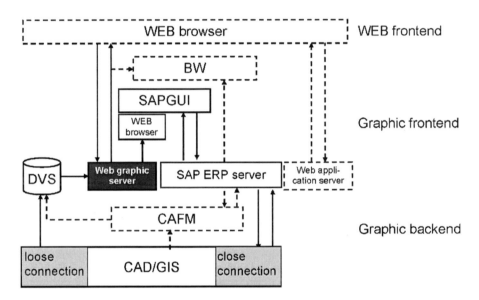

Fig. 11.14: Example of an architecture with optional components

Here in the interface, an RFC destination is implemented, which passes on calls from SAP to the CAD system. The coupling of the CAD systems is realized by Microsoft COM technology. For integrations with the Unix world, web services (see chapter 3) that allow access to the interfaces described above are recommended..

11.4.4.4 AN ERP SYSTEM AS BASIS FOR AN INTEGRATION WITH CAD SYSTEMS

Due to its widespread use in the ERP world, the following considerations are restricted to SAP and its integration with CAD. The remarks made here can also be partly adapted to other ERP systems.

11.4.4.4.1 CAFM FUNCTIONS IN STANDARD SAP

In this section, a general understanding of SAP's approach to facility and real estate management is given.

From an economical view, real estate is resources, such as materials, or a work force in construction and services. It is procured, sold, or torn down, causing utilization costs and generating proceeds. Figure 11.15 tries to express this life cycle from an economical view. The corresponding explanations refer to available SAP functionalities in the individual periods of the life cycle of the real estate.

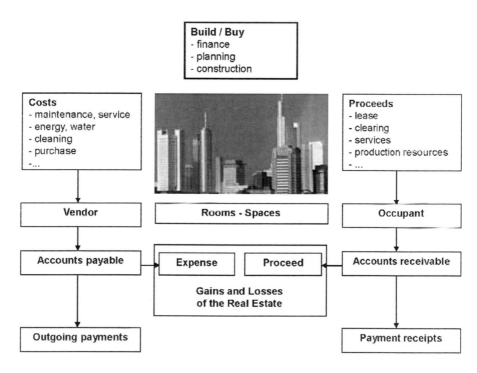

Fig. 11.15: Life cycle of a real estate from economical viewpoint

Each real estate desire begins with the question of financing. Investments can be planned and prepared with the investment management component (IS). The purchase of properties can be completed actively with the land use management (LUM) component of the real estate (RE) module. Planning the building is not the responsibility of SAP, although in the material management (MM) module and in the service procurement

(SRV) module, functionalities are present that, while not reaching the complexity of specialized planning tools, can be utilized effectively. Finally, building construction can be controlled with the project system (PS) module, even if PS focuses on the financial aspects of the project. In addition, interfaces to specialized planning tools are available.

Real estate creates costs, particularly in maintenance, cleaning, and repair, as well as various space-related services. Maintenance is accommodated in plant maintenance (PM) module, and procurement in the purchasing module. Apart from this user view, SAP also has supplier view support. In the customer service (CS) module apart from the maintenance processes, the invoicing of the completed work to the user is also done. Additional services can be handled by the sales and distribution (SD) module.

The core of the four modules is the common master data view of material, equipment, and the technical place. Materials and/or services are bought or sold. Functional locations denote objects that have a fixed location, that have to be maintained, and that can be structured down to the room level. Equipment is movable objects that can be allocated to functional locations. This master data can be used for the modeling of building objects that need to be maintained.

Real estate income is generated by leasing, which is pursued in the real estate (RE) module. Originally, not much more than a bookkeeping tool for rentals, it now offers as master data an architectural model for the buildings and field parts. In addition, RE supports the user view and thus the processes of renting. In particular, the combination of leasing and renting corresponds to the actual conditions of many enterprises characterized as corporates. In addition, there are the company's processes of internal leasing and/or renting. The space allocation in RE/FX supports space utilization optimization with the goal of vacating spaces in order to externally lease, sell, or terminate rental contracts.

All these processes are completed in business relations between suppliers and customers/tenants. Suppliers and customers/tenants are administered in most ERP modules as partners that have a connection to accounts payable and/or debtors in the bookkeeping FI module. Through the individual process steps, documents are produced automatically, which fulfills the commitments from received invoices by payments. If proceeds surpass the expenditure, one can regard the real estate as an economic success. Benchmarks should provide positive results. The fact that an enterprise breaks even is just as important for permanent success. The process chain of FM ends there.

The controlling is also of fundamental importance for the management in the economic sense. The controlling (CO) module differentiates between cost-center and cost-category controlling. Costs can be planned accordingly and recorded by an auxiliary account assignment (that is, the cost center is quoted in the invoice document). This functionality occurs in all ERP modules and permits control of the efficiency of the real estate and facility management.

In the meantime, the complementary systems became ever more important for operating a SAP system. Today, the integration of those systems has become much easier. In the following section, the integration of SAP with CAD is considered. Thereby the only CAFM functionality according to GEFMA guideline 400 that cannot be fulfilled by the SAP standard is satisfied.

11.4.4.4.2 CAFM FUNCTIONS IN SAP WITH CAD INTEGRATION

A CAD integration offers a qualitative and quantitative measurable benefit to the users. From the qualitative standpoint, the user acceptance and the precision of master data are most important. The supply of correct quantities, on whose basis contracts or orders are then locked, is certainly the quantitatively highest benefit of employing CAD.

A mouse click in the graphics not only causes an adjustment of master data, but can affect the financial stream.

The alignment of data between CAD and SAP probably represents the most important reason for CAD integration. The quality of the master data increases with CAD integration.

However, it quickly becomes very clear that the supply of accurate data geometry to SAP is not the only reason for CAD integration. Many processes orient themselves very strongly at the location and the geometrical condition of the objects (e.g., rooms, equipment, assembly groups). This is considered a requirement for all CAFM software. For the users of SAP, this is usually the largest hurdle in handling SAP.

In this case, the extension of the SAP user interface (SAPgui) by a CAD interface is advised. By using this interactive graphical interface, a user can do the following:

- Identify SAP master data by clicking into the drawing.

- Color/highlight graphic objects such as areas based on the characteristics and conditions of associated SAP master data.

The value added by such a CAD integration results in the support of the following CAFM processes: -

- Leasing

- Move management

- Procurement (e.g., of cleaning)

- Maintenance management

- Sales and customer service (invoicing of FM services for the operator)

Initial data alignment. Initial data alignment is used mainly for the migration of the CAD data into SAP master data. In enterprises where up-to-date CAD drawings are available, it is suitable to provide SAP with those data.

The support of data acquisition by CAD integration can take place in different ways:

- SAP master data is already available and will be connected automatically with the CAD objects and updated during initial data alignment.

- SAP master data is missing and will be produced automatically on basis of the CAD objects during initial data alignment.

- SAP master data and the CAD objects are compared and a difference list is produced. The determined differences are then converted manually in SAP.

Compared to the time an enterprise would spend on manual determination of the data, the employment of the CAD integration leads to savings of hours, days, weeks, months, or even years, depending on the size and quantity of the CAD drawings. Investments in CAD drawing standards and quality would pay off after the migration of the CAD data into the SAP master data.

Data update. Since the objects contained in the CAD drawings are not static in the long term, the corresponding changes need to be updated in the SAP master data.

After initial data alignments is made from CAD objects to SAP master data, a CAD integration is able to transfer changes of the CAD objects to the SAP master data easily (see figure 11.16). There are different possibilities for arranging such a process:

- Fully automatic

- Semi-automatic

- Manually with support

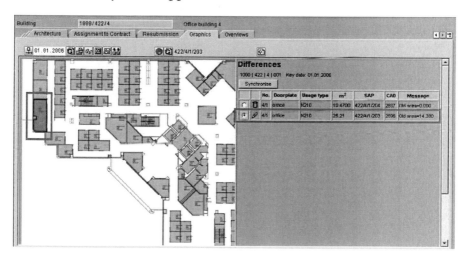

Fig. 11.16: Difference list and synchronization basis after a renovation

Production of topical maps. As soon as a CAD integration is completed, this linkage can be used for graphic evaluations and therefore provide topical maps.

Graphic evaluations (color coding of polygons according to the properties of the characteristics of the linked SAP object topics) are based on the standard SAP search mechanism. This SAP standard mechanism is used for all color coding based on characteristics of the SAP object belonging to a certain area.

Leasing. The complex process of leasing is supported in SAP by the RE module. The extension of the SAP GUI by a CAD interface offers a higher control comfort for the user and the access to the current measurements of rooms.

If the CAD integration offers the possibility of space coloring based on leasing data, the user can already determine the vacant rooms graphically before letting (see figure 11.17).

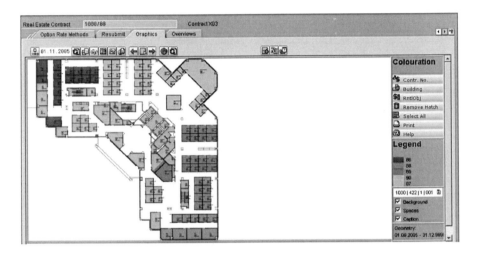

Fig. 11.17: Display of vacant and leased spaces

By a mouse click on an area in the CAD, the areas that can be rented are selected and connected with a renting object as well as assigned to a lease contract.

Move management. Contrary to leasing, SAP does not offer an independent module for move management. However, allocating organizational units to spaces is possible with the real estate management module.

For moving,

■ the master data of the person must be worked on (using module HR) or

■ a business partner can be assigned to

— a space/job of the architectural module
— a renting unit/renting space in the RE module
— a functional location in the PM module.

To administer location, equipment in the SAP module PM can be located or removed in a "functional location."

Through a CAD integration, it is possible to provide in SAP an individual move transaction. Consequently the user can place the different SAP objects using the graphical interface in the CAD or can remove existing placements by mouse clicks.

To facilitate for the user a placing of persons or facility objects, the CAD surface also offers possibilities for the coloring of spaces (e.g., according to the current tenant) (see figure 11.18).

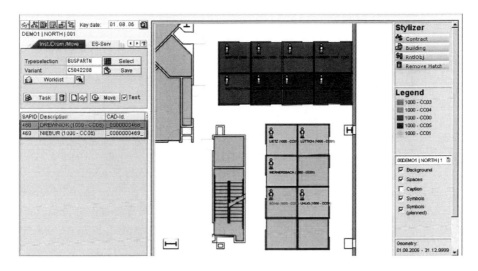

Fig. 11.18: Move planning

Additionally, the following actions can be released in a move transaction in SAP:

- Change the address of business partners

- Generate service notifications and orders in PM for move execution

- Adapt lease contracts

- Update key indicators for controlling

- Internal cost allocation of used spaces

Procurement and sales. Procurement and sales are core competencies of SAP, which also offers various possibilities for the procurement and sale of FM services. Through integrated CAD support, the necessary but laborious determination of quantities can be drastically simplified. The objects concerned can be selected by a simple mouse click, and the necessary quantities can be extracted from the CAD objects under consideration.

Although the functionalities of SAP for the classical offer, assignment, and treatment of accounts of construction works and supplies are only possible with restrictions, less complex FM services can be procured or sold with SAP.

Maintenance management. It is frequently necessary to visualize facilities and equipment components in a layout plan in order to determine locations and to produce layout plans for external service providers. CAD integration can also clearly facilitate the generation of messages/tickets when problems arise. Telephone messages left upfront by the user of a property are frequently available but leave minimal information. However, in most cases, the location where the problem or fault was detected can easily be determined. With the help of CAD, the rooms and locations of facilities can easily be displayed. A message can then be generated directly from the CAD interface. Some fields of the message can be supplied with data coming from the SAP object, which is connected with the selected space (polygon) or the selected symbol.

11.4.5 CAFM SYSTEM WITH COUPLING TO A BMS

Different information from the building management systems (BMS) flows directly into the FM processes. The connection of BMS software and CAFM software forms a substantial basis for regular evaluations of medium consumption and running times of machines, and for handling unplanned deviations from standard operation.

On the basis of transferred metering readings of consumption media (see figure 11.19), cost allocations and additional cost charges can be provided. In addition, machine runtimes are provided for planning the maintenance of technical building equipment.

Deviations from the standard operation (e.g., temperature, pressure, and humidity) are disturbances and release appropriate fault reports.

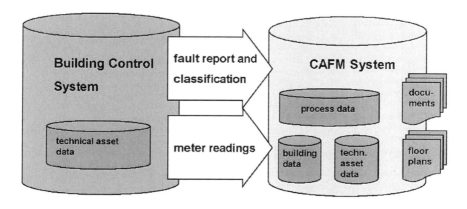

Fig. 11.19: Example of a CAFM system from a CAFM and a BMS software

11.5 DATA STORAGE

Depending upon the origins of CAFM software, represented above, substantial data storage takes place both in databases and in graphic models.

Relational data models are the most common variant for data storage. To support the object-oriented approach, some CAFM database kernels are equipped with an object-relational modeling possibility. A few CAFM systems on the market are based on object-oriented database systems.

Graphic data storage still commonly takes place in the 2-D or 3-D CAD models (see section 3.4) of the graphic cores of CAFM systems. Frequently, in the appropriate CAD systems, one or more layers are assigned to the tasks of FM. However, there is a trend toward storing graphic data in a database system as well.

Documents or further structured data can then be provided as directory trees with appropriate documents or in the form of standardized data structures such as XML (eXtensible Markup Language (Disterer et al. 2003).

As soon as more than one procedure for data storage is involved in a CAFM system, rules need to be made for which data source represents the leading system in each case.

11.6 INTEGRATION OF CAFM COMPONENTS

11.6.1 INTERFACES IN CAFM SYSTEMS

As described in the preceding sections (see figure 11.5), interfaces are often necessary for existing software as a requirement for balanced information and knowledge management in FM. For a general classification, refer to section 4.2.2.

Since these interfaces need a complete database, however, they usually play a rather minor role during the beginning of the CAFM implementation phase. A realization often takes place only in a later development phase. Hence, it is most important to provide a concept ensuring a clear delineation of tasks and feasibility. The correct interface concept with the defaults and definitions for

■ information distribution,

■ interface flexibility, and if necessary,

■ standardization of data exchange

is one of the success criteria for an efficient CAFM system.

The range of the expenditures necessary for interfaces can vary substantially based on the implemented CAFM functionalities, the processes, and the complexity of the IT infrastructure.

Every now and then it can be necessary to provide a special workflow concept for the analysis of internal operations. Which process steps can be mapped onto which software application and which data needs to be exchanged between the systems should be documented. Furthermore, it is important that, after data transfer from the source system, the necessary functions in the target system can be triggered to enable further automated data processing.

For example, automated work order forwarding to certain colleagues is possible, if the intended recipient does not react in a specified period. A second example is the blocking of rooms or equipment in a room reservation system if a building or a repair action is going on. After a verification of the maintenance action is made in the CAFM software, the blockage is waived automatically.

A more extensive discussion of the interface problem, with more detailed technical explanations as well as a recommendation regarding the approach for the interface definition and integration can be found in the GEFMA guideline 410 (NN 2007a).

11.6.1.1 DATA EXCHANGE FORMATS

Alphanumeric data. For documents, which are to be transferred as text files to a CAFM software, the following formats are recommended:

- ASCII

- Portable Document Format (PDF),

- Rich Text Format (RTF),

- MS Word (DOC), or

- Standard Generalized Markup Language (SGML)and/or other formats based upon XML like the Internet standard HTML (Hyper Text Markup Language)

ASCII is the simplest and permanently most readable format. For other formats, if necessary, the version which can be used for the exchange is to be specified.

The exchange of tabular data is recommended:

- Separately in form of structured texts, for example, in the format CSV (comma separated values), i.e. text fields separated by semi-colon, tab or similar separators,

- MS Excel (with definition of the version), or

- Via open database interfaces based upon SQL, such as ODBC or JDBC.

If based upon SQL, different from a conventional file transfer the relations between tables as well as administration information (e.g., rights of access) can be transferred.

Geometrical data as pixel graphics. This concerns among other things the import of building drawings, which are available only on paper to be transferred by scanning to a raster graphics file, as well as graphics, which are already present in the raster format, such as digital photos. With those graphics a visualization of the spatial situation is already possible; however no detailed evaluation such as determining areas from floor plans. The cause consists of the fact that a raster graphics represents only a number of isolated dots (pixels). Usual file format types for raster graphics are, among other things,

- raster formats (e.g., TIFF, BMP, JPG, PCX, RLC) and

- metafiles (e.g., WMF, EPS).

Geometrical data as vector graphics. Here the contents of the file are based on graphic elements (e.g., straight lines, polylines and circles) with coordinates and attributes (such as type of line, line width, color, layer).

Vector data forms the basis of CAD drawings and models. Typical CAD systems read and write data in common, however not standardized formats (so called industry "standards") including the following:

- DWG (Autocad DraWinG—a binary format)

- DXF (Drawing eXchange Format—ASCII)

- DGN (Microstation DesiGN file)

File formats vary with each release version of the respective CAD programs. For data transfer the version must always be indicated.

For an exchange with other CAD systems as well as other design and visualization programs the exchange format DXF was created by the AutoCAD developer Autodesk. This is a proprietary format, which is protected as registered trademark of Autodesk and is not subject of standardization. In the context of a data exchange DXF supplies very different results, i.e. some characteristics of the original drawing are usually not transferred correctly. With each new version of AutoCAD the DXF format can also change. Therefore, with DXF data exchange an indication of the corresponding AutoCAD version is indispensable. Currently, DXF cannot cope with all requirements imposed by FM.

Object data with geometry. The above problems are resolved in principle with the IFC standard (Industry Foundation Classes) developed by the International Alliance for Interoperability (IAI). Here objects are defined (walls, windows, and doors) and provided with a set of attributes, for example, manufacturer, material, geometry and maximum opening angles of windows and doors. This also includes relations between objects (e.g., a door exists within a wall opening).

The IFC standard also contains specifications for objects that emerge only during the operation of a building such as technical equipment, furnishing and space allocation.

The physical IFC data format is originally based on the industry standard STEP and is available now also in the XML format. An IFC based data exchange supplements at present conventional methods with proprietary data formats. The practical use is already proven in a set of large scale projects. Thus, the IFC standard represents at present the most promising method for the object and geometry data exchange.

11.6.1.2 EXAMPLES OF INTERFACES AND DATA EXCHANGE

Data acquisition from building design and execution of construction. The first goal of CAFM software, when considering a new building, is the acquisition of current graphic and alphanumeric data of the building design and execution of construction for FM. This requires detailed specifications for architects, specialized technical planning, and information for companies regarding formats, qualities, and indicator classifications (e.g., drawing numbers, building/room numbers, asset numbers) so that the information can be used later. These specifications for inventory documentation should be fixed when awarding a contract.

Data to be transfer usually includes the following:

- Geometrical data (e.g., portfolio of buildings, rooms, and other spaces)

- Room data (e.g., room equipment, data of space use)

- Asset data (technical equipment, such as elevators, HVAC, and security systems)

- Other FM-relevant data

Data exchange during the operation phase. The range of data exchange in the operation phase depends on the tasks of the CAFM system and the workflows to be supported. So, necessary data from the building design phase, including execution, must be exchanged with external contractors. Further, the extent depends on the external systems that must be integrated.

"Typical" external (legacy) systems and/or applications of software, which are used in many enterprises and therefore to be applicable for a data exchange, include the following:

- Materials management software

- Document management systems (e.g., orders, descriptions, diagrams)

- Reservation systems (e.g., parking lots, conferences, equipment)

- Geographical information systems (GIS)

Here a clear, non-overlapping differentiation cannot be made, since the employment of ERP software, the following specific software components could already be integrated in the ERP system:

- Software for financial accounting, cost calculation, and administration of orders

- Software for bidding, assignment, and accounting

- Maintenance management systems (MMS)

Data exchange with building management. As an example, the acquisition of data from a building management system (BMS) into CAFM software will be considered. Important data from BMS include the following:

- Data point addressing pattern

- Maintenance messages from limit value transmitters

- Fault signals

- Operation hours and/or period of operation limit values and load cycles

- Counter consumption data

The volume and cycle of the data transfer must be specified individually for specific projects. Accordingly, a monthly reading is sufficient for the acquisition of counter-consumption data into the CAFM system (among other things, as the basis of the later operating cost account).

A further relevant data exchange can result, for example, in the case of the employment of the following technical systems:

■ Access control systems

■ Personnel information systems

■ Telephone and video conference systems

In the field of building management systems, many proprietary specifications exist, so that we find a variety of individual integration solutions. However, there are also standardization efforts. Typically, the OPC interface (OLE for Process Control) for MS operating systems is to be mentioned. For the provider, this allows independent exchange of data between the different systems. The BMS vendor or third-party vendor must install an appropriate OPC server to establish a physical connection to the field devices (data points).

Interfaces to MS Office products. Interfaces to MS Office products are a "must" for each CAFM software product. This is especially valid in the implementation phase of the acquisition of data, which usually exist in Office formats such as Excel. Examples are room equipment catalogs, cleaning tables, meter overviews, and contracts.

In the operating phase of the CAFM system, a flexible reporting mechanism is important. Here it must be possible to export the CAFM data very simply (e.g., to Word or Excel). It is left to the user whether and in which form further processing takes place outside of the CAFM system.

11.6.1.3 DATA SECURITY AND INTERFACES

The variety of possible interfaces puts high demands on the CAFM software, since it is supposed to enable an integrated and enterprise-wide solution. Therefore, besides the interface concept, a security concept must also be provided, which regulates exactly which special data is subject to special security requirements and preventive measures (see section 5.1). Apart from providing a software-internal user authorization concept, the following questions related to data communication are also to be treated:

- Which data are being transferred to which computers by which networks?

- Which damage can occur if certain data is read and perhaps manipulated by unauthorized persons?

- Which computers with which data have to be protected?

- Which encryption and authentication methods are to be used?

- How is response behavior affected during data communication?

- Which information and events are to be logged while taking into account data protection?

- What is the residual risk remaining?

Data security also includes an appropriate data backup and data archiving system. An interface solution involves not only the CAFM software but also the interconnected external systems. These are to be included into the concept. It needs to be clarified, in detail, which software with which data in which cycle with which storage duration are to be considered. This also concerns the procedure of transferring data back. If it is not possible to perform data transfer automatically, the procedure must be described in detailed checklists, administrators are to be instructed, and respective tests are to be conducted to verify proper functioning.

11.6.2 CAFM SYSTEM WITH INTEGRATION BY DATA WAREHOUSE

Another way to integrate the different FM-relevant software components and systems on the data level is to build a data warehouse (DW). Whereas the employment of a data warehouses for use in areas such as marketing, sales, and production is very common, their use in FM is still in its infancy (Eppenberger and König 2003; May et al. 2007).

A data warehouse system (DWS) consists of a superordinate database that unites information from different software applications within an enterprise as well as appropriate data and user interfaces. A data warehouse is focused on periodically collecting, editing, and retrieving topical, standardized, long-term, and time-referenced data from different data sources (Disterer et al. 2003; Chamoni and Gluchovski 1999). It enables evaluations that cannot be provided from the different single applications as easily. In particular, by using suitable key indicators, valuable insights can be gained into the FM processes.

The organization and evaluation of the data take place on the basis of a particularly adapted data structure. The results are made available in detail, quickly, consistently, and company-wide if necessary. A data warehouse can offer, among other things, the following functions:

- Supply of historicized, consolidated, and correct data

- Only one information system (uniform data source)

- Simple access via web browsers

- User-friendly, easy-to-handle user interface

- Generation of reports

- Ensuring simple and efficient distribution of reports

- Flexibility in formatting reports

- Large possibilities of data evaluation

- Graphic design and layout of reports

- Simple visualization of CAD drawings

- Simplification of workflows

A data warehouse (see figure 11.20) is modeled in a multidimensional way (Eppenberger and König 2003) and serves the long-term storage of historical, settled, validated, synthesized, operational, internal, and external data. The functional application fields are represented in figure 11.20 in tabular form on the left side. They result from the corporate view as a collaborative system, in which different fields of activities can be differentiated. There are three functional areas:

- Market performance function—*marketing and sales.* It places customer satisfaction into the center of their actions.

- Market performance function—*production.* This is where the real market performance is produced, it needs the necessary infrastructure and capacities, and it must specify the range of the relevant factors of application.

- Supply function. It ensures the supply of the enterprise with necessary resources—the factors of production. These factors can be infrastructure, energy, information technology, or human resources.

The enterprise is split into a functional and an analytic part. The functional part is composed of the respective application software systems, to which numerous FM-relevant software components belong. The analytic part, which supports the management with strategic information, enables three-dimensional views of analyses and inquiries as well as the different relations between economic key figures.

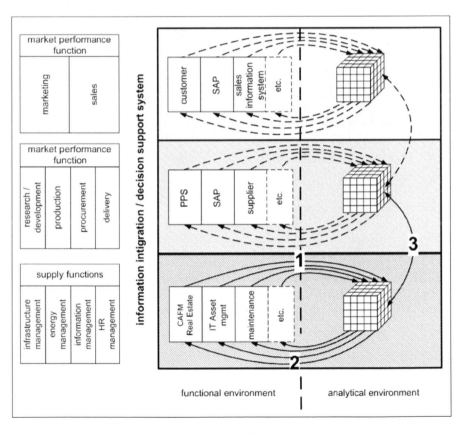

Fig. 11.20: Structure of a data warehouse

A data warehouse within FM functions as follows:

- The data is imported from the FM-relevant software systems (see figure 11.20).

- It is also possible to retransfer the consolidated data again into these systems to increase data quality.

- To provide information to the higher-level functional areas, it is possible to exchange information between the analytic systems.

Despite all advantages of data warehouse projects, there are critical *success factors* that must be considered. These are, among others,

- Functioning internal communication

- Commitment of the management

- Acceptance by the users

- Certain size of enterprise and/or data volume

- Suitable time of DWS introduction

- Corporate-wide utilization of the system

To be able to use a data warehouse efficiently and optimally, intensive preliminary discussions and an exact analysis of the process operation must be conducted, and a clear strategy for the enterprise must be set. Therefore, it must be clarified which sources of information the users require for their activities. For each source system, its own special interface must be established.

Further advantages of a data warehouse are its site-independent access and the user-friendliness. All typical analysis and representation possibilities such as lists, diagrams, and graphic plans are part of the DW solution. In this case, a simple and configurable browser user interface is available.

However, the high initial investment costs are problematic. The tangible financial benefit of a data warehouse project must be proven to the enterprise's decision makers (see chapter 8).

11.6.3 CAFM SYSTEM WITH INTEGRATION BY MIDDLEWARE

Depending on the FM task, it is possible that a part of the necessary data is already available in proven FM-related IT components. The main challenge is gathering data from different sources and making them available for the different FM processes.

For such an integration task, middleware is a key component of the CAFM system. In the technical literature, this data integration is also referred to as Enterprise Application Integration (EAI).

The substantial advantage of this approach is the concentration of data for new tasks, without requiring a new data acquisition or processing. Such a development can be achieved either on the basis of the existing CAFM program or by using an additional CAFM middleware (see figure 11.21).

With the help of the middleware, different data sources and CAFM software components are merged. A CAFM object, for example, a room, is then described data source independent in the integration level. For example, a visual impression could be provided by a photo, equipment by an XML-based inventory model, contracts by text documents, objects' sizes by a service-oriented software, and financial data from an ERP system.

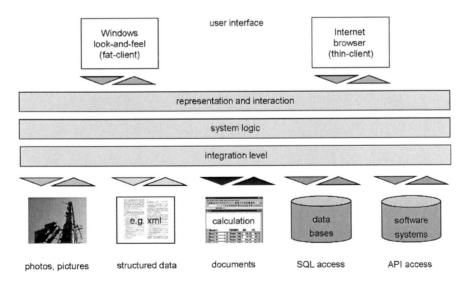

Fig. 11.21: Architecture of a CAFM system with an integration of data, logic, and user interface via middleware

Apart from the data integration of different software components, middleware can have business logic that integrates across different subsystems. This business logic allows the mapping of FM processes, which uses the functionality of the middleware and if necessary the functionalities of individual CAFM software components. In this way the middleware offers a workflow across different software systems.

A representation and an interaction based on the business logic can be established in a unified user interface of the middleware. In this way, it becomes possible for both the processes and the data from the integrated software components to be presented to a user in a single-user surface.

One of the possibilities for a uniform and universal usable user interface is provided by the HTML standard. The data and processes of the middleware can be called and displayed in any Internet browser. Usually, this does not require any additional installations of client software.

A substantial challenge with the setup of a middleware-based CAFM system is in the establishment of a user administration. This must refer both to the logic of the middleware and to the integrated CAFM software components. The user administration of one of the integrated systems is not suited for this, because this concerns only one specific process, not the overall FM tasks.

In a user administration across different software systems, the roles, groups, and associated access rights to the FM processes are defined. Each user, who is assigned to different roles and groups, is granted the appropriate access rights. From the user administration of the integrated individual systems, further properties can be assigned to the user (see figure 11.22).

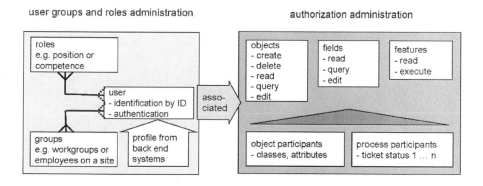

Fig. 11.22: User administration in a CAFM system with several software components

11.7 CAFM AND INTERNET

11.7.1 OVERVIEW OF THE APPLICATION SCENARIOS

Numerous tasks in FM have much in common with Internet/intranet-based solutions. In FM the facilities are usually in many different locations, and numerous persons participate in the activities around these objects. Therefore, various data is required. These challenges can be coped with efficiently by Internet/intranet-based IT solutions.

Most CAFM solutions on the market today dispose of certain web-based functionalities. In the simplest case, this covers the generation of web-enabled data, among them the export of HTML documents, which can be viewed in any browser.

A further web ability is the generation of a CAFM system's user interface completely in HTML. Sometimes the functionalities provided can be used only by certain types of browsers.

Completely web-based CAFM solutions include all internal and external users into the workflow. Such CAFM solutions result in substantial cost savings through time reduction during information acquisition, smooth communication between the involved users as well as process-accompanying documentation. By integrating the existing systems, a customized software solution is derived.

A web-based support is particularly suitable for the following essential FM processes:

- Acquisition and provision of FM data

- Administration of floor plans and design drawings

- Provision of documents

- Establishment of reporting

- Generation of requests for proposal and/or bids

- Handling of unplanned job,

- Generation of bills of quantities (e.g., for standard performance)

- Pursuit of job execution

- Billing of job performance of clients and contractors

11.7.2 AVAILABLE SOLUTIONS

Facility management tasks require working with extensive alphanumeric data and documents. For this reason, Internet/intranet-based CAFM solutions usually include both database and document servers. These data and documents are provided to the different web-based modules via an application server (see figure 11.23).

Typically, the provision of FM-relevant basic information in an information portal and on top of this on different functional components is part of an Internet/intranet-based CAFM system. In the following, the benefits and the functionalities of some currently available solutions are presented.

*Information portal.*In an information portal, the different property-related information is made available. Access for different user groups is controlled by an integrated concept of roles and rights. This guarantees that users have access only to the information they are allowed to. The necessary data is made available to the users by the integrated database and document servers.

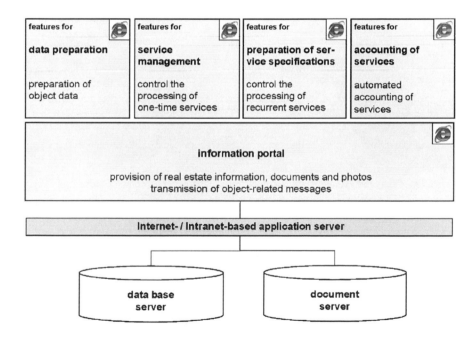

Fig. 11.23: Internet/intranet-enabled CAFM solutions integrate database and document servers

Frequently, content management functionalities are integrated in an information portal, which allows a comprehensive and individual configuration of the information portal by the user. In this way, project-specific document archives and an individual reporting systems can be established (see figure 11.24).

When using an information portal, effort during the provision of information can be reduced considerably. A comfortable search function enables fast access to the desired information. The integration of stakeholders such as owner, operator, tenant, and internal and external service providers into FM offers numerous advantages: reporting of and working on faults using the Internet reduces the process time and enables a process-accompanying documentation. At the same time, customer satisfaction increases with the delivery of good and fast service.

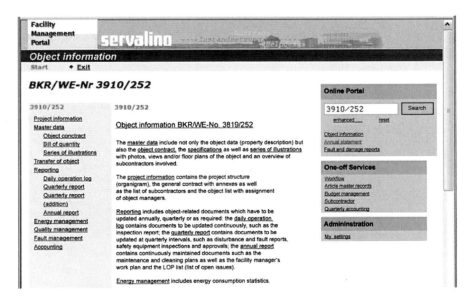

Fig. 11.24: Internet/intranet-based information portal with reporting system

Data preparation. With a web-based data preparation, a software solution is available with which FM raw data can be prepared systematically for further use in the target data structures. This procedure ensures a high return on investment for FM data collection.

The data acquisition allows the validation of collected data via an Internet portal regarding plausibility, for example, values, value ranges,

mandatory fields, physical dimensions or internal dependencies, and adherence to the defaults of an import specification. The examined data can
be displayed in lists at any time. If all data complies with the quality criteria, it is prepared for import into the target system. Here data is grouped
as required, completed by keys (necessary for database tables in the target
system), and exported in a format suitable for the target system. Target
systems can be, for example, CAFM or ERP systems (see figure 11.25).

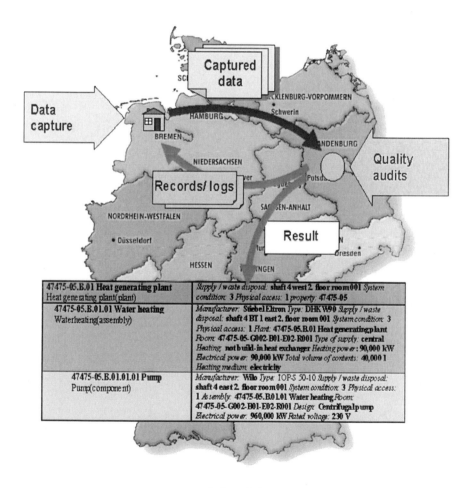

47475-05.B.01 Heat generating plant Heat generating plant(plant)	Supply / waste disposal: shaft 4 west 2. floor room 001 System condition: 3 Physical access: 1 property: 47475-05
47475-05.B.01.01 Water heating Waterheating(assembly)	Manufacturer: Stiebel Eltron Type: DHK W90 Supply / waste disposal: shaft 4 BT 1 east 2. floor room 001 System condition: 3 Physical access: 1 Plant: 47475-05.B.01 Heat generating plant Room: 47475-05-G002-B01-E02-R001 Type of supply: central Heating: not built-in heat exchanger Heating power: 90,000 kW Electrical power: 90,000 kW Total volume of contents: 40,000 l Heating medium: electricity
47475-05.B.01.01.01 Pump Pump(component)	Manufacturer: Wilo Type: IOP-S 50-10 Supply / waste disposal: shaft 4 east 2. floor room 001 System condition: 3 Physical access: 1 Assembly: 47475-05.B01.01 Water heating Room: 47475-05-G002-B01-E02-R001 Design: Centrifugal pump Electrical power: 960,000 kW Rated voltage: 230 V

Fig. 11.25: Web-based data preparation

Service provision order service processing. A cost-optimized and efficient completion of activities necessary for the operation of real estate is a crucial

success factor for efficient FM. This is valid in particular for the processing of unplanned activities, whose costs constitute a high portion of the total cost.

Administrative effort is reduced to a minimum by the Internet/intranet-based execution of the business process. Unplanned activities can be supported, starting with a fault report by a tenant, followed by placing an order by the owner, and finally ending with completion of the task and a cost statement by the service provider (see figure 11.26).

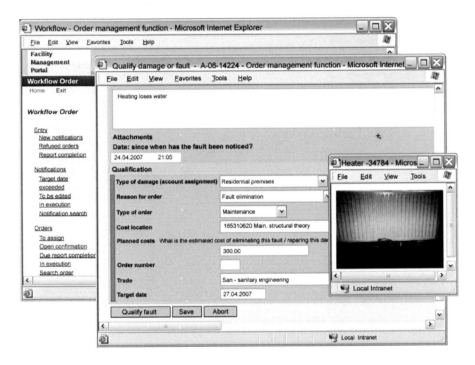

Fig. 11.26: Web-based order handling

All process steps can be supplemented by accompanying images and documents. In this way, logging of faults detected and orders completed is possible.

The transition of an order from one state to the next is logged with a time stamp in a journal, so that the up-to-date processing status and the history of an unplanned activity can be seen at any time. The reporting person can get information on the processing status of his or her message;

service providers can track the handling of the order; and the costs incurred are transparent to all parties.

In numerous processes, during which a coordination between different persons is necessary, orders can be handled iteratively (e.g., during the placement and acceptance of services) (see figure 11.27).

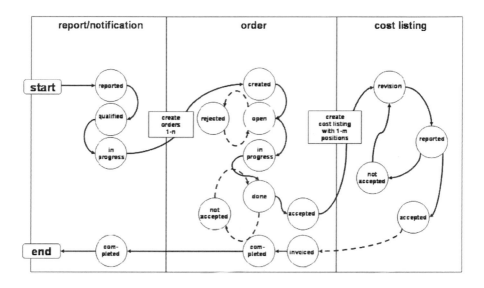

Fig. 11.27: Process orientation during handling of unplanned services

Generation of bills of quantities. Bills of quantities form the basis of any standard service. The generation of bills of quantities is fundamental for the bid, award, and accounting process.

This requires the joining of data for buildings, technical equipment, and exterior installations with sample bills of quantities and thus enabling the automatic generation of bills of quantities.

Depending on targeted application, bills of quantities can be provided with or without quotations. Bills of quantities without quotations are used for bids, where the suppliers need to specify prices only for the given service positions. In this way, different offers can be compared quite easily. The bills of quantities can be produced as a PDF document, in the HTML format, or in a standardized data format (see figure 11.28). Bills of quantities with quotations can be used directly as appendices of contracts.

These bills of quantities can be presented in the respective information portals both completely and sorted by trades or budget items.

Items – Plant 47475-05.B.01 Heat generating plant

Item no.	Quantity	Unit	Description	UP	Sum
19.1.1	3	Item	04.04.01.02.01 – Safety valve maint. + serv. This only applies to a function text. Calibration is carried out if paid for separately according to effort. Due to the danger of causing leaks, in the case of coolant circuits, function testing is only conducted in the course of repairs or overhauls. **Service Level Agreement: 3 Cycles** Visual inspection　　　　　1,00 p.a. Technical servicing　　　　1,00 p.a.	No UP	0,00 €
19.1.2	3	Item	06.09.01.01.01 – Water heater maint. + serv. **Service Level Agreement: 3 Cycles** Visual inspection　　　　　12,00 p.a. Technical servicing　　　　1,00 p.a.	No UP	0,00 €
19.1.3	1	item	06.09.02.01.01 – Wall-mounted hot-water tank maint. + serv. **Service Level Agreement: 3 Cycles** Visual inspection　　　　　12,00 p.a. Technical servicing　　　　1,00 p.a.	No UP	0,00 €
Sum items plant 47475-05.B.01 Heat generating plant					

Fig. 11.28: Section of an online generated bill of quantities

Performance accounting. Services completed must be accounted for on the basis of framework contracts, service catalogs, and work performance records. Accounts take place as single or aggregated accounts at different times (e.g., immediate, monthly, quarterly, annually).

An online portal can support performance accounting with an automated accounting of standard and unplanned services. Existing framework contracts and standard price agreements are used as the calculation basis for lump-sum accounting and accounting obligated to produce proof. The accounting periods are specified individually.

If the functions of performance accounting and execution are combined, online performance records of internal and external contractors can be transferred directly to the account process. The prepared billing data can now be output as customized documents (e.g., invoices) in PDF format.

For the visualization of the performance accounts, both object-related and activity-related costs and/or accounts can be provided online (see figure 11.29).

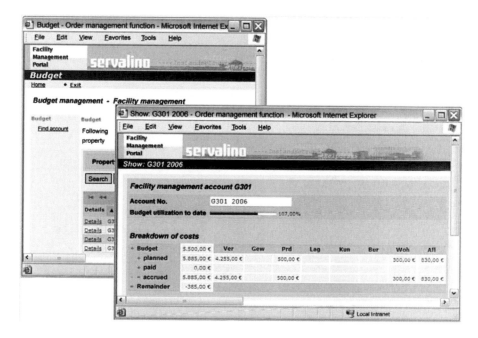

Fig. 11.29: Internet/intranet-based review of budgets

11.8 SUMMARY

Today, more than ever, a CAFM system is expected to support the processes in facility and real estate management efficiently.

The situation of the users is characterized by a broad spectrum of requirements. On the one hand, many organizations have just begun to automate their FM processes with appropriate IT support. On the other hand, numerous companies and institutions already have experiences in the organization and utilization of IT systems in FM. In these cases, highly specialized teams have very specific requirements for CAFM solutions. Some of them have already implemented their second or third CAFM software package.

On the vendor side, the spectrum of available software is not less complex. A few years ago, the vendor market was expected to consolidate itself to a few large players and products. However, this did not happen. Quite the opposite is true. Software in CAFM systems ranges from standard office suites, over proven CAFM software, up to integrated special solutions including ERP and BMS and using Internet/intranet technology. The decision for the employment of standard CAFM software or of a combination of various FM-related software components can be made only based on the needs of an individual enterprise.

In this chapter, the requirements for a CAFM system were defined along with some CAFM software examples. These examples were composed of various software components, and some integration solutions were presented in detail.

12

SELECTION OF CAFM SOFTWARE

*Joachim Hohmann, Russ Burlew, Kevin Janus, Nicole Lobb,
Michael Marchionini*

12.1 GENERAL

In section 6.1 this question was answered: "Why CAFM?" The facility
management process differs significantly from that of the core business as
it relates to production and administrative functions. It is this basic difference that determines each step of the decision-making process during
the introduction of a CAFM system.

The implementation of a CAFM system highlights the connection
with IT and the expectations associated with such a tool. CAFM, however, does not solely guarantee cost savings through efficiency; but in
conjunction with a professionally minded staff, it can add more influence
to the overall efficiency of an organization's core business.

Facility management requires detailed knowledge of the specific infrastructure of a given facility and how the related business processes can be supported by IT (e.g., in space management, maintenance planning, lease administration). These considerations lead to a system that is responsive and quickly delivers information in support of these functions using a database to be interpreted by the FM professional. The size, number, and complexity of the facilities and related processes are an important consideration in selecting the best-fitting CAFM software for a specific organization. The complexity of the facility is often determined by its use or main function (real estate, buildings, controls, etc.).

By utilizing a method of proper design, implementation, use, and management, the CAFM system can provide information on demand that will incur an overview of the current facility operating conditions, and be able to provide deeper insight into specific areas of the facility as required. The CAFM tool should provide the user with an effective interface that allows quick analysis of data being monitored and assists in determining a clear set of actions to correct a deficiency and validate that the correct action was taken. This can become an invaluable tool for evaluating and managing complex real estate or building management issues.

The basic condition for a successful selection of CAFM software is the understanding of the particular organization's requirements and objectives. One should also consider any existing system(s). It has to be stressed at this point that the selection process for CAFM software must support the core business and processes being supported by the FM department (see chapter 13).

CAFM software requirements are described (Hoppe and Marchionini 2002) by the following:

- Features

- Technologies

- Customizing

Evidently, the database represents the foundation for the requirements, which are divided into inventory data, process data, and other data.

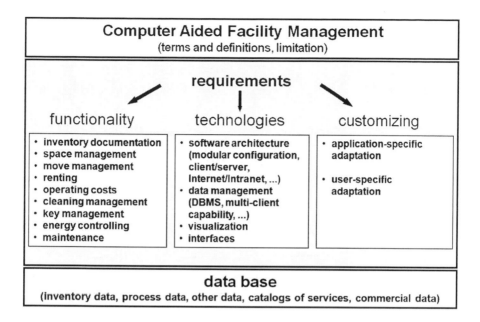

Fig. 12.1. Requirements of CAFM software

This chapter on the selection and implementation of a CAFM software corresponds strongly with chapter 13, which covers strategies of introducing CAFM into operations.

12.2 FUNCTIONAL SPECIFICATIONS DOCUMENT AS A BASIS OF A REQUEST FOR PROPOSAL

One of the first steps should be to compile conceptual guidelines for a professional CAFM implementation (see section 13.2), which include required methods and tools. Examples of such goals on this list could include the following:

■ Fast and secured access to a digital inventory of real estate holdings for all relevant and authorized entities of the organization

■ Optimization in space management, particularly with the development of occupation and space concepts, including move planning

- Preservation and/or increase of value of buildings and facilities by appropriate maintenance strategies and modernization

- Energy management through monitoring, collection, and trending of data, affording real-time reaction to events of substantial deviation from norms

- Transparently monitoring of costs of real estate operation through use of appropriate key figures with the objective of influencing control and a reduction of costs

- Support of the assignment of facility services by accurate quantification

- Support of management decisions for budget planning by reliable key figures and indices

12.2.1 DESCRIPTION OF PROJECT

One of the substantial features of CAFM software is the support of FM processes (NN 2007b). That is, CAFM software must support the user in a suitable form with customer-specific workflows and customization according to the existing operational and organizational structure.

The description of the project with a realistic representation of the relevant FM processes and workflows is an indispensable resource for later success and reference. This is an opportunity for the enterprise to identify existing deficiencies and the need to modify processes. It is a prerequisite for the software vendors to have an accurate and complete overview of the project and its environment in order to be able to calculate their quote realistically.

The following are suggestions, but not limits, of the points to emphasize in the project description:

- Organizational objectives and procedures toward FM, yet in support of the mission statement

- Existing IT environment and compatibility from both hardware and software perspectives

- Analysis of the data currently being used, including any prior records that should be subtracted and any additional information that needs to be implemented with the new system, paying particular attention to the structure, extent, relevance, and quality of the data

A thorough and comprehensive description of the project also protects against an overload of inquiries by vendors throughout the bidding process.

12.2.2 PERFORMANCE SPECIFICATIONS

In the project description, CAFM support and functional requirements should have been formulated. The main application areas (NN 2007b) were introduced in detail in chapter 7 and are listed here again:

- Inventory documentation

- Space management

- Cleaning management

- Move management

- Energy management

- Operations and maintenance

- Locking and access management

- Asset management

- Contract management

- Lease administration cost controlling and allocation

- Cost allocation

The above list contains suggested examples, and a specific list should be developed tailored to the organization the system will be supporting (see NN 2004a). According to individual requirements, processes can be added or removed. In addition, it is important that these processes are formulated as accurately as possible, meeting the detailed requirements.

The determination of necessary content and capabilities of the CAFM software is recommended in order to classify the type of CAFM software. In GEFMA guideline 400 (NN 2007b), the following are found:

That a CAFM system represents an individualized and thus specifically customized comprehensive solution for an enterprise and/

or an industry to support the processes of the facility management organization.

A CAFM system can consist either of an off-the-shelf CAFM software, or the combination of mono-functional software tools or other standard or individual software. If necessary it has to interface with the commercial enterprise software and building management systems.

12.2.3 IT REQUIREMENTS

Fundamental technological requirements should be defined and examined for compatibility with the organization's existing IT infrastructure and for future developments.

The software architecture, delivery (e.g., use of CAFM over the Internet/intranet), as well as data storage and retrieval and visualization are key issues (see chapter 11).

In principle, CAFM software should be available for multiple users, supporting the simultaneous access by many users. The CAFM software must be developed modularly so that only the actual modules needed are acquired and licensed accordingly. The modules should be constructed in such a fashion that they support workflows. The ability to alter and supplement the software at a later time is a necessary consideration for the end user.

Today the support of Internet/intranet technology querying and reporting jobs should be a minimum requirement (e.g., for failure reports, service requests, etc.). This technology allows a larger community to benefit from the CAFM system. Therefore, an indispensable feature is an operating system that distinguishes between levels of access to the software, granting varying degrees of access from read-only to submit-only to the allowing alterations and changes within the system itself. Typically this is controlled through the assignments of accesses associated to specific logins.

The physical retention of data takes place within the framework of the database management system (DBMS). The relevant requirements for a CAFM software basically result from the already existing products in the organization. Although it is common for a particularly large organization to have different databases in use, an enterprise should attempt, if possible, to have a uniform DBMS so that nothing further in connection with CAFM needs to be purchased.

The choice of a relational, object-oriented, or object-relational database management system is not critical at this juncture (see section 3.3). Independent of the physical data retention, the relevant data at the surface of the CAFM software must be object-oriented interpretable. An example would be the linking of attributes associated with renting/leasing and related documents or reports relevant to the attribute, in this case property/equipment being rented or leased.

Database access should be made using standard query languages such as SQL or Open Database Connectivity (ODBC) and permit the freedom of choosing the DBMS for the user. Data retention should take place with redundancy contentions and the ability to automatically align distributed databases.

Besides the DBMS, an important basic component is visualization. Visualization methods permit a clear and understandable representation of the complex FM data, structures, and processes. The visualization method of data must be adapted to the intended purpose and user group. CAFM software can contain a CAD kernel with reduced operation functions for FM-relevant data being graphically represented and basic manipulation features as well as graphic support for FM processes.

For data importing/exporting (industry), standard graphical formats (raster and vector format) should be supported (see section 3.6).

12.2.4 INTERFACES

Typically, CAFM software is integrated into the IT landscape of the organization, thus careful attention to details of compatibility, etc., must be adhered to in order to avoid costly and time-delaying issues (see section 4.2 and NN 2007b).

CAFM software that allows the importing of data serves either the alignment of the master-data file or the exchange of transaction data from differing data formats (ASCII, Excel, etc.). Flexible integration of data formats is a necessary feature of the software, allowing limited but different data record structures to be captured. For the exporting of data, similar requirements are valid.

The many kinds of data transfers (NN 2007a), particularly online links, play an important role in other FM-relevant software systems, such as building automation and the commercial enterprise software.

This requires a comprehensive look at or use of the Extensible Markup Language (XML).

12.2.5 DATA ACQUISITION AND TRANSFER

The acquisition of the necessary data and respective transfer into the database of the CAFM system are crucial success factors of each CAFM introduction. These are described in more detail in chapter 10 and in GEFMA's Guideline 430 (NN 2007c).

12.2.6 CUSTOMIZING

The requirements for customizing a selected CAFM software should be formulated in detail, during which the following have to be distinguished:

- Application-oriented adjustments

- User-referred adjustments

The definition of CAFM requirements should be done with the intent of obtaining clarity as well as recognizing what adjustments have to be expected and what resources are available with the proper knowledge and training on the system. If the vendor has to make the adjustments or customizations, he or she should be provided all necessary information to calculate a quote.

Application-oriented adjustments. As a rule, CAFM software has to be adapted to the specific data, structures, and processes of the enterprise or industry. The emphasis of the adjustments or customizations can include the following:

- Generation and configuration of interfaces to other systems, like the organization's commercial IT or building automation

- Change and/or extension of the data model (object classes, properties, relations)

- Additional data fields within the input masks (i.e., for FM object attributes)

- General blockage or deletion of individual data fields within the input masks

- Additional input masks

- Modification of standard reports concerning contents and layouts

- New generation of reports

User-referred adjustments. In a multiuser system, flexibility of the rights granted and access options of individual users are necessary. This takes place on two levels:

- *Data access rights:* These contain restrictions of access for certain objects (data records) and attributes (data fields). A hierarchical restriction of access (i.e., complete building of all-inclusive hierarchically subordinated objects) should be supported.

- *Program access rights:* These contain restrictions of access to certain menu options and functions and are in addition to the data access rights.

12.3 STANDARDIZED PROCUREMENT AND RFP

The selection of a software fitting the overall concept is very important (but not crucial in itself) for a successful implementation of a CAFM system. Despite the complexity and the large number of efficient programs and products offered on the market, the product selection should not become the dominating and the "all-important" factor of a system introduction. Often the quality of the concept already determines the success or failure of a project.

Often, too much attention is paid to procurement (i.e. finding the suitable software and an efficient implementation partner). This becomes clear in negative examples, where

- an organization invests too little into the conceptual stages and customization development, but extends the procurement process over several years with the result that senior management stopped it, due to management uncertainty, or

- the implementation team puts too much time and effort into extensive process analysis and customization with external consultants, only to have too little budget left, ultimately (and dictated by this budget shortfall) resulting in installing just a "mini-CAFM."

In the following, a procedure (Hohmann and Marchionini 2006) is presented based on appropriate standard tools that support a standardized procurement, evaluation, and selection process:

- Product requirement specifications

- Procurement document

- Evaluation criteria matrix

- Vendor query

- Price inquiry

- Product presentation scenarios

- Decision support matrix

- Business case

12.3.1 GENERAL FORM AND CONTENTS

The following general procedure assists with determining software selection. As a rule, the pre-selection of efficient products and a competent installation partner should be based on use of market reviews, references, recommendations, etc., which are then summarized in a limited RFP (Request for Proposal) from all bidders. This should include the following:

- Project description

- Product requirement specifications

- Background on bidder

- Default for the bidder's representation

- Default for the basic requirements list

- Default for the price inquiry

These documents should be sent to the bidders in hard-copy form as well as digitally. This will provide clear understanding during the evaluation process through side-by-side comparisons. The contracting method/terms, milestone dates, and other partners on the project and their respective roles should also be in writing. Detailed statements should address the following:

- Contracting method/terms

- Explicit permission process for out-of-scope procurement

- Address and time frame for expected delivery of the product

- Form of the delivery

- References to the handling of the bidder-submitted information

- Default references to form, date, and specific demands by requestor

- References to the availability of seeing the product demonstrated in "live" use

- Pertinent dates for the bidding process/contract award

- A hard cost or at a minimum a "not to exceed" price

- Furnishing of example data

- References upon request, held in confidentiality

At this point, it has to be mentioned that in many organizations, either corporate or public policies apply to procurement processes, which might differ significantly from what is described here.

12.4 SUMMARY

During the selection and introduction of an organization's CAFM system, there may be uncertainties about the project's goals, priorities, and procedures to apply.

This chapter, in particular, offers an outline for the process. The suggestions made are for general purposes. Only an individually tailored plan should be formulated for any given project.

In summary, the criteria for successful decisions follow this time frame:

- First, the facility department's objectives must be aligned with those of the overall organization.

- Second, a detailed framework of the overall concept and the requirements for implementation has to fulfill.

The CAFM software selection is only one part of the entire project. The project must be appropriate in its means and dimension, based on the complexity of the facilities.

13

IMPLEMENTATION STRATEGIES FOR CAFM

Michael May, Robert Burns, Chris Keller, Nicole Lobb,
Michael Marchionini

13.1 OVERVIEW AND ISSUES

The successful implementation of a CAFM system is far more than just the procurement of CAFM software. It is an extremely complex process that should affect the entire organization of the enterprise within which it is implemented. The successful implementation of CAFM requires consistent, dedicated focus, management, and leadership from initial analysis through implementation to continuous improvement throughout the life of the system.

CAFM implementation is usually a long-term process. The factors affecting the length of the project are the size, complexity, and use of the real estate portfolio. Successfully managing a real estate portfolio requires both long-term strategic planning and successfully executing specific daily tasks. These endeavors require the engagement of the staff at all levels, from operations to senior executives. Crucial to the success is a carefully managed project with realistic and obtainable strategic milestones. The milestone objectives are a balance between process change, automated tasks, workflow, and readily available, high-quality data.

The CAFM implementation strategy needs to take into account the dynamic nature of both the use and the management of a building. This necessitates constantly reviewing the objectives of the project and the technical solution to verify that they continue to be valid and synchronized. New business requirements, continuous process improvements of the inhabitants of the facility, and the ever-changing physical building will introduce new requirements and require optimization adjustments to existing objectives throughout the life cycle of the project and the facility.

The implementation of CAFM is under no circumstances to be equated with the acquisition of a CAFM software. The enterprises that have taken this approach usually end up with a failed project and expensive shelfware. The projects fail primarily due to a misalignment between the business objectives and the technical solution. A properly designed and executed strategic implementation plan mitigates this risk.

13.2 PROJECT PLAN

The project plan (schedule) is to be compiled immediately following the compilation of the requirements list and the breakdown, as possible, into allocated individual stages of development. It is the basis of budgetary and capacity planning, and it demands a software vendor statement for feasibility.

A possible project plan in a very rough structure is described below (see also the checklist in appendix 7). With regard to the following suggestions for project planning, the X in the date represents the date of placing the order for procurement and installation of all CAFM components.

1. Installation of the first stages of development: Implementation of initial software modules on a given number of computers and user training; initial pass at introducing at least one sample building with CAD drawings and attributes to further refine the accuracy of the performance specifications (final definition of the attributes

compellingly necessary in this phase) covering production, CAD drawings and equipment records.

Time frame: X + 1 months

2. Structure inventory documentation: Productive use of the detailed modules formulated in stage one of development for a defined number of users. Organize the interface between the CAFM software and other existing enterprise software, such as ERP, etc.

   Time frame: X + 3 months

3. Installation of a functional system around the modules of the second stage of development, again with focus on the user training, additional computers/users, and modules. Implementation and test of first objects, such as maintenance agreement, HVAC component, or inspection document.

   Time frame: X + 7 months

4. Further development of the inventory documentation according to any additional modules, and productively use of these modules.

   Time frame: X + 12 months

5. Extensions of user access. Integration of additional Internet-inquiry stations. Rollout to remote locations.

   Time frame: X + 16 months.

The suggested schedule represents a first orientation. With problems that occur and/or experiences throughout the individual phases, lessons should be learned and changes/deviations explored as long as they support the original project objectives.

13.3 STANDARDIZED PROCUREMENT AND RFP

The selection of a software fitting the overall concept is important (though not in itself crucial to the project) for a successful implementation of a CAFM system. Despite the complexity and the large number of efficient programs and products offered on the market, the product selection should not become the dominating and the "all-important" factor of a system introduction. Often the quality of the concept already determines the success or failure of a project.

Often, too much attention is paid to the procurement marketing (i.e., finding the suitable software and an efficient implementation partner). This becomes clear in negative examples, where

- an organization invests too little in the conceptual stages and customization development, but extends the procurement process over several years with the result that senior management stops it due to management uncertainty, and

- the implementation team puts too much time and effort into extensive process analysis and customization with external consultancy, only to have too little budget left, ultimately (and dictated by this budget shortfall) resulting in installing just a "mini-CAFM."

In the following, a procedure (Hohmann and Marchionini 2006) is presented based on appropriate standard tools, which supports a standardized procurement, evaluation, and selection process:

- Product requirement specifications

- Procurement document

- Evaluation criteria matrix

- Vendor query

- Price inquiry

- Product presentation scenarios

- Decision support matrix

- Business case

13.3.1 GENERAL FORM AND CONTENTS

The successful implementation of CAFM can be realized only by properly designing and executing a strategic plan that includes at least the following phases (NN 2007d):

- Conception

- Product and vendor selection

- Implementation

- System development and use

Fig. 13.1 represents an outline of the operational sequence, in of a typical CAFM system implementation. The individual steps are depicted in detail in section 13.2.

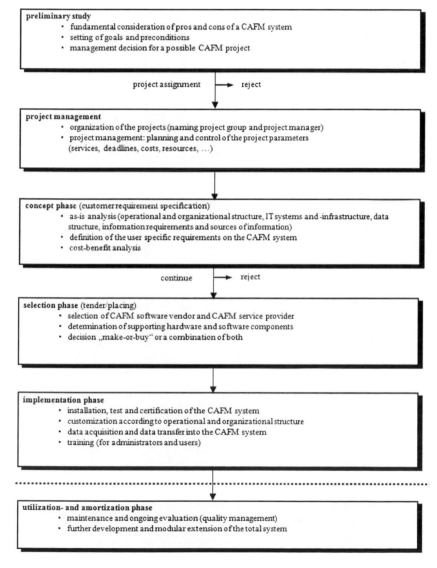

Fig. 13.1: Operational sequence of a CAFM system implementation

This complex project task diagram shows very clearly that the introduction of CAFM cannot be owned or implemented by an individual department. The directive to implement a CAFM project must come from the top of the organization. If CAFM only delivers cost reductions, increases in service quality, and employee satisfaction, then it could be conceived and implemented by one department. However, properly executed CAFM adds significant value by increasing the productivity of all employees using the facility and therefore increases the organization's competitive advantage. Realizing this potential added value requires integrating senior management strategic objectives and the processes to achieve these objectives from several departments with the project objectives. Senior leadership can be very helpful in creating the impetuous for the project team to preserve and maintain the focus and level of effort necessary to see a long project through to its successful conclusion. It is not unusual for these types of projects to take a year or more to implement.

During the system implementation, numerous problems can arise (May 2001b). If left unresolved, these problems can quickly escalate synergistically and combine to impact the project negatively, even to the point of failure. The most frequent causes of problems during the implementation of a CAFM project include the following:

- Lack of expertise or knowledge, especially concerning project and organizational goals, processes, data migration, existing systems, and the long-term IT strategic plan or the rollout strategy

- Inefficient or outdated FM processes; automating bad processes just increases the efficiency of delivering poor services

- Incorrect representations or expectations of the value of the project

- Inaccurate, inconsistent, or incomplete data to populate the system

- Existing IT solutions that are not optimal for integration

- Missing, incomplete, or incorrect data standards.

- Stakeholders from all organizational levels (operators to managers to senior management) need to be included in all project phases (conception, selection, implementation, development, and use) in order to ensure proper alignment between objectives, processes, and the solution

- Inadequate funding. Most CAFM projects require a higher upfront cost with a relatively sharp decline to a steady-state maintenance level of spending. Inadequate funds or inadequate cash flow can adversely affect the project.

- Unusual, complex, or changing existing conditions can lead to higher cost or a poor solution within the budget. The existing conditions include IT, FM. or departmental processes, datasets, IT infrastructure, organizational hierarchy, organizational propensity for change, and team composition.

- Poor rollout strategy (e.g., based on the technology rather than the processes)

- Ineffective data development process. Missing, incomplete, inaccurate or poorly timed and coordinated acquisitions of the data are some of the causes.

- The system selected has inadequate integration interfaces to other systems, requiring custom integration to be developed. (e.g., ERP, BMS, laser measuring, BIM, etc.).

- Changes in the organization's processes or objectives.

- Adoption resistances by the staff. This can be caused by lack of properly preparing the staff for the requisite process changes, by not setting expectations to match the solution, or by misalignment of the processes, objectives, and solution.

The following (section 13.4) has some references that help mitigate or avoid these problems.

The procurement procedure, which includes the RFP process and the acquisition of the CAFM system, is described in detail in chapter 12.

13.4 THE CAFM IMPLEMENTATION PROCESS

The CAFM implementation process consists of five phases:

1. Conception phase

2. Selecting a consultant (optional) phase

3. Software and vendor selection phase

4. Implementation phase

5. System development and use phase

13.4.1 CONCEPTION PHASE

The system and project objectives are designed and specified during the conception phase. This phase consists of identifying the primary project focus, defining the project goals and objectives, conducting needs analysis sessions, developing the functional specifications, writing the tactical and implementation plans, and producing a cost benefit analysis.

During the conception phase, it is advisable in most cases to consult with a competent and experienced adviser who can either lead the project during this phase or lead the entire project. This adviser must possess practical project experience in successfully executing these kinds of projects in the past.

Workshops and interviews are the best way to accomplish this task, even if there is documentation for the existing processes. The interviews should include stakeholders at all levels within each primary function, from daily operators to mangers to senior level. The size of the groups will be determined by the number and complexity of the primary functions, the culture of the organization, and the personalities of the stakeholders. During these interviews, the end-user requirements, the processes used, and the technical environment will be reviewed, documented, and reconciled with each other and the project goals to develop a functional specification.

13.4.1.1 PRIMARY FOCUS

This phase includes the analysis and evaluation of the existing conditions and project objectives for the purpose of developing the CAFM strategic plan. Some of the tasks for this phase include the following:

- Definition of the primary goals and objectives for the project

- Education of the project team

- Investigation of the enterprise strategy and the CAFM user

- Identification of required documentation and people to interview regarding FM processes

- Process analysis for recognizing weak points

- Identification of any staffing resources issues regarding staffing requirements for the CAFM project

- Identification and prioritization of IT support requirements

- Review of organization structure (org chart)

- Definition of required real estate information and facilities information

- Identification of the IT resources requirements and the sources of information for the FM processes

- Analysis of the existing IT environment as well as the necessary interfaces

- Review of the organizational IT and FM IT strategic plans

- Utilization of required experts

13.4.1.2 GOALS AND OBJECTIVES

Since the facility and naturally also the CAFM system must make a valuable contribution to the organization, the CAFM system must base its goals and objectives on the core business strategy. The facility management strategy must take into account the company targets and planned developments. Therefore, senior management of facilities must have regular interaction with the senior management of the enterprise. Integrating the strategic FM plan with the enterprise strategic plan allows the FM department to respond in a timelier manner to changing business requirements. Prompt responses to new or changing business requirements also require the close coordination and alignment of the IT, FM, and enterprise strategic plans.

The CAFM strategic plan should be derived from the FM strategic plan, which in turn is derived from the enterprise strategic plan and will need to be coordinated with the IT strategic plan. The alignment of these plans should ensure continuous project support from all levels within the organization.

The goals and objectives of the CAFM project need to be developed as the first step in the project. See initial project analysis (see figure 13.1). The project team that develops the goals and objectives should be comprised of the core project team and the key stakeholders. This team should be interdisciplinary and have representatives from all primary FM functions and organizational levels. The project team should have daily operators, managers, and senior management represented. It also needs to have a strong leader, who may be within the organization or a consultant. In either case, there must be a strong project champion from within the organization who can provide senior management-level support throughout the duration of the project.

The goals of the project are summarized in product requirement specifications (functional specifications). The goals and objectives and the corresponding designed solution are then developed into functional specifications and the RFP (if required). The RFP should specify the required hardware, software, services, and data development requirements.

The goals and objectives are unique for each organization. They are based on the key concerns of the enterprise, and the corresponding solution is tailored to those specific needs. While no two CAFM implementations are exactly the same, there are typical goals that can be abstracted:

- Fast and secure accesses to digital inventory information of the real estate portfolio for all relevant and business critical facilities

- Optimization of space management (moves, adds, changes)

- Preservation or increase in value of the buildings, technical plants, and building systems by replacement, maintenance, and preventive maintenance plans

- Energy consumption optimization through energy management and process management tools and plans

- Management of the costs of the enterprise real estate portfolio through internal value metrics and external benchmark metrics

- Support of building improvements and maintenance services with condition assessment and performance metrics

- Management support through the budget by having the budget based on linking facility budget items to organizational cost benefit analysis through value analytic metrics

The following section describes the subsequent CAFM implementation phases.

13.4.1.3 ANALYSIS PHASE

The analysis phase has the most diverse issues to be examined of all the phases. These have considerable influence on the CAFM project. The issues include at least the following:

- The FM organization

- The FM processes

- The user requirements

- Project resources

- The IT environment

- Evaluation of the data for input

Systemic institutional issues related to organizational or cultural deficiencies cannot be solved through CAFM. The analysis phase helps to identify them and can help reduce the impact on the FM department by using the CAFM system to isolate the interaction points.

The FM process analysis is one of the most important parts of the CAFM implementation. Through the analysis, the identified deficiencies become the starting point for improving the FM processes through automation. Without knowledge of the life cycle, quality, and costs of the current FM processes, an economic analysis to determine the value of implementing the system is impossible. The information for conducting a process analysis is typically not available and must be developed by means of interviews.

According to the extent and complexity of the FM processes, different process analysis methods and procedures can be used. Particularly for larger enterprises, established approaches and supporting IT tools exist (Corsten 1997).

Even if the following remarks read as very academic, this approach for large enterprises is crucial for the successful implementation of a CAFM system (see also chapter 4). The process analysis should represent activities and task sequences that are organized with a logical connection and have a distinct beginning and end. A process represents a repeatable sequence of activities with measurable input and creation of value and output. The assigned and required resources for the process must also be examined.

Complex processes are divided into subprocesses, whereby the clarity and comprehensibility of the life cycle and connections can be improved. The definition of the different subprocesses includes the definition of detailed steps and their connection, the required personnel, as well as the necessary information (source, format, system).

Numerous methods for analyzing and notating large complex processes are available. The process logic can be illustrated through the following (Corsten 1997; Scheer 2001):

- Flow charts

- Program structure charts

- Class diagrams (by means of UML)

- Event-driven process chains (EPCs)

Alternatively, a simplified tabular representation can be used initially and then expanded as complexity warrants. With all notation forms, it is critical that the description includes sufficient detail.

Finally, the different operational sequences are to be analyzed by both the people executing these tasks and their managers. External advisers are often used to help with process identification and analysis. While the internal knowledge is critical and can be provided only by enterprise staff, the objective view and varied experience of an external adviser is often very helpful.

The processes are analyzed for potential improvement. Some processes may have become obsolete or redundant, especially if automated.

Well-defined functional and technical specifications need to be derived from the process analysis. These requirements must accurately reflect the needs of the users of the system. If they are not, the system will be rejected by its daily users. This part of the processes is critical, and it is almost impossible to devote too much attention to it. The specifications must be developed from both the daily users and management. Daily users must accept the system and realize tangible benefits from the task automation, or the system will fail.

One result of the analysis phase is a realistic estimate of project resources. The resources include not only financial, hardware, and software but most importantly the appropriate project team. The CAFM project will be as successful as the team is qualified and motivated. The project team must have a leader who understands the importance of the team and has the experience and qualifications to lead them through the complexities of the project.

The IT enterprise environment needs to be included in the analysis. This should include not only hardware and software infrastructure, but also technical support expertise. Existing systems including database servers, CAD, ERP, and HR systems need to be considered in evaluating CAFM systems.

Integration with legacy systems needs special consideration. These systems need to be discovered and understood. Some of these may be ERP, CAD, GIS, and/or BMS systems. The analysis should include both a short- and long-term cost benefit analysis of different kinds of integrations, including a bi-directional interface, a one-way feed, a stand-alone system, or replacing the system through the CAFM project. The integration can be part of the initial implementation or can be implemented in a future phase. Sometimes the initial integration is a onetime manual feed to initiate the system and followed up with an integration in the next phase. This approach works well if the data doesn't change much or if the required update duration is several months.

The hardware systems will also be evaluated. This includes the workstations and the servers. Some or all of these may need to be upgraded to run the new system(s) efficiently. This is also an opportunity to upgrade systems based on the current IT technology plan of the enterprise. Coordinating the installation of the CAFM systems with the enterprise IT strategic plan projects is critical.

Finally, the investigation of the available data required for the CAFM system to determine the effort of obtaining and maintaining the system is a critical requirement. Data acquisition and long-term maintenance are the most cost-intensive processes of the CAFM system.

The analysis should document the sources, types, and field mapping of all data sources for initial population and for integration. It should also evaluate the data for consistency (validation), accuracy, and completeness.

13.4.1.4 CAFM FUNCTIONAL SPECIFICATIONS

Based on the FM processes identified during the analysis phase, the functional specifications can now be developed. The overall system design must address specific users and their processes. Most CAFM systems are modular in nature, and each module is divided into major process categories. Larger projects are typically rolled out a module at a time. While these modules may seem independent (especially from an organizational perspective), the systems are fully integrated from both a data and a process perspective. One of the key elements that need to be addressed during this phase is onetime initialization activities, such as data development. If the project is large enough to need multiple rollouts, the success of each rollout will facilitate the subsequent rollouts by building acceptance, momentum, and continued support from senior management.

An important component of the concept phase is the formulation of the substantial requirements for the different CAFM modules regarding the following:

- The required functionalities and the processes they support

- The desired integrations with other enterprise systems

- The system requirements (hardware and operating systems) based on the IT environment

The CAFM functional specifications will be developed into full technical specifications which will ultimately provide the specifications for the hardware and software system requirements for the RFP.

13.4.1.5 CAFM TACTICAL AND IMPLEMENTATION PLAN

A basic condition for a successful implementation of a CAFM system is a realistic tactical and implementation plan. The plan needs to include required tasks and their duration, sequence, and priority. The design of the plan should include balancing functions and processes from the perspective of achieving quick, provable results. The organization has to provide continuous support for the duration of the rollout. For larger, more comprehensive systems, this can be a year or more. Stages during the conversion can include:

- Selection of competent vendors or implementers of CAFM software (on the basis of market reviews, conference visits, seminars, and individual presentations)

- Selection of a service provider for implementing CAFM software (RFP)

- A pilot approach for implementing the system with the goal of optimizing the configuration and implementation of the system

- Implementation of the first stage of development, including training and data acquisition and rollout

- Continuous development of the system

CAFM systems and their environments are subject to constant change. Immediately following the successful implementation of a given module, new requirements and continuous improvement initiatives require making adjustments and enhancements to the system. This dynamic is an important criteria in CAFM software selection.

13.4.1.6 COST BENEFIT ANALYSIS

The last step of the conception phase is to conduct a cost benefit analysis. While most stakeholders and the technical designers would like to automate every function, this is not practical or cost-effective. Each function needs to be evaluated for its efficacy in delivering more value than it costs. Inherent conflict between costs and ease of use and functionality need to be balanced.

Please refer to chapter 5 for a detailed description of the ROI cost model. The calculation of the necessary expenditures should include the following cost elements:

- Consulting (concept, project support)

- License costs of the CAFM software

- Hardware costs

- System installation

- Customization, configuration and programming, and interfaces

- Training (user and administrator)

- Data acquisition (initial population, conversion of existing, and continuous maintenance) and data governance

- System maintenance (software maintenance)

The necessity (e.g., external consulting, hardware costs) as well as the extent (e.g., dataset, number of users) of the individual cost elements are critical to know if the project needs to be scaled back or implemented over several budget cycles.

The decision for implementing a CAFM system is based on clearly presented and realistic cost information that also includes the priority of each item and the value returned of each item (see chapter 8). From this information, the necessary metrics can be determined for the ROI.

13.4.2 SELECTING A CONSULTANT (OPTIONAL)

When deciding to implement a CAFM system, an educated team member should be involved. When a system is developed, implemented, or updated with new features, there are several important areas to consider:

- Needs of the CAFM system end users

- Existing processes affected by proposed changes

- Changes to the data architecture

- Effects on third-party applications

- Overall project timeline

- Quality and accuracy of the work performed

- Inclusion of work in an existing change management system

- Additional support needs

One may choose or have access to a member within the facility who is capable of planning and performing each stage in the selection and implementation of the CAFM software. Otherwise, it may be beneficial to involve a specialized consultant(s) who is experienced in these areas, is able to break down the project into manageable chunks, and can then actually perform the needed work. Before you select a consultant, it is important to understand the different types of work to be performed.

Should you select an independent adviser who doesn't implement software but manages the initial selection phase of the project? Or do you choose an independent adviser who specializes in a particular software package? Or perhaps a combined approach? In this last scenario, one might use a completely independent consultant to define the needs and perform the product selection, as well as a product-specific consultant who specializes in the implementation and performs the actual work.

13.4.2.1 A NEUTRAL PARTY

An independent consultant can create a specification that documents the functional requirements of the system and weighs the importance and cost of each area. This information can then be used to create a selection matrix used to make the final software selection.

After the selection process, the role of this neutral consultant changes. He or she may be retained as a project manager, be offered additional consulting and quality control, or be removed from the project altogether.

13.4.2.2 SOLUTION-SPECIFIC CONSULTING

In contrast to the neutral consultant, the solution-specific consultant can offer a depth of knowledge as to how his or her particular package addresses each area of need. The advantage here is that problems can be addressed quickly and other comparative projects using the same product can be used for reference. The success of this approach depends entirely on the ability of the consultant to understand the needs and overall goals of the end user.

13.4.3 SOFTWARE AND VENDOR SELECTION PHASE

13.4.3.1 SOURCES OF INFORMATION FOR CAFM SOFTWARE

The selection software that meets the specified criteria is critical for a successful implementation. The product selection is, however, only one of many important required steps of a CAFM implementation and should therefore be weighted correctly. (The detailed software selection process is covered in chapter 12.)

There are many reliable sources of information on CAFM systems that the potential user can use. Manufactures all have sites for learning about the capabilities of the product and getting some examples of case studies and references of successful projects. There are qualified product and market reviews available from technical periodicals and publishing houses. There are many articles and presentations on the Internet as well.

Many of the top brands are represented at tradeshows or industry conferences like IFMA, APPA, AIA, Corenet, NFM&T, and FM. CAFM implementation specialists can also provide a wealth of information in the form of customer references.

Creating and a Request for Information (RFI) can also be a great source of information. While vendors can provide a lot of specific information about their product, they will not be highlighting their deficiencies. Product deficiencies are the key success determinant. Soliciting consultants that specialize in CAFM implementations but do not specialize on one system can provide a wealth of information about several products, including both their strengths and weaknesses.

Properly evaluating the systems requires some knowledge of the systems. Visiting trade shows and conferences provides an opportunity not only to gain this knowledge but also to be able to compare several systems in a short time, allowing one to go back and forth between different manufacturers and compare the products.

13.4.3.2 SOFTWARE DEMONSTRATION WITH USER DATA

The software presentation needs to be focused on the critical functions required for the project and should include sample data that is the same for each software demo. This will help to equalize the comparison and make it easier for the evaluators to evaluate the systems properly and fairly. The systems should be evaluated based on a fixed, detailed checklist. The checklist and demo should cover the following points:

- Clear presentation of the required functionalities

- Scenarios in the sense of process workflows

- Compliance with the existing IT environment, including operating system, database system, network environment/intranet

- Use of the enterprise's data (drawing, room numbering, equipment, organizational structure, location information, etc.).

- Desired prototypical analysis tasks

The demo should cover the following main categories:

- Functionality

- Technology

- Software architecture

- User-friendliness

This will allow for a direct comparison of each vendor and system. Working with a precise checklists is crucial. The conversion of the user's data tests the vendor and system's efficacy in developing the initial dataset.

13.4.3.3 MAKE OR BUY

Before an RFP is developed, the question of whether to make or buy should be discussed. This concerns both the purchase of software licenses and the purchase of appropriate services such as inventory data collection. The key points for a decision include the following:

- Range and complexity of the functional requirements formulated in analysis phase and described in the requirement specifications

- Conformity of these requirements with the software products available in the market

- Quantity and quality of the already available inventory data

- Capacity and qualification of the enterprise's IT resources

The CAFM case study examples presented in the appendixes 1 through 6 include systems that have been developed using either the make or the buy strategies. Either strategy can be successful.

13.4.3.4 RFP

The RFP should be well defined and limited to the specific functional requirements developed in the conception phase.

The RFP process is addressed in more detail in chapter 12, so this section will focus only on the formulation of the requirements (performance specification) for the RFP.

- The requirements list should be based solely on analysis and concept phases. While it is critical to take into consideration future requirements, the RFP should address only those functionalities that can be achieved within the project timeline and directly support the project objectives or are necessary for base functionality of the system. The functional specifications need to be prioritized based on being required by the system, directly supporting the project and enterprise goals and a favorable cost benefit analysis.

- General inquiries should be avoided. These are often misleading and/or subject to varying interpretations by the respondents. Examples of general inquiries to avoid include

  - Use of Internet technologies (Y/N)
  - Object orientation (Y/N)
  - Interface with building automation (Y/N)

All too often in practice, RFPs are too broad and comprehensive. They focus on future and potential needs rather than the specific requirements developed in the analysis phase. This tends to generate responses that are much too high for the actual budget and will make it difficult to reduce the scope with revisions. It is much easier, more accurate, and more cost-effective to release a conservative scope and expand to the requirements to meet the budget, especially if the requirements are prioritized.

It is assumed that all established providers of IT solutions have expertise in the implementation and support of facilities business automation and can develop, implement, and support integrations between systems, including ERP systems.

In addition to the CAFM software, the RFP should include all services, including consulting, configuration, customization, integrations, training, data development, system support, and data governance.

A substantial part of the bidding procedure is the evaluation of the presentations and offers. Appropriate criteria are in chapter 12.

13.4.4 IMPLEMENTATION PHASE

13.4.4.1 TRAINING

The necessary training courses are to be specified in a special training course plan that should be specific to the user's needs. The training should include the following:

- Using the system (operators perspective)

- System administration

- Operation of the implemented interfaces

To avoid an information loss, the potential users should be trained directly before beginning to use the modules and the new processes planned for it. Otherwise, in a very short time the acquired knowledge might be lost, which will result in additional expenditures for retraining. The ideal approach to training is to base each class on user-specific tasks and to use their data. The pilot project can be used to fine tune the training program (training on the job).

13.4.4.2 PILOT PROJECT

Prior to rolling out CAFM for all FM functions enterprise-wide, a pilot project should be implemented. It should be selected carefully and should be comprised of an existing building that has a readily available and comprehensive dataset. This will reduce the cost and time of the pilot by avoiding the development of missing data.

The primary goals of the pilot project are the following:

- To demonstrate the necessary process support with suitable IT tools

- To prove the adaptability of the software to special demands of user

- To determine the IT support requirements for the individual FM business processes

- To examine the usefulness of the available data

- To determine the long-range data development requirements

- To prove the feasibility and operability of the interfaces to the IT systems existing in the FM environment

- To develop a long-term strategic plan for continuous improvement.

13.4.5 SYSTEM DEVELOPMENT AND USE

13.4.5.1 DATA GOVERNANCE

The value of a CAFM system is largely determined by the quality, quantity, and relevancy of the stored data. In principle only the data essential to conduct daily business and form long-term strategies should be collected and maintained.

For quality assurance, it is necessary to regularly examine the relevancy of the data. The data should support the processes and the metrics for continuous improvement and quality assurance. Often the processes or the metrics change requires an adjustment to the dataset being maintained. There are several kinds of data to be maintained in the system: supporting data (e.g., list of cities, list of space standards, list of departments); transactional data (e.g., work orders, invoices); asset data (e.g., list of equipment, buildings, rooms, employees); and data required for metrics and strategic planning. Some of this data is alphanumeric and some is graphic (images, drawings, BIM model). Some of the data is manually created, while some is fed from a different system through an integration, and some is generated as a part daily activities. All need to be validated either though the system or by manual review using exception reports. Owners need to be identified and held accountable for the quality, completeness, and relevancy of their data.

13.4.5.2 GRADUAL SYSTEM DEVELOPMENT

The development of a CAFM system is characterized by a regular extension of the functionality of the system. This is accomplished either by introducing new modules or extending existing modules.

The business requirements driving these changes may include one or more of the following:

- Replacement of existing IT tools with new FM modules

- Development of interfaces between existing enterprise solutions (IT integration)

- New processes

- New metrics

- New business goals and objectives

- Changes to organizational structure or FM department responsibilities

- New strategic initiatives

All changes to the system must be designed and implemented from a holistic system design while taking into account data governance efficacy and security.

13.4.5.3 FM ASSET INVENTORY DATA

Asset inventory is typically developed following two methods: rapid development and gradual development. Some of the assets need to be developed quickly (and indeed may need to be developed prior to the system rollout). Some of the asset data may be developed or improved over time. For example, a complete list of buildings may need to be developed prior to system rollout, but the corresponding floor plan drawings may be developed over time, and some noncritical buildings may never have drawings. Another example is developing an equipment list for preventive maintenance. Most organizations start with the larger and more critical pieces documented prior to rollout and add the rest of the equipment based on a prioritized list or while conducting PMs on the equipment. This allows for a more efficient data-collection process. The decision to develop the asset inventory data over time is a balance of business priorities, cost, availability of quality data, and how critical the data is to the functionality of the system.

13.4.5.4 DEPARTMENT

With the increasing development of the CAFM system, its attractiveness for the user organization rises. Visibility of the system and its value increases as the information from the system is used in presentations and meetings. More and more people will request access to the system and its information. This access needs to be granted and managed with alacrity. Noncritical stakeholders need to be granted limited access to control data quality (e.g., they may have read-only access) and overall system integrity (e.g., they may have limited access to only the complete and verified datasets). Nothing will destroy the credibility of a system faster than having an executive find an error in the data. It will then be assumed that much of the data will have errors.

13.5 IMPLEMENTATION STRATEGIES

13.5.1 INITIAL CONSIDERATIONS

Defining the tasks necessary for implementing CAFM is quite complex and requires special expertise for a successful outcome. The implementation strategy needs to take into account the available resources in the context of the overall goals and the time frame to complete the project.

Different implementation approaches (May 2001b) have been successfully used in practice. The choice of the implementation strategy depends on different factors:

- Scope and complexity of the project

- Budget

- Time frame

- Available expertise

- Authority of the project team (senior management support)

- Organizational culture

If the project team does not possess the expertise to achieve the project goals, a consultant should be hired to participate. The role the consultant plays needs to be defined clearly. Just hiring a consultant will not be sufficient to ensure success. The consultant has to be positioned properly on the project team. He or she may be hired to lead the project, manage the project, give technical advice, or to be a moderator for the project team to balance the project goals with the technical solution (a trusted neutral adviser).

Essentially there are two fundamental approaches to implementing CAFM:

- Analytic approach

- Pilot approach

The best approach cannot be determined at the very beginning of the project. Once the parameters of the project are defined in the analysis phase, the best approach can be identified.

13.5.2 ANALYTIC APPROACH

The analytic approach, which is in most cases selected, is comparable at the beginning stages with the methods of classical project management. The goal is to achieve the most comprehensive solution while minimizing both cost and risk. This analytic procedure is, in most cases, preferred. However, it is cost intensive and time consuming. Periods of up to two years to complete the conversion are not rare.

The analytic approach to the initial implementation follows these steps:

- Analysis of the existing conditions
- Goal definition
- Feasibility study
- Cost/benefit analysis
- Implementation plan
- Functional specifications (product requirement specifications)
- Design of the data model
- Data acquisition (develop supporting data and base drawings)
- CAFM RFP
- CAFM system acquisition
- Implementation (configuration, customization, and integrations)
- Training of the stakeholders
- Pilot project
- Data transfer (data feeds)
- Evaluation and adjustment based on lessons learned from the pilot
- Extension to the rest of the enterprise

These stages can partially overlap temporally based on special circumstances.

13.5.3 PILOT APPROACH

The primary advantage of this approach is that the system is up and running quickly, showing fast results. The risk is that the system may need to be modified while it is in use, which can be disruptive. This approach assumes that the project team is very familiar with CAFM systems or already owns a robust system, and will select the system without extensive, cost-intensive investigation of the different FM automaton products available in the market. Knowledge of the systems can be obtained through comprehensive demonstrations, interviews with existing users, and visiting industry or manufacturer's conferences where user case studies are presented. Additional information can be obtained through articles or attending product user meetings.

The pilot approach requires the following steps:

- Establishment of a small project team

- Development of project goals

- Early decision for a CAFM system and experienced vendor

- Definition of a visible pilot dataset (usually a typical building of medium complexity)

- Focus on key important enterprise issues (goals)

- Installation of the software (e.g., starting with an evaluation version)

- Training the personnel during the conversion of the pilot dataset (training on the job)

- Parallel the analysis of db structure, interfaces, data collection, and report creation during the pilot project

- Evaluation of the project (ease of use, tools, methods, personnel)

- Decision for continuation (e.g., continue with the project rollout, adjust the system, or abandon the effort or approach).

This beginning can be realized in a visible time and cost framework. Results should be obtained in one period of at a maximum of three to six months. In the most unfavorable case, it is recognized that with the selected software, the desired goals are not attainable. In this case the project must be ended before the costs of the project escalate further. In this way, the risk of a wrong decision remains small. This beginning is only recommended, if there is a high level of confidence in the selected software.

Conceptually, both approaches can be combined into one. This could be accomplished if the full analysis is performed prior to selecting the system. The system selection can follow the pilot. Minimal configuration and system modification can be performed and a more robust pilot project can then be implemented.

13.6 SUMMARY

The introduction of a CAFM system is a very complex procedure that requires both good planning and extensive expertise in project management, in information technology, and in facility management.

During the implementation of a CAFM system, a set of errors can lead in the long run to the failure of the project (May 2001a). Some of the key reasons for the failure include the following:

- Unclear goals (which can lead to a misalignment between the objectives and solution)

- Unclear team responsibilities

- Inefficient FM processes

- Absence of senior management support

- Too much ambition for the available project resources

- Insufficient vendor capabilities (e.g., poor financial health, lack of experience, buggy software)

- Insufficient synergies between departments (not enough participation of multiple departments)

- Missing common perspective between the user, provider, and implementation consultant

- Too rigid an organization (lack of resources, unrealistic expectations, unwilling to change)

- Software not user-friendly

- Software missing required functionality

- Underestimation of the level of effort for data development and maintenance

- Excessive demands or resistances of the staff

- Insufficient funding or resource (time) allocation

The following is a list of suggestions for a smooth and successful selection and implementation of a CAFM system (see also May 2005 for tips for a successful CAFM implementation):

- Participation of senior management from the outset

- Analysis and documentation of the FM-relevant enterprise processes

- Clarifying the required information as well as by whom, where, and how it will be developed and maintained

- Definition of the range of applications (with priorities) to be included in the CAFM implementation

- Development of sufficiently detailed product requirement specifications before evaluating capabilities of the existing commercial systems

- Definition of a pilot project that will produce quick, quantifiable results and will validate the system's ability to be scalable, to be easy to maintain, and to meet all project objectives

- Selection of cost-effective data acquisition technology

- Use of both a development and test environments for implementing changes to production with minimal disruptions

- Examination of the quality of manuals, training curriculum, and other materials

- Test of the ease of use of the system

- Calling of references of the software provider and/or service provider

- Inclusion of sufficient technical support

The successful realization of project objectives can be achieved only if the enterprise provides the appropriate framework for the project. There must be adequate time, effort, and expertise applied to the initial process and existing system analysis. The project team must be comprised of people with appropriate qualifications and expertise. The team must be given the proper authority from senior management. Senior management must provide unwavering and complete support throughout the duration of the project. The objectives must be clearly defined. The specifications for both the system and its implementation must support the objectives and be derived from the analysis of the existing systems, processes, data acquisition, data maintenance, and available resources to implement and then maintain the system.

The value of the system plays an important role in the long-term decision of implementing CAFM (chapter 8). Both quantitative and qualitative factors need to be evaluated to determine the value of the implementation.

The CAFM implementation must support the FM processes from the very beginning of the implementation. Knowledge of the cost, life cycle, and quality of the current FM processes are critical in evaluating the value of the implementation of a CAFM system. Unfortunately this information is usually unknown and must be collected laboriously through interviews, workshops, reviewing standard operating procedures (SOPs), etc. Opportunities for process improvements and for optimizing the implementation are recognized only through the analysis of the processes.

In summary, the successful introduction of a CAFM system is both challenging and an interesting task, which requires both management experience and extensive, detailed knowledge of the entire project team.

14

IT-BASED STRATEGIC SPACE OPTIMIZATION IN FM

Michael May, Michael Marchionini

14.1 THE CHALLENGE

In this chapter, we show how CAFM functionality can be improved considerably when integrating classical CAFM information management with mathematics-based simulation techniques. This example is thought to encourage more research and development in this direction.

At present, cost reduction in real estate and facility management is a hot topic. While energy consumption is a major focus, it is often overlooked that a much larger potential lies in an efficient use of the available space. Space allocation is tedious work and a great challenge for a facility manager, and it can have a considerable economic impact on the entire organization. Space allocation is not only an operational task in areas such move management, but it also is an issue in strategic planning.

Currently, this endeavor is approached manually, using CAD tools and spreadsheets at best. Consequently, the results are questionable and far from optimal. This is due to the tremendous complexity involved in the task. The inherent mathematical problem in the space management is the Quadratic Assignment Problem (QAP), known as one of the most intricate discrete mathematical problems, belonging to the well-know class of NP hard optimization problems.

To date, there are no known algorithms that solve these kinds of problems in an efficient manner. For example, the running time of these algorithms is (only) polynomial dependent on the problem size. It is a great challenge to develop new technologies that assist in this very complex optimization process, taking into account that much of the information needed in this task is already available in CAFM systems. Only a few efforts have been made so far to solve this type of optimization problem satisfactorily (May et al., 2009).

Here we will present a novel approach toward automating this difficult assignment task. In a research cooperative, the University of Applied Sciences HTW Berlin and the ReCoTech GmbH have developed new mathematical models and procedures that allow an approach toward automated space optimization in large real estate portfolios. The procedure assigns departments and people to available spatial resources (in one or many buildings) while taking into account preconditions like shortest distances and adjacencies of organizational units. The software developed generates different variants of space allocations and evaluates their quality based on criteria such as reduction of cost, time, number of necessary reallocations, and/or communication traffic. In this way, the FM is able to set free valuable space in one site and to utilize office space more efficiently in other.

With this technology, cost reductions can be achieved in a comprehensible and objective way. The approach presented is independent of any specific CAFM systems and uses standard data formats, thereby improving the applicability of the new technology.

14.2 UNUSED POTENTIALS

The following example aims at clarifying the possible effects of a space reduction (see table 14.1), as possible with the technology presented in this paper.

Let us assume a real estate portfolio with 1,000,000 square feet of rental space and an average rent of $1.65 per square foot per month and average operating costs of $0.50 per square foot per month.

Table 14.1: Example of cost saving when reducing rental space

	Annual costs	Annual costs when saving 10% of operating costs	Annual costs when saving 3% of rental space
Rental costs	$19,800,000	$19,800,000	$19,206,000
Operating costs	$6,000,000	$5,400,000	$5,820,000
Total	$25,800,000	$25,200,000	$25,026,000
Savings		**$600,000**	**$774,000**

Even if the assumed values differ in some cases or a leasing situation is not given, the basic statement remains: the optimization of space usage provides an extremely high saving potential. In addition, a majority of the facility managers will confirm that the saving of 3 percent of necessary space can be achieved much easier and faster than the saving of 10 percent of the operating costs.

14.3 SPACE UTILIZATION OPTIMIZATION

The objective of space utilization optimization is usually related to complex strategic business goals. An automated optimization procedure must take into account the following:

- Available spatial structure

- Actual spatial needs and constraints

- Communication needs and intensities within the organization and the resulting requirements for proximity of individual organizational units

Following are examples of resulting tasks:

- Allocation schemes for new buildings and new occupancies

- Space concentration with the goal of vacating unnecessary areas for subsequent utilization by selling, leasing these spaces, etc.

- Space concentration with the goal of providing space for organizational units to move in from other locations

Figure 14.1 illustrates the space optimization tasks.

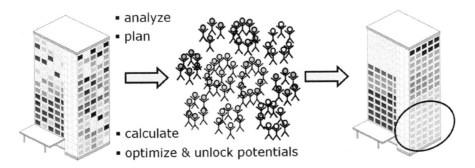

Fig. 14.1: Strategic space management with substantial optimization potential

Although the economic consequences of an efficient space-utilization planning are obvious, so far suitable technologies and IT-supported procedures are missing.

Thus allocation schemes today are still accomplished by the responsible facility and/or space managers either manually or with the help of classical IT tools such as CAD or CAFM. These IT tools are limited to the manual (interactive) planning of a single floor or group of floors. An automated generation of allocation proposals or the simulation of different scenarios does not exist. Optimized space planning for complete sites is not possible at all.

Investigations revealed that with the exception of a GIS-based approach by NASA Langley Research Center (NN 2009), an applicable IT solution for an automated space-utilization optimization does not exist, particularly with consideration of communication relations and intensities within the organization. Early developments from the 1980s and 1990s, which followed the classical Stacking and Blocking Approach (Brauer 1992), did not get beyond prototype solutions. The reason for that is the enormous complexity of the (combinatorial) optimization problems to be solved, ranking among the most difficult in discrete mathematics.

14.4 THE MATHEMATICAL PROBLEM

The allocation problem under consideration belongs to the class of layout/placement/location problems (May, Nerlich, and Weese 1988). In general, it is about assigning a certain number of objects in an optimal way to a number of locations/facilities, considering certain constraints and relations between the objects to be placed.

The fields of application reach from chip design in microelectronics over the creation of plant layouts and the ergonomic design of keyboards up to the automatic generation of graph drawings in computer graphics and graph theory.

The mathematical background for the creation of optimal allocations is the so-called Quadratic Assignment Problem (QAP), which was examined for the first time by Koopmans and Beckmann (1957).

The complexity of these problems results from the combinatorial explosion of the allocation possibilities of organizational units to spatial resources. The allocation of 10 organizational units (e.g., employees, teams, departments) to 10 spatial units (e.g., areas/rooms, space groups) already results in $10! = 3,628,800$ allocation possibilities. In reality, exact algorithms already fail concerning a size of >15. With 70 organizational units, which represent a usual problem size in real life, the number of the possibilities rises to an incredible 10^{100}.

Mathematically the formulation of the QAP reads as follows:

Let $o_1,\ldots,o_n$, be $n>1$ objects (e.g., persons/groups), which are to be assigned to n locations (e.g., areas/groups of rooms) $v_1,\ldots,v_n$, the transportation volume (e.g., also communication flow) c_{ij} between the objects o_i and o_j and distances d_{kl} between the locations v_k and v_l, i.e. $d_{kl} = D(v_k,v_l)$, whereby D is a distance measure (metric).

We seek a cost-minimal assignment of the n objects to the n locations:

$$\min_{\pi \in S_n} \sum_{1 \leq i < j \leq n} c_{ij} d_{\pi(i)\pi(j)}$$

where π denotes the set S_n of all permutations of $\{1,\ldots,n\}$. The goal function results as the sum (double sum) of all weighted distances between the communicating objects, where the weighing factor c_{ij} describes the communication volume or the communication intensity between o_i and o_j.

According to state-of-the-art mathematics, no algorithms exist that can solve such (NP hard) problems accurately within acceptable (polynomial) computing time. In addition, there are numerous constraints defined by the user that must be formalized likewise. For the practical solution of the actual problem, only good approximation methods (heuristics) can be applied.

The QAP is a simplified version of the space allocation problem under consideration in this chapter.

14.5 THE SOLUTION

Heuristic procedures are approximation methods that cannot guarantee an optimal solution for the problem, but seen from a practical viewpoint, they supply sufficiently good and efficient solutions. Such procedures are usually based on iterative or constructive approaches. Within the iterative procedures, an existing initial solution is gradually changed, so that an improved allocation is finally achieved. In some procedures, each iteration step improves the result; others accept a temporary deterioration, whereby attention must be paid to the requirement that the algorithm must terminate in acceptable computing time.

The problem with this approach is the immense computing time and the massive dependence of the result on the initial allocation. Constructive procedures, which usually work according to the bottom-up method, develop a solution step by step, where initially a starting object is selected and allocated, and all others are placed subsequently considering the constraints imposed. Such a "greedy" algorithm usually results in a local but not global optimization. Often good allocation decisions in the initial process of a constructive algorithm result in relatively poor decisions in later phases of the procedure.

Consequently, a new approach was derived, based on the divide-and-conquer paradigm. A divide-and-conquer algorithm works by recursively breaking down a problem into two or more subproblems of the same type, until these become simple enough to be solved directly. The solutions to the subproblems are then combined to provide a solution to the original problem. In our case the approach essentially consists of controlling the size problem (combinatorial explosion) by grouping suitable rooms into room groups/blocks on the one hand and on the other hand employees to teams/clusters. Thereby problem sizes are created, for which the developed algorithms can generate good solutions even on conventional PCs.

Forming space blocks and employee groupings of manageable size (see figure 14.2) enables an iterative procedure, allowing an allocation on the site level as well as on the room level. This top-down approach makes the task technically solvable and resembles strategic human thinking and problem solving.

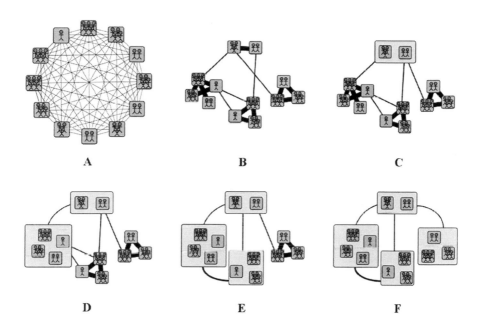

Fig. 14.2: Grouping of individuals/teams in clusters with respect to communication relations during an iterative process (A-F)

Here the intelligent user is required with his or her ability of pattern recognition and strategic thinking. The facility manager is deliberately and actively integrated into the process. He or she is given the possibility of dividing the building into spatial units and the organizational structure into teams/clusters. Furthermore, the FM is allowed to assess the results after each iteration and to influence the further process of the calculation. This method enables a stepwise restriction of the problem size and thus the result is optimally tailored to the specific task.

14.6 MODELING THE BUILDING STRUCTURE

An important challenge concerning automated allocation planning and the related space management is the transformation of a CAD drawing or building model into a formal description, on which the mathematical optimization procedures mentioned before can be based. A suitable way to display the spatial structure of a building is space graphs (May and Lost 1998), modeling the relative position and accessibility of areas. The vertices symbolize rooms and linking elements (doors, passages, stairs, elevators, etc.), and the affinity of areas and linking elements are the edges of the space graph. A space graph models the relative position and accessibility of the rooms, even throughout the borders of floors and buildings. A similar way of modeling spatial structures is provided by the space syntax (Hillier 1999).

Seen from a mathematical viewpoint, the building structure is modeled by a bipartite graph G(U,V,E). U denotes the set of the rooms (vertices), V the set of the linking elements (vertices), and E the set of the allocations of rooms and linking elements (edges). Figure 14.3 (May and Lost 1998) shows an example space graph based on a sample floor.

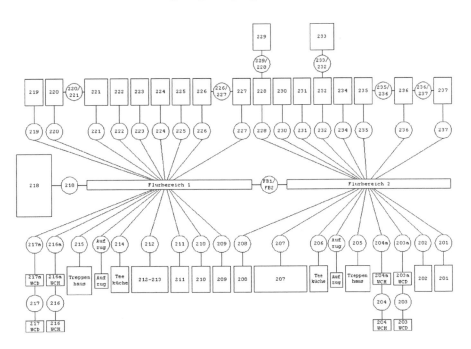

Fig. 14.3: Section of a structural model of a building as a space graph

A special challenge here is the automatic generation of this space graph from graphical data, which can usually be supplied by CAD or CAFM systems. At the same time, the room sizes (areas) needed for the optimization are determined from the CAD drawings. Furthermore, the space utilization for each room (e.g., according to national standards classification) can be derived (if necessary also from alternative data sources, such as Excel sheets).

On the basis of the space graph and with the help of shortest paths algorithms, it is now possible to determine the true distances d_{ij} (see definition of QAP) between two rooms $u_i \hat{I} U$ and $u_j \hat{I} U$, which obviously differs much from the "normal" Euclidean distance. Today such algorithms are also used in modern navigation systems.

14.7 RESULTS

A technology and a software tool that provide automated allocation optimization for real estate portfolios have been developed. The methodology developed is able to generate very quickly alternative allocation variants according to the given optimization criteria, like space requirements and proximity between certain organizational units. The task of the user is now to determine the "best" of the variants provided. An efficient visualization and selected KPIs support the user in making a final decision.

Figure 14.4 shows an automatically generated allocation variant with consideration of intercommunication between individual teams of the organization (May et al., 2007a; Marchionini and May and Marchionini, 2008) in a graphical form.

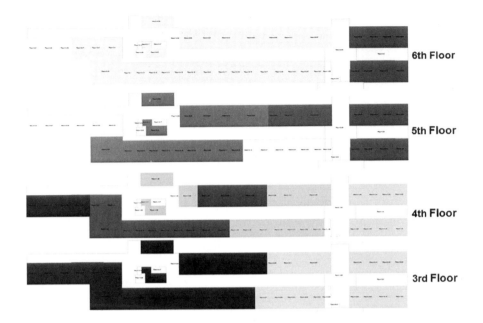

6th Floor

5th Floor

4th Floor

3rd Floor

Fig. 14.4: Computer-generated allocation variant

The same color (gray level) stands for groups/teams, which ought to be accommodated in spatial proximity to each other. The distribution of a team (e.g., over two floors) can be more favorable than assigning the whole team to one widespread floor. The spatial proximity of such groups can be forced by specification of their communication intensities.

Compared to the minimum conceivable (theoretical) space requirement of 100 percent (sum of all spaces needed without consideration of available room sizes), the automatically generated variant needs only 1.76 percent more space. It must be emphasized that the solution generated fulfills all space requirements (constraints) imposed.

Such requirements can be defined by some possible settings, for example,

- Specific pre-allocation

- Change of space requirements of individuals

- Definition of projected space (buffer space)

They give the user the possibility of controlling the procedure. With the possibility of assigning individual priorities/weights to criteria, such as

- occupancy rate,

- compactness, and

- communication relations,

the user can "control" the results of the optimization algorithms.

In addition to the optimization achieved by the software, the project partners have stressed the following benefits:

- Dealing intensely with the actual situation with the aim of modeling the data made previously hidden problems transparent in the early stages of the project

- Comparison between different planning scenarios highlighted useful strategic possibilities of a different use of predefined room types

- Using an objective technology to apply the same criteria to all space optimization tasks eliminated subjective prejudices

14.8 SAMPLE PROJECT: MUNICIPAL ADMINISTRATION BUILDING

As part of a major restructuring effort, the city authorities of the German city of Recklinghausen needed to evaluate the relative merits of two main scenarios concerning the future use of Building A as well as the investigation of two refurbishment options and their effect on each. The following question had to be solved: How many (and which) departments fit into Building A,

- if the archives are refurbished as offices, and

- if the attic is refurbished and used as office space?

Two planning scenarios were considered, in which we looked for a new distribution of all office space according to either of these goals:

- Exclusive use as a city administration building

- Exclusive use as a citizens services center

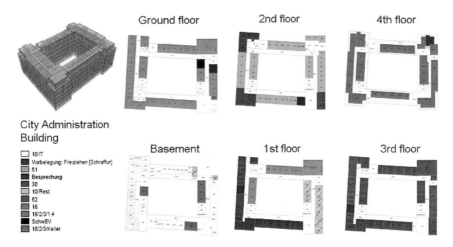

Fig. 14.5: Computer-generated allocation variant with
detailed planning of departments

As a result of the optimization (see figure14.5), over fifty persons were added to the office building. This also meant a reduction of planned investment for a new building by 3.9 million dollars.

Other projects are being conducted in the industrial and health sectors.

14.9 SUMMARY

A new computer-based technology enabling strategic and automated space optimization for real estate portfolios of any size regardless of their location was presented. Initial data is taken from existing CAD and/or IWMS/ CAFM systems and automatically transferred into formal building models (space graphs). The optimization procedure produces comprehensible allocation variants in a short time. The results are provided in alphanumeric (list) format but can also be visualized using the initial CAD data. In this way the results can easily be understood by the user and could be modified if desired. Furthermore, they can be handed over to classical IWMS/ CAFM systems to be used in subsequent processes, such as detailed relocation planning (on the level of individuals or individual workplaces).

This approach shows how CAFM functionality can be enriched by incorporating model-based simulation technologies. More innovations of this kind are expected to arise over the next years thereby increasing the value and efficiency of CAFM technology for their users.

15

THE INTERNATIONAL FM/IT RELATIONSHIP

Michael May

15.1 IT—AN ENABLING TECHNOLOGY FOR FM

The efficient utilization of information technology—and Computer-Aided Facility Management in particular—has proven to be crucial for FM organizations both in the private and the public sector around the globe. We have experienced more than two decades of using IT and in particular CAFM systems to document and to control facilities and facility processes. We have seen a tremendous development over the last ten years,: not only is there a wide variety of more than one hundred tools and systems available on the market worldwide, but the number of IT applications in FM is continuously growing. CAFM systems are developing into efficient information tools for supporting FM processes. Numerous software packages following different approaches, providing different functions and varying results have been used for years.

Therefore, IT is widely recognized to be an enabling technology for facility and real estate management.

Despite this promising development, there are numerous factors hindering the widespread success of IT and related CAFM tools. CAFM is still far from being the standard tool and technology that office tools or ERP systems have become. Also, not all projects conducted can be considered as being successful. Potential users are uncertain about the ways to implement IT in FM, especially about the efforts and benefits related to that process. Consequently, the worldwide market lags far behind expectations.

15.2 IT AND FACILITY MANAGEMENT

The relationship between IT and FM has not developed homogeneously in different parts of the world. The acceptance and progress of CAFM is closely related to the general state of IT development in that country or region.

The term CAFM comes from the United States and suggests that it refers to a software application. In principle we can assume that CAFM is frequently used and highly developed in the countries where FM ideals have been entrenched for a long period (e.g., in the U.S., Great Britain, Germany, The Netherlands, and Scandinavia). Therefore, it is also not surprising to find a large number of CAFM installations and strong local vendors in these countries. Internationally, there are often substantial differences in the current state of implementation and technologies employed as well as the respective objectives of the CAFM tools.

Many of the problems in the planning and implementation of a CAFM project seem to be general. However, more than two decades after the first CAFM systems appeared on the market, there are still no clear guidelines on how to implement them efficiently and no clear factors leading to success. This frequently causes poor decisions, unnecessary cost overruns, and frustration. Due to a lack of experience, knowledge, and tangible results, users often hesitate to introduce adequate IT tools in their organizations.

There is still uncertainty concerning the procedures and achievable effects. This is closely related to the lack of recognized CAFM implementation frameworks (models). From an economic point of view, it is very important to support the process of implementation in order to avoid wrong decisions and unnecessary investments. Implementation strategies and formulae for success are especially of great interest.

There is also a considerable degree of uncertainty on a global scale about the terminology used in IT-FM (Hohmann et al. 2008). Some of the terms related to IT (systems) in FM are used synonymously; others express subcategories or were introduced as registered trademarks by vendors to differentiate their products from their competitors. This includes terms like CAFM, CIFM, CMMS, TIFM, and IWMS.

It seems that, after all, the term CAFM best fits the support of IT for FM. In accordance with other CAx terminology (like CAD, CAM, CAQ), the focus is on the general IT (computer) support of the application field under consideration. Consequently, CAFM describes the support of FM processes and users by information technology. This understanding is typical for Europe, but there are other interpretations that originate from the early days of computer support in FM. They consider CAFM to be the use of computer-assisted methodologies (including drawings, database reporting tools, and spreadsheets) to manage large amounts of facility-related information. This is definitely an important feature of CAFM but does not describe the holistic approach that IT support in FM stands for.

For the newcomer, the variety of terms and products can be confusing. And the interpretation of different terminology varies from region to region. As an example, the term Computerized Maintenance Management System (CMMS) is usually used for computer systems that assist in planning, managing, and analyzing maintenance processes. For instance, in some parts of the world, as in Scandinavia and Australia, this term is frequently used for what we understand by CAFM.

The term facility automation is not only used for CAFM-related processes and systems (Lunn and Stephenson 2000) but also for a wide range of building automation tasks. Therefore, the use of Facility Automation System (FAS) may cause ambiguity.

Finally, we note Integrated Workplace Management System (IWMS), a term created by Gartner (Bell 2005). An IWMS is considered an enterprise platform that supports the planning, design, and management of an organization's physical asset base. IWMS systems assist organizations in optimizing the use and administration of workplace resources, one of the most valuable of which is the management of a company's real estate portfolio. Other areas of functionality include lease administration, space management and maintenance management. This shows that IWMS comes very close to the European understanding of Computer-Aided Facility Management.

CAFM, based on the latest developments in information technology, represents the support and realization of the FM concept throughout the entire real property life cycle. CAFM represents the application of computer systems, including hardware and software, to support FM functions efficiently. CAFM software systems back up the specific processes of FM and the persons involved in those processes. Thereby, all relevant data occurring during the life cycle of facilities and related processes is captured, used, and analyzed electronically. In addition, CAFM software has to provide a number of primary functions (NN 2007b) to meet the requirements of FM fully.

In many cases, during the introduction of FM, the hope of resolving inherent FM problems just by implementing an IT tool is a false hope. If the necessary preliminary enquiries, planning, and strategic decisions are missing and there is a lack of involvement by personnel and management stakeholders, then the implementation of FM is doomed to fail. In addition, the software becomes an expensive investment.

15.3 INTERNATIONAL DEVELOPMENT OF IT IN FM

The first IT applications for FM-related tasks appeared in the 1960s, even though we did not recognize facility management as a profession during that time. Specific problems, especially in design and construction, were already supported by IT, and the first attempts to deal with computer-supported space management appeared. Graphical user interfaces did not yet exist, but mainframe computers were already providing some computational power.

Using the term *facilities planning* (Brauer 1992) methods were developed for the design and evaluation of floor plans and related layouts, whereby mathematical procedures from the field of operations research were used. These were singular applications for use only in large organizations, since computer resources were extremely expensive. Interestingly, CAFM took its starting point from this limited application of the computer in FM, whereas today's developments in CAFM focus more directly on the automation of FM processes.

In the 1960s, the first database applications appeared. They supported simple planning and information management tasks, such as space planning and inventory. However, they remained isolated and were too expensive for most companies.

With the advent of the PC in the early 1980s, computer programs could be used for the first time by a wide variety of employees. In particular, office tasks (office automation) like word processing and spreadsheet programs became widely used. In this manner, simple FM activities could be supported. Usually, these were specialized solutions for individual organizations.

Also, Computer Aided Design (CAD) systems gained acceptance in supporting complex design tasks. They became generally accepted as an important data supplier in facility management. Thus the automatic determination of space areas, the color coding of different space uses, or the localization of inventory provided a suitable decision basis in space management.

Soon the importance of combining graphic with textual information was recognized. The approach of linking and evaluating alphanumeric data with graphic objects in a CAD system did not result in the success expected, because only very limited "reporting" potential (usually list generation) existed; consequently the CAD files were overloaded with alphanumeric information.

Later the two apparently different worlds of graphic and alphanumeric data were combined by coupling CAD systems with database systems (DBS) in a bidirectional way. This resulted in FM-specific software packages covering only very limited fields such as space management or move planning. Modularization of software was not yet implemented to a large degree. Also, these systems could not easily be adapted to the ever-changing requirements in the organizations they supported. Frequently, the operation of those systems was complicated and nonuniform from a user's perspective.

Especially in Europe, many software developers came from the AEC (architecture, engineering, and construction) industry; the holistic understanding of FM was hardly developed at that time.

A further step in the second half of the 1990s was the concentration on data management and processing. Thus CAFM software was developed on top of a database system. CAD as well as other IT systems now played the role of a data supplier for the CAFM application. For the visualization of the graphic data, either viewer programs or "mini" CAD systems or kernels (usually 2-D) were used.

The software was developed in modules and could communicate with other applications via appropriate interfaces. There were, however, great differences concerning user-friendliness and flexibility.

First, software providers tried to waive the artificial separation of graphic and textual data as both data types were administered equally in the DBS. Thus all favorable mechanisms of a DBS could be used, such as data security and transactions. Still, these were systems especially developed for specific CAFM tasks. The problem of the integration into the IT environment of the user was not yet solved satisfactorily.

The role of design data and its interaction with FM processes changed dramatically with the advent of Building Information Modeling (BIM) (Eastman et al. 2008). Though the original ideas were already derived in the 1980s in Europe, the breakthrough of this technology did not occur until recently, when BIM was adapted by the leading CAD software providers especially in the United States. Large organizations are beginning to require BIM models for their building projects. For example, in the U.S. federal government, BIM is a requirement for projects at the U.S. General Services Administration, the U.S. Army Corps of Engineers, and the Department of State.

BIM is a sophisticated software technology that provides a complete 3-D digital representation of a building or subsystem. BIM provides both a visually accurate model of a building and a database for recording the breadth of information developed and associated with building components. Beyond being a software tool for drawing and documentation, BIM offers a platform for enhanced interdisciplinary collaboration, the capability to manage change, and the ability to extend information support throughout the life cycle of buildings (Sabol 2008). BIM incorporates a universal, open data standard to allow full and free transfer of data among various platforms and applications.

Recently, a next-generation IT system for FM appeared. This concerns web-based integration platforms, which include mobile communication possibilities and interoperate with other IT systems (e.g., ERP or BMS) on the level of the operating systems, the programming languages, or the applications. In this case, middleware and EAI (Enterprise Application Integration) as well as Service Oriented Architectures (SOA) are used (May 2006).

The availability of FM information in the Internet/intranet enabled CAFM applications to be visible globally in an organization and beyond for the first time. This increases their added value considerably. Thus today nearly unlimited application opportunities exist for the CAFM technology.

A further development consists of integrating mobile computers such as PDAs (Personal Digital Assistants), smartphones, or tablet PCs with CAFM databases. This communication takes place, for example, via Wireless LAN (WLAN) connections or by means of data alignment via docking stations. We speak of Mobile Facility Management" solutions. In addition, technologies such as RFID (Radio Frequency Identification) for reliable identification of objects in buildings are becoming more and more popular (Schauer and Marchionini 2006).

While in the past, the focus of CAFM software was clearly on data acquisition, storage, and evaluation, the interest shifted to the modeling and control of FM processes. Here we differentiate between manual, semiautomatic, and automatic process control (May 2006).

In addition to intelligent query tools, filter mechanisms and rights of access semiautomatic process control also includes notification mechanisms, for example, depending on certain attribute values, the user receives a personal report or work order.

However an automatic process support is possible only if the CAFM software possesses an integrated workflow component. By a workflow, it is possible to map a process directly into software. The software then controls the processes, and all users receive exactly the information and orders within the processes for which they are responsible.

Above all, an integrated workflow management system offers the possibilities to structure and control the FM processes.

15.4 STATE OF THE ART IN INTERNATIONAL IT USE IN FM

Worldwide, we can basically differentiate between four regions (continents) where CAFM has gained a more or less substantial impact on FM strategy and operation:

- North America

- Europe

- Asia

- Australia

In these regions are differences in the state of using and developing CAFM technologies. If we take Europe, for instance, we find a decreasing level of using IT in FM (and in FM development as well) from north to south and west to east.

Many of the leading software vendors are based in the United States. However, the greatest variety of software products can be found in Europe (already more than fifty in Germany). Among them we can find many software products that are mostly present in just one or a few countries. So far there is only one CAFM player from Europe active in the global market.

Currently, the Asian IT/FM market clearly has the biggest potential. Consequently, the leading U.S. providers have enforced their activities, especially in China, India, and Japan. But we also find some local CAFM software developers in Asia, such as in Japan and Hong Kong. There is a similar situation in Australia, where FM and CAFM have gained momentum over the last years. This was mainly due to the Australian "FM Action Agenda" (NN 2008b). Besides the international market leaders, some local software vendors focus on specific topics, such as sustainability, and offer corresponding modules within their packages.

Concerning integration issues, CAFM in North America has already acted for many years as an integration platform for various FM-related IT systems, including ERP, building automation, and mobile applications. A variety of integration techniques from data to application integration are available. This trend is rather new in Europe but has gained momentum in large, private organizations and is slowly penetrating the public sector. In Asia and Australia, integrated IT/FM solutions are rarely found.

Here most projects concentrate on specific modules/functions like space management or maintenance management.

Though building management systems (BMS) are widely in use, the interoperation with CAFM tools is not yet standard. Frequently the proprietary formats and protocols of the BM hardware providers are used to integrate BMS and CAFM systems. These are usually customized solutions that can hardly be transferred to other projects. The trend is toward open, standard IP-based supervisory networks.

Most IT tools from North America and some from Europe are FM business-process oriented. That means these systems allow structuring and control of FM processes via integrated workflow tools. However, many projects in Asia, Australia, and in part of Europe are more data-centric than focused on processes. This still originates from the days when CAFM was purely a data-acquisition and management technique.

As mentioned earlier, BIM is one of the latest software technologies to assist in the interoperability of software systems throughout the entire life cycle of buildings from design and construction to operation.

Graphical representations of buildings and their components have always played an important role in CAFM applications. Hence, almost all software products have an integral CAD kernel (in most cases just 2-D) or interface with the systems of the leading CAD software vendors. Rework is often necessary to make CAD files, delivered from project construction documents, applicable to FM (Sabol 2008). The benefit of graphics to the facility manager was sometimes questioned. Obviously, there are FM tasks, such as space and move management, in which visual information supports the imagination and decision making of FMs. But generally much effort was focused on data acquisition, especially CAD drawings. The situation has changed with the advent of BIM. With BIM, graphical representations do not just serve visual purposes but are specific views on the general building model. Compared to 2-D/3-D CAD files, building information models provide completely new opportunities, such as interoperability of software systems and improved FM process efficiencies.

In the United States and parts of Asia and Europe, BIM is already widely established in the design and construction phase. Full integration of BIM into CAFM systems and full exploitation of building information models in FM can be found very rarely. In Europe the first CAFM products have been fully integrated with BIM technology and show impressive results; however, most of the classic CAFM providers still ignore this important topic or use it just to a minor extent. In Asia we find an active BIM community (e.g., in Hong Kong, Korea, Singapore, the Philippines), that even organizes its own international BIM conferences. However, there is not much indication of BIM use with CAFM. In Australia the situation is similar. BIM is pushed by some academic institutions and was promoted by the FM Action Agenda.

The use of mobile technologies with CAFM is standard in North America and parts of Europe. Many applications—such as maintenance management, troubleshooting, location-based services, and/or mass notifications during an emergency evacuation—are able to benefit from this innovative technology.

With some delay, all major technological trends in FM will spread to all regions mentioned.

15.5 GENERAL PROBLEMS AND OBSTACLES

Despite differences in the level of technology used and the pace of implementing and adopting new technologies and tools, there are a lot of problems and obstacles that seem to be quite common in the different continents and regions, including that following:

- FM and hence CAFM has not yet reached the C-suite in many organizations. As a consequence we note a lack of management commitment, frequently resulting in project failure.

- Many organizations have not yet formed a specialized FM department and consequently miss the opportunities that new technologies can offer to the FM.

- Some projects are lacking an ambitious and well-prepared project team. CAFM cannot be implemented successfully by a project leader running his or her daily business in parallel to the CAFM project.

- Often we see just a small number of CAFM users who benefit from the complex information base. Web-based solutions provide access to (selected) FM information for everybody. This leads to a much broader acceptance and usability of CAFM technology.

- Frequently FM is considered just from a specific (isolated) perspective, such as a technical or economic viewpoint. This is also reflected in many CAFM projects, which concentrate on isolated application fields (e.g., space management, maintenance management, lease management), thereby neglecting the holistic approach of FM.

- Sometimes we note coordination and competency problems among the participants of a CAFM project (user, software vendor, or implementation partner and consultant). This relationship must be based on trust and efficiency.

- Project teams are often too ambitious and strive for too much progress in an unrealistic time frame. Clear priorities based on expected efficiency and quality gains must be set.

- Users underestimate the effort to acquire and maintain FM data. They want to capture too much data, not always knowing the reasons they need it and the benefits of it. Here, less is more. It important not only to choose the most efficient data acquisition technique but also to establish a clear procedure on how to maintain this data. A strict data-quality assurance policy must be established.

- Often CAFM software is isolated from the organization's IT infrastructure and existing software systems, such as ERP systems. IT integration—on whatever level it may be accomplished—is the key to success.

- In many cases CAFM is focused on data rather than processes. Consequently those approaches concentrate on information related to (mainly static) structures and objects but can hardly support dynamic procedures. Leading CAFM software vendors have therefore implemented workflow management technologies into their products.

- To date, CAFM software is hardly interoperable. So far there is no easy way of migration from one CAFM system to another. This is a challenge to the software developers and should be a requirement of the users. BIM/IFC may be one path toward interoperability in Computer-Aided Facility Management.

- There is a lack of independent information sources regarding efficient implementation models and strategies. Knowledge-based IT systems like FM-ASSIST (Buettner et al. 2008) are starting to emerge as an innovative technology that helps organizations to implement (CA)FM based on a unified approach and knowledge. Those systems are able to provide assistance similar to what usually is done by an IT/FM consultant.

- Usually, it is very difficult for the user to differentiate between the various software products on the market. For the sake of quality assurance, first approaches toward CAFM software certification based on functional checklists have been established successfully in Europe (Opi et al. 2011).

- Well-educated CAFM specialists are still rare. Even in most curricula of university FM programs, the relationship between IT and FM plays a marginal role. The use of certain software systems is taught rather than the fundamental ideas behind that category of application software. Here the responsibility of and need for action by educational institutions and FM associations cannot be overstated.

16

CAFM TRENDS AND OUTLOOK

Maik Schlundt

16.1 TRENDS IN FM/IT

CAFM trends are linked to developments in facility management and information technology. Furthermore, ongoing developments in the IT sector influence CAFM. New IT technologies are checked for CAFM and implemented if considered suitable. One example is the development of RFID technology that replaces bar codes to simplify inventory management.

When we look at various developments within the IT sector, it becomes obvious that they are marked by new technologies in the field of software and hardware. For CAFM, a growing automation is key, especially in the field of data, information, and knowledge management.

In the following, new developments and trends are outlined.

16.1.1 NEW SOFTWARE TECHNOLOGIES

Among the latest IT trends are, for example, cloud computing and application virtualization.

Cloud computing is nothing really new, but has recently been promoted as a new concept. The idea is that applications can be started directly from the Internet, so they do not have to be installed on the desktop PC. As a result, no resources from servers or administrators must be provided, because this is the task of the software provider. For CAFM solutions, this is quite interesting, because it saves costs for hardware and administration. Cloud computing means distributed applications and a flexible allocation of processing power.

Another recent trend is the so-called application virtualization, which are programs packed together in a software container and made available as an executable file (.exe). Therefore, instead of being installed on the computer, the application must only be copied. Thus, the installation of clients is considerably simplified.

The issue of integration is still a major concern, particularly the integration of CAFM software into the existing IT landscape. Web services already provide many opportunities. Linking Web 2.0 technologies and using hosted applications—for instance, information services like Google (Google Earth or Google Maps)—is an interesting topic. Web 2.0 applications such as Google Earth provide simple and user-friendly interfaces; therefore, the demand for training programs decreases. Some CAFM vendors are already starting to integrate this kind of user guidance into their own systems, or they provide an opportunity to connect to existing navigation tools

Another upcoming issue is the interoperability of CAFM systems with information services that provide regulations and guidelines for facility managers. The latest versions of important documents become available, which is a big advantage. If this had to be organized by a company, it would require a lot of time and effort. With this new development, however, all the extra work could be outsourced easily.

In addition, linking information and data—for example, via mobile phone positioning using GPS and combining this piece of information with objects in a map—could make data collection in CAFM much easier. This could be used for finding property, buildings, and the exact locations (coordinates) on the map.

There are also a lot of trends and new developments in the field of knowledge management. With Web 2.0 tools like wikis, the documentation of CAFM software for tutorials or instructions becomes possible and easier through cooperation. For example, you can create up-to-date software manuals because you can write support calls directly into a wiki. In the field of management of ideas, wikis can also help when discussing innovations online with great flexibility.

Building Information Modeling (BIM) is more often used in large projects. The concept is becoming more and more common in the building industry and consequqntly CAFM. BIM can utilize the IFC format for data management and integration. As a result, the FM receives a very high data quality because of a building information model.

Decentralized data collection is also an exciting topic. With Web 2.0, users can add information about buildings and related facilities; therefore they can make use of so-called collective intelligence.

Process management, especially workflows, is playing an ever more important role in service companies, for example, for the effective implementation of FM standard processes.

16.1.2 NEW HARDWARE TECHNOLOGIES

The decreasing cost of hardware and other developments have an influence in this field. For example, there is an increasing supply of wireless technology for building automation, such as counter and controlling devices that operate with a wireless connection, often using GSM connections in areas that are hard to access.

Mobile devices, such as netbooks or tablet PCs are lighter than traditional laptop computers, have a longer battery life and better performance, and are therefore perfect for helping FMs access data on the spot. There is also a trend toward paperless office management by means of ebooks. Because of the new INK technology (electronic paper), these have clear screens and look like real paper. These devices are energy-efficient and suitable for long-term use on the move. However, existing devices do not have enough features and functions yet for everyday use, such as flexible search functions within documents and way to quickly browse pages. With an increase in functions, consumer is likely to increase, so ebook applications for accessing project documents, manuals, and reports are likely in the near future.

16.2 IT/FM IN 2020

In 2020 IT-based FM systems will have turned into automated, integrated, and process-oriented hardware and software systems. These sophisticated systems will link all FM processes with the main line of business.

CAFM software consists of decentralized modules that can be controlled by any device via a standardized interface. All-in-one devices have already penetrated the market, especially pocket-size controlling devices (similar to netbooks) that come with special glasses and ear buds.

As a consequence, the mobile facility manager will be connected around the clock and, thanks to IT support, will be able to do every task efficiently. Data will be collected either via flying sensors that carry measurements or special glasses that automatically provide live recordings on the spot.

Thanks to the full integration of all IT/FM modules, creating and controlling workflows will become a piece of cake. Therefore workflow automation will be implemented easily.

As soon as 2020, intelligent meeting rooms that can adjust the room temperature on their own or intelligent lamps that switch off automatically as soon as the building is empty will become operational. The room temperature will be perfectly adjusted to needs and will be highly energy-efficient.

In short this will lead to the following:

- An almost perfect accuracy of inventory data

- Software that introduces the user to itself in about ten minutes

- All-in-one devices that create a higher quality of work—facility managers will have one device that is a phone, calendar, and central-object database for addresses, facilities, etc.

- Better collaboration thanks to open systems and mutual trust

- Flexible, object-oriented graphical databases

Companies have realized that synergies can be created only via cooperation. In addition, cooperation is the key to long-term success that guarantees the survival of humankind and a high living standard.

APPENDIX 1:

CASE STUDY BB&T

Kevin Foley

A1.1 CORPORATE OVERVIEW

BB&T Corporation, the fourteenth largest financial holding company in the United States, has expanded rapidly since the late 1980s by acquiring sixty community banks and thrifts, more than eigty-five insurance agencies, and thirty-five non-bank financial services companies. A financially sound institution, BB&T operates retail banks in the Southeast and Mid-Atlantic regions of the United States. The company also has a large insurance brokerage operation and owns an array of specialized non-bank financial service companies across the United States and Canada.

A1.2 REAL ESTATE RELATED DATA

The company's Support Services Division also grew rapidly to keep up with the responsibility of managing all real estate properties. The company's banking network operates 1,500 retail branches ranging in size from 1,000 to 20,000 square feet, with an average size of 5,000 square feet. Data centers, operations, processing, and back-office functions occupy 70 so-called "corporate" buildings with a total of 3 million square feet. When you include BB&T's non-bank businesses, the company occupies nearly 2,500 locations totaling more than 13.5 million square feet.

A1.3 FM GOALS AND POLITICS

Over the last couple of years, BB&T increased its focus on organic growth as a viable way to grow its core banking business. In 2006 and 2007, the company constructed seventy-one De Novo banking locations and acquired new sites to accommodate future growth. In the back office, intense focus on efficiency was creating increased amounts of vacant space. At the same time, regulatory changes and the expansion of online initiatives fueled demand for office space in new markets. The company realized that it needed a solution that would help track all its acquisition activities and also allow it to utilize back-office space more efficiently. The company set a conservative goal to reduce occupancy expenses by 500,000 dollars annually over the first few years with the new system.

As the organization grew, FM became increasingly complex. Methodologies and data sources had become increasingly fragmented into silos; therefore, BB&T needed to consolidate information to become proactive in managing physical assets. After an intensive evaluation of Integrated Workplace Management Systems (IWMS), it chose Planon as the application that best satisfied its requirements.

BB&T was in the process of centralizing maintenance, janitorial, and landscaping services in its banking network. Partnering with an outside service company led to the consolidation of vendors and many changes for internal employees. To help measure service levels, the leading vendor offered its own proprietary system and personnel for managing work orders. This led BB&T to introduce an additional help desk for bank employees; it also meant that the company was dependent on the vendor for performance reporting. BB&T needed a way to manage its own information on maintenance history and service levels.

A1.4 LEGACY SYSTEMS

Prior to the integrated approach, BB&T's Support Services Division used a number of Access databases and Excel spreadsheets to track information. The result was a massive duplication of effort to keep simple property data up-to-date across various systems. The company utilized an externally hosted real estate management system, but this solution was not updated with internal data and had no interaction with the Accounts Payable department. BB&T had also customized a third-party procurement tool to manage maintenance work orders. This system was not equipped to handle future growth and became difficult to support due customization of the product.

A1.5 THE CAFM/IWMS PROJECT
A1.5.1 PROJECT IMPLEMENTATION

In the summer of 2007, BB&T implemented its first phase of the IWMS for all processes related to facilities projects, planned, and reactive maintenance. This made it possible for all employees of the bank to submit service requests, report maintenance issues, and order products via the Employee Self Service Portal (ESS). Employees can check the status of their requests and orders at any time and interact with Support Services directly through the Portal. Orders are routed directly to external service providers and can be managed in the vendor's own back-office system via an interface to the IWMS database. The interface allows vendors to follow up on calls, request additional information, provide quotes and estimates, and ultimately complete their work orders and initiate the invoicing process. The BB&T Support Services staff can easily obtain the status on any outstanding orders and measure vendor performance as it relates to SLA agreements.

The next phase included the integration of the IWMS's mobile solutions. Using these solutions, maintenance staff and technicians can receive and update the status of work orders, enter working hours, enter costs, and enter parts used during reactive and planned maintenance activities.

BB&T completed its implementation of the solution in July of 2008, and it is already recognizing the benefit of an integrated approach:

- Over 28,000 BB&T employees have access to the Employee Self Service Portal and have the ability to place service calls or order assets.

- Over 300 BB&T employees work with the ProCenter Java client. Employees at 40 external vendors are also working with the system via this client.

- Over 120,000 facilities and reactive maintenance orders and over 27,000 preventive maintenance orders have been created in the system thus far.

- The Lease Administration module is managing over 1,500 locations.

- Approximately 40 million dollars in invoices will be processed yearly on reactive maintenance alone. This figure is expected to reach several hundred million dollars as additional tools were added in June of 2008 to manage construction projects.

A1.5.2 PROJECT SCHEDULE

Period	Activity
12/5/2006	Decision for the project
01/22/2007-07/10/2008	BB&T-IWMS implementation project
01/22/2007-02/02/2007	Phase 1: Project startup
02/05/2007-03/06/2007	Phase 2: Project initiation
02/08/2007-02/13/2007	Kickoff meeting
02/13/2007-06/30/2008	Phase 3: Implementation
02/13/2007-03/12/2007	Preparation
03/14/2007-04/17/2007	Develop implementation plan
02/20/2007-06/30/2008	Module implementation
02/20/2007-05/22/2007	1.0 Base data and load (existing DBs and spreadsheets)
02/20/2007-06/04/2007	2.0 Design services / space and move management configuration
05/22/2007-08/27/2007	3.0 Strategic vendor management configuration

05/22/2007-08/29/2007	4.0 Support services helpdesk configuration
10/15/2007-11/20/2007	4.0.A. Implemented vendor interfaces and batch invoicing process maintenance processes
10/22/2007-12/18/2007	5.0 Integrate support for purchasing processes in maintenance, design, and move processes
10/22/2007-12/18/2007	6.0 Integrate support for warehouse / assets & inventory management in maintenance, design and move processes
11/05/2007-02/29/2008	10.0 Extended maintenance functionalities
06/18/2007-09/07/2007	Analysis RE work packages 7.0, 8.0, 11.0, and 12.0
11/05/2007-06/30/2008	7.0 Implementation standard property management / replace AMT
03/03/2008-06/30/2008	8.0 Implementation extended property management
03/03/2008-06/30/2008	9.0 Implementation project management
07/01/2008-07/09/2008	Phase 4: Closing the project
07/18/2007-07/09/2008	Communication plan
03/07/2007-07/10/2008	Implement system administration organization
01/22/2007-05/30/2008	Project monitoring tasks

A1.6 RESULTS AND LESSONS LEARNED

The IWMS system replaced both of the work-order systems used by BB&T and also its leading service provider. Through use of the Employee Self-Service module, BB&T was able to consolidate two help desks into one and realize efficiency savings that nearly tripled the company's internal goal. Additionally, BB&T now has capability to report on service levels and maintenance history unlike ever before.

On the real estate side, BB&T tested the IWMS's space management tool by loading CAD drawings for approximately 3 million square feet of corporate office space. In a pilot space study, BB&T discovered a vacancy rate of over 20 percent in a key corporate market. The amount of vacant space exceeded the estimates of BB&T's space planning team. Accurate occupancy information will allow the company to strategize future growth plans to improve utilization of existing assets, which could potentially result in millions of dollars' worth of cost avoidance. Due to the early success, BB&T plans to expand the use of the space management tool to include an additional 11 million square feet of retail bank and other office space.

BB&T rearranged the implementation schedule to accommodate pending expirations of contracts for its legacy systems. Although the project was completed on time, BB&T later decided that a more disciplined approach should have been followed. Installation of one function at a time across the entire organization and allowance of time for immediate enhancement would have improved initial user satisfaction and eased the transition.

Integration of data is likely to be a challenge for any organization wishing to implement an IWMS, and BB&T was no exception. Entire project team meetings had to be devoted to seemingly simple tasks such as a decision on which database would supply property addresses. Once data integration issues were resolved, the company turned to facility managers to gather equipment listings, location histories, and planned projects, which had never been consistently recorded in an electronic format. The expansion of a knowledge base continues to require extensive input from the field.

Facility management professionals often have varying technical backgrounds, and BB&T found that it is crucial to plan training appropriately for the audience. User acceptance is directly correlated to an individual's comfort level with other computer applications. In addition, communication to the entire organization about the status of the two-year project could have helped prepare users who were not integrated until the later stages of the project.

APPENDIX 2:

CASE STUDY GENERAL DYNAMICS C4 SYSTEMS

Patrick Okamura, Deborah Schneiderman

A2.1 CORPORATE OVERVIEW

General Dynamics is a market leader in the areas of business aviation, land and expeditionary combat vehicles and systems, armaments, munitions, and shipbuilding and marine systems. General Dynamics C4 Systems develops and integrates communication and information systems and technology for a myriad of U.S. government programs, allied nations, and select commercial customers globally. As a prime provider of "network-centric" products and systems, General Dynamics seamlessly and securely connects users—from the network core to the tactical edge—with the information they need to decide and act. Its world-class capabilities create high-value, low-risk solutions for use on land, at sea, in the air, and in space. Based in Scottsdale, Arizona (see figure A2.1), General Dynamics C4 Systems employs over ten thousand worldwide and specializes in command and control, communications networking, computing, and information assurance.

A2.2 REAL ESTATE RELATED DATA

General Dynamics C4 Systems is a facility housing research, light manufacturing, and office space for approximately 4,600 employees. The majority of the 1.6 million square feet exists across two separate buildings.

The site's first building was constructed in 1957 by Motorola and housed its Integrated Information Systems Group (ISSG). This group worked with defense and government customers to develop technologies, products, and systems for secure communications and integrated communication systems. When Motorola opened on McDowell Road in the late 1950s, it was considered Scottsdale's first major employer. Eventually, with thousands of employees, the company's presence helped drive the development of modern Scottsdale, stimulating the construction of new housing, schools, and retail centers. General Dynamics later acquired ISSG in 2001, assuming ownership over the existing facilities, which housed approximately three thousand people. Since the sale, the employee population at the Scottsdale site has increased approximately 26 percent over the last eight years.

Fig. A2.1: General Dynamics Scottsdale Campus, Hayden Building

A2.3 FM GOALS AND POLITICS

To address the growing employee population and related space needs, the facility manager for General Dynamics C4 Systems in Scottsdale was approached by executive management to research, identify, and implement a CAFM system that could gather, maintain, track, and organize the site's space data as well as integrate with other systems already in use in the organization.

At the same time, another initiative at the company was underway to attain a second Leadership in Energy and Environmental Design—Existing Buildings (LEED EB) certification for its Hayden Building, the LEED EB/OM (Operations and Maintenance) certification.

As organizations begin to realize the environmental impact of their office buildings, LEED has taken on greater importance, becoming an internationally recognized green building certification system. In the United States, for instance, buildings account for the following:

- 72 percent of electricity consumption

- 39 percent of energy use

- 38 percent of all carbon dioxide (CO_2) emissions

- 40 percent of raw materials use

- 30 percent of waste output (136 million tons annually)

- 14 percent of potable water consumption

General Dynamics C4 Systems had been incorporating sustainable practices for several years and led the corporation in these efforts when it began its first LEED EB certification process in 2003. Developed by the U.S. Green Building Council (USBGC), LEED EB recognizes organizations that have achieved and maintained sustainable standards for their office buildings. Organizations are rated on criteria such as cleaning, maintenance, chemical use, indoor air quality, energy and water efficiency, recycling, and exterior maintenance programs. To qualify, candidates are rated on a checklist of these various conservation requirements, with quantifiable results needed to receive LEED rating.

However, at General Dynamics C4 Systems, the absence of an enterprise-wide tracking system resulted in time-consuming, sporadic data collection, making a second certification a seemingly out-of-reach goal. Therefore, the key to a successful LEED EB/OM certification process for a building was greater access to data.

A2.4 THE INITIAL SITUATION

As in many organizations, the FM team used traditional methods of space tracking—manually manipulated data using a spreadsheet program. This process took countless hours to assess space needs accurately. A more efficient method to track space and occupancy and manage internal customer space requests was needed. Improved visibility into these elements also could help maximize the use of the site's facilities.

From a technical perspective, the FM team wanted an open system that could integrate data from a diverse set of existing systems, such as human resources; finance; and the department's existing Computerized Maintenance Management System (CMMS). Also, as a group that continuously seeks process improvements, the FM required a highly configurable system that could map to existing requirements and easily be configured to support process changes.

A2.5 THE CAFM PROJECT

A2.5.1 REQUIREMENTS OF THE CAFM SOLUTION AND SYSTEM SELECTION

In 2007 the Leonardo Academy, an environmental thinktank and sustainability leader, identified that CMMS systems were key in assisting with LEED EB/OM certifications. This confirmed the FM team's finding two years earlier when USGBC certified General Dynamics's Roosevelt Building as the first industrial facility in the world to receive the LEED EB certification. The FM team had successfully integrated its CMMS program to support the LEED EB certification needs by tracking a variety of preventative maintenance tasks, including equipment/systems performance; maintenance quality and consistency levels; and equipment reliability. In addition, the CMMS program allowed the department to access and assess maintenance-equipment performance history. Integrating the CMMS and energy management system, the FM team was able to monitor equipment/systems energy efficiency and consumption levels as well as assess energy consumption trends.

To achieve LEED EB/OM certification of the second main facility in Scottsdale, however, the FM team saw the need to incorporate a CAFM system to manage user requests. This allowed General Dynamics C4 Systems to provide responsive and efficient service to the organization, streamline communications and reporting, and better track service-request information.

The CAFM system selected was user-friendly and configured to connect space and occupancy data to floor plans. To support sustainability initiatives, the FM team tracked maintenance-related activities, including equipment efficiency, performance, and reliability, through its CMMS system. For the tracking of sustainable initiatives, such as indoor air-quality maintenance activities and materials with recycled content, the FM team used spreadsheets. The team also considered its CAFM as an alternative method for gathering sustainability data. Therefore, the CAFM tool was reconfigured to assist in tracking these initiatives. This ensured that ongoing sustainability efforts and related initiatives, such as cost savings and cost-avoidance opportunities, were identified and properly documented.

In addition, the sustainability information was then integrated with the spatial and other data and can be easily viewed on the floor plan, which allows the team greater visibility into sustainability initiatives and their results (e.g., immediate access to room/area data associated to sustainable materials, features, and amenities). This integration has provided additional data, including the following:

- Architectural features such as natural lighting, light shelves, and R factors

- Paint and carpeting specifications (e.g., color, manufacturer, and dye lots)

- Area infrastructure capacity (electrical/HVAC/connectivity)

- Equipment specifications and related maintenance data

- Green-cleaning schedules

- Upgraded lighting and comfort controls

Once the organization realized the benefits of integrating CAFM features into supporting its sustainability initiatives, the enthusiasm to create and introduce innovative concepts escalated. Various groups within the FM team introduced their own recommendations on how to store and use pertinent data. As they brainstormed, a transformation occurred: the engineering and construction team discovered that proper commissioning practices could be used to minimized operations and maintenance service calls and reduced energy use; the strategic space planning team discovered it could profoundly impact the volume of construction debris and recycled content materials depending on how site interior renovations were proposed; and the building site and tenant services team discovered the success of its green-cleaning initiatives could be extended into the construction-scope programming phase.

In addition, the CAFM system tracked the company's initiative to reduce its carbon footprint related to employee commuting. System enhancements support the facilities team's initiatives to do the following:

- Assign telecommuting status to participating employees to track reduction in commuting

- Identify workstations to validate use of telecommuting

- Track assigned lockers and locations of staff that commute by bicycle and require shower facilities

- Track car/vanpool assignments and users

- Track alternative fuel vehicles

Fig. A2.2: Water conservation monitoring

A2.5.2 SYSTEM ARCHITECTURE

The cost of implementing a CAFM system at General Dynamics totaled approximately 50,000 dollars. The system that General Dynamics C4 Systems operates is an integrated, web-based software package that runs on the organization's intranet. The system, which can be accessed by all or assigned employees through a web browser, is comprised of three core modules:

- Space management

- Strategic planning

- Asset management

And four extensions:

- Move management real estate

- Portfolio management

- Facility maintenance management

- Project management

The FM team selected a CAFM system that interacts with Autodesk's DWF format drawings and also has the ability to be integrated with AutoCAD through an administrative tool. This capability is particularly critical to the space management core module as key information is simultaneously updated between the CAFM database and the facility AutoCAD plans. In utilizing DWF files, the CAFM system recognizes that facilities managers, and certainly office workers and other potential CAFM product users, are not always CAD users. Accordingly, the interface between FM and its CAFM system was designed to be user-friendly for non-CAD users. DWF files are easy for all users to view and review. The resulting DWF files are easily manipulated by a non-CAD user who may perform a task such as assigning a new employee to a vacant desk.

A2.5.3 PROJECT SCHEDULE

Period	Activity
03/2005	Decision for the project
04/2005	Developing the RFI
06/2005	Interviews
08/2005	Short-listing candidates
09/2005	Initial implementation
10/2005	Full implementation
06/2006	Integration with CMMS System
06/2007	Integration with Energy Management Program
06/2008	Integration with Sustainability Initiatives

A2.6 LEED EB: OPERATIONS AND MAINTENANCE (OM) CATEGORY ASSESSMENT

LEED EB: Operations and Maintenance (OM) is measured in six categories:

- Sustainable sites

- Water efficiency

- Energy and atmosphere

- Materials and resources

- Indoor environmental quality

- Innovation and design process

Certification is awarded by achieving the credits that meet or exceed the predetermined point threshold. To that end, the FM team discovered that CAFM software could be leveraged by FMs to document and realize the impact of sustainable choices. Additionally, the integration of CAFM software can facilitate LEED EB/OM documentation within the specific LEED categories.

Energy and Atmosphere

The CAFM system's implementation supported General Dynamics' strategies in the energy and atmosphere category in the following areas:

- Commissioning and retro-commissioning data

- Energy usage by business/product area

- Energy-efficient equipment and modifications

- Lighting upgrades

- Building loads

- Hyperlink to CMMS to confirm equipment specs and maintenance information

As a result of the tracking, energy consumption was reduced through several procedures. This included a 25 percent reduction in lighting, accomplished by equipping areas with lighting controls and use of high-efficiency lighting. The CAFM system also allowed the FM team to develop supporting reports on commissioned areas, demonstrating energy reduction in power usage, scheduled infrastructure refurbishments, and high-efficiency lighting upgrades.

Water Efficiency

The CAFM system facilitated the FM team's tracking of water efficiency category elements in the following areas:

- Track and monitor low-usage equipment and systems (see figure A2.2)

- Provide fixture specifications

- Identify low-flow water fixtures

- Track history and features of remodeled restrooms

- Hyperlink to CMMS

Recycled-Content Material

In measuring recycled-content material (see figure A2.3) installed within the site, the FM team calculated materials incorporated in the facility and additionally identified nearly five hundred tons of construction-waste diversions from local landfills and a 10 percent increase in material reuse. This was evidenced in the following categories:

- Ceiling tile
- Carpeting
- Glazing
- Millwork
- Increased material reuse
- Other recyclables
- Minimal disturbance to interior environments

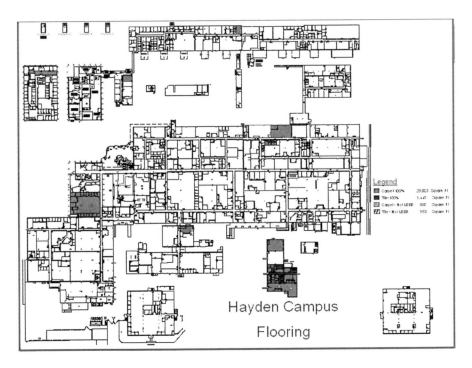

Fig. A2.3: Hayden Building Recycled Content Material Installation

Indoor Environmental Quality

Utilizing the CAFM software, the FM team tracked and measured the effectiveness of indoor environmental air-quality monitoring systems and design strategies such as the following:

- Designated smoking areas

- CO monitors

- Day views and lighting

- Ventilation capacities

- Area renovations and retrofits

- Filtration specifications and performance

- Comfort survey data

- Green cleaning/products data

Innovation—Option 2: Innovation in Operations

General Dynamics C4 Systems applied for Innovative Credit for the concept of incorporating a CAFM system to support sustainability initiatives in the following areas:

- Track and monitor the site's sustainable materials

- Manage recycled materials and content

- Support the site's sustainability strategic plan

- Gather and track data to support LEED recertification required every five years

Ultimately, the FM team used the CAFM software for tracking in a cross section of checklist items required for LEED certification, including the following:

- Tracking restroom upgrades

- Tracking materials with recycled content

- Green seal and label materials

- Lighting

- Recycling centers

- Area renovations and retrofits

- Demolition and reconstruction data

To streamline sustainability efforts revealed by the CAFM system, the FM team also expanded its recycling efforts to include electronic equipment, and reduced the need to drain and refill fire risers. The FM team also reduced housekeeping costs, predemolition audits, and post-construction cleanup costs and materials. The expanded use of the CAFM system has assisted facilities in multiple situations and resulted in the following organizational benefits:

- Increased department collaboration

- Minimized emotions in decision making

- Developed supporting policy and procedures

- Expanded creativity

A2.7 RESULTS AND LESSONS LEARNED

The implementation of the CAFM system introduced several benefits to the facilities team, such as the ability to do the following:

- Initiate an entire site as-built drawing

- Validate actual space availability

- Confirm department space assignments and allocations

- Identify vacant, assigned, and occupied space

As General Dynamics C4 Systems approached its second certification effort in Scottsdale, the FM team expanded the tracking of sustainability initiatives to include the CAFM system and apply it to the LEED EB/ OM certification process. The implementation initiated a complete site as-built drawing, which quickly revealed that current CAD plans were inaccurate. Connecting the space management database to the floor plans enabled the visualization of space use, showing a significant amount of vacancies that were previously unnoticed. At the time, General Dynamics was well underway in planning for a new multimillion-dollar facility to accommodate projected space needs, when the FM team's CAFM system confirmed that approximately eight hundred employees could be added at the present facility. Within the first forty-eight hours of implementing the new system, the company realized an immediate savings of approximately 65 million dollars (the amount allocated for the new building), as well as offsetting enormous amounts of embodied energy emissions produced during the fabrication of related construction/building materials for the proposed building.

Additionally, by negating the facility expansion and its associated costs, the FM team achieved sustainability-related savings. For example, in 2006, one year after achieving LEED EB certification of the Roosevelt building, the FM team recorded the following approximate sustainability savings:

- 4 percent reduction in annual energy usage

- 20 percent reduction in annual potable water usage

- 250,000 dollars in infrastructure modification cost avoidance

- 38,000 dollars in maintenance-labor savings

- 35,000 dollars in recycling refunds

In addition, by maximizing its access to data and the CAFM system's capabilities, the FM team

- Discovered new opportunities to expand the use of data

- Assisted in capital and strategic planning

- Integrated current databases so facilities personnel could access current and accurate data

- Removed emotions and ambiguity from decision making

- Input relevant and applicable sustainability data and information

CAFM systems are typically designed for use within the building envelope, spanning exterior wall to exterior wall. The General Dynamics

C4 Systems FM team has proposed that the system extend its scope and span the site sidewalk to sidewalk. With such an expanded scope, the FM team could access a more comprehensive set of supporting documentation required to recertify in the future with LEED EB/OM, including the exterior documentation for site sustainability, reference materials, and additional sustainability information and data. The FM team maintains that if it could access information from an expanded database, it could possibly achieve a 30 to 35 percent savings in future recertification labor resource needs.

Expanding the system to reach sidewalk to sidewalk would allow the FM team to use the CAFM technology in the sustainable sites category to track

- Heat islands

- Parking

- Drainage information

- Low-water use vegetation

The results can be summarized as follows:

- A leader in sustainability efforts to reduce its carbon footprint, General Dynamics C4 Systems received the LEED EB certification for its Roosevelt Building in 2005.

- As part of its efforts to achieve a second certification, LEED EB/OM, General Dynamics C4 Systems implemented a CAFM system. The new system confirmed that more employees could be added at its present facility. The company realized an immediate savings of approximately 65 million dollars (the amount allocated for the new building), as well as offset enormous amounts of embodied energy emissions produced by new construction.

- Introduction of a CAFM system also generated enthusiasm to create and introduce innovative concepts. Various groups within the FM team introduced their own recommendations on how to store and use pertinent data related to sustainability.

- The second main facility on the Scottsdale campus, the Hayden Building, was certified LEED EB/OM in November of 2009.

- The Roosevelt Building is expected to be recertified LEED EB in 2012.

APPENDIX 3:

CASE STUDY ST. MARY'S GENERAL HOSPITAL / GRAND RIVER HOSPITAL

Geoff Williams, Roger Holliss

A3.1 CORPORATE OVERVIEW

A3.1.1 ST. MARY'S GENERAL HOSPITAL

St. Mary's General Hospital is a 151-bed adult acute care hospital located in a 350,000-square-foot facility in the heart of Kitchener, Ontario. St. Mary's is one of Ontario's top performing hospitals and is nationally recognized for providing safe, high-quality, and innovative acute adult care.

As the Regional Cardiac Centre and Regional Centre of Excellence for Thoracic Surgery, St. Mary's serves a population base of more than 750,000 people in Waterloo Region and the counties of Wellington, Grey, and Bruce. The hospital's four areas of clinical focus include cardiac and respiratory care, general medicine (emergency and inpatient), and surgical services. The hospital has an operating budget in of 130 million dollars and has more than 1,200 staff, 800 physicians, and 400 volunteers working toward the common vision of becoming the safest and most effective hospital in Canada, characterized by innovation, compassion, and respect.

Established by the Sisters of St. Joseph of Hamilton in 1924, St. Mary's has been transforming to the meet the needs of a diverse and growing community for more than eighty-five years.

A3.1.2 GRAND RIVER HOSPITAL

The current Grand River Hospital consists of the former Kitchener-Waterloo Hospital and Freeport Hospital. K-W Hospital was first established in 1895 as the Berlin-Waterloo Hospital. Seventy patients were cared for in its first year. The thirty-bed facility had one operating room, a handful of nurses, and a dozen physicians. Freeport Hospital first began as a tuberculosis sanatorium. Following medical advances and altered treatment of tuberculosis after World War II, Freeport began admitting chronic care and rehabilitation patients. By 1970 the Freeport Sanatorium became Freeport Hospital.

While Grand River Hospital has a rich history of quality caregiving, its future will be even more impressive. It will provide new and expanded services to meet the rapidly growing community's health care needs. By 2011 it will be redeveloped to include the following:

- A new inpatient oncology unit with an increase of six patient beds

- A new ambulatory care center

- A new mental health unit that includes a crisis assessment facility, day hospital, and child and adolescent inpatient psychiatry unit

- A new, spacious intensive care unit with an additional eight patient beds

- A new brachytherapy surgical suite to treat appropriate cancer patients by administering radiation internally

- A new and expanded fracture clinic

A3.2 RESTRUCTURING OF HEALTH CARE IN ONTARIO

Because Ontario has a public health-care system, there was a provincial mandate to create a commission called the Health Services Restructuring Commission (HSRC) in 1996. This commission had a four-year mandate, which was to

1. make decisions on restructuring Ontario's public hospitals, and

2. make recommendations to the Minister of Health and Long-Term Care on reinvestments in and restructuring of other parts of the health system and other changes required to support restructuring generally, and the creation of a genuine health services system in the province.

The commission made far-reaching recommendations that effectively marked the beginning of change in the landscape of Ontario health care. For community hospitals such as St. Mary's General Hospital and Grand River Hospital, there was restructuring to allow each corporation to focus on its strengths and not compete for patients and health-care staff. Subsequent to the commission's report, Ontario enacted the Local Health System Integration Act of 2006 (LHIN), which are meant to be an important part of the evolution of health care in Ontario, moving from a collection of services that were often uncoordinated to a true health-care system. SMGH and GRH are part of the same LHIN and have started the process of harmonizing services so they do not duplicate efforts. For these two facilities, this includes a joint Integrated Director of Engineering and Bio-Medical Services.

A3.3 REAL ESTATE RELATED DATA

A3.3.1 SMGH

St. Mary's General Hospital was a typical Ontario community hospital leading into the millennium. It had a two building site occupied approximately 250,000 square feet with a central plant and an eleven-storey bed tower. At this point, planning was well underway to almost double the facility size by 2008, and decisions were being made using fragmented, conflicting, and nonexistent information.

A3.3.2 GRH

Grand River Hospital is a much larger organization spread out over two campuses occupying a combined 1 million square feet in 2008 but scheduled to grow to over 1.2 million square feet by 2010. With an additional 250,000 square feet slated to be renovated, GRH was bracing for a tumultuous construction process as the building needed to remain fully operational at all times. GRH also had a number of FM/IT implementations that failed because they had difficulty integrating the solution into day-to-day operations and also because of lack of staff buy-in.

A3.4 THE INITIAL SITUATION

Under the leadership of the Integrated Director of Engineering and Bio-Medical Services, efforts have been made to develop common platforms, services, and service offerings between the two organizations. However, in the process of developing common platforms, there were a number of tremendous holes in documentation and information found. In an effort to right the ship, and recognizing that "you cannot manage what you can't see," SMGH and GRH underwent an exercise in bring together disparate information.

The inheritance of two aging facilities was a daunting task. In both organizations there is what was vernacularly known as The Room, which was the place to store but not index or catalog documents, drawings, specifications, and maintenance manuals. The difficulty with The Room— beyond its lack of organization—was that there was no tracking of the chronology of projects that had occurred in the facility and, as a result, information on one drawing set did not always agree with documentation on another. This disparate information led to a high degree of personal frustration on the part of the management team along with a concern over making decisions around information that could not be relied on.

A3.5 THE CAFM PROJECT

In building a CAFM roadmap, a core group of staff put together both short- and long-term requirements of the CAFM system. The first order of business was to begin to reconcile the building information (drawings, documents, and data) so that informed operational decisions could be made moving forward. During this process, the entire team was engaged to promote an idea of ownership among staff members so that when the implementation was completed, the team could hit the ground running as contributors to the system.

Once the roadmap was complete, the idea of putting together a "proof of concept" that overhauled mission-critical documentation inside a CAFM solution was put forward. As an initial venture, the medical gas, heating, and domestic plumbing systems were chosen as the highest priority, and a service provider (Seawood Solutions and Services Inc.) was to implement this phase of the project. The SeawoodFM product is a web-based, turn-key solution that allowed SMGH and GRH to focus on operating the building while a team of professionals both gathered information and implemented the system on the organizations' behalf.

After the "proof of concept" phase, SMGH and GRH set a goal of ensuring these new tools and systems became part of the FM team's daily tasks and not an add-on. Only once this was achieved did the two organizations begin to develop a long-term implementation plan that followed the approach outlined below:

1. Gather what you know (existing documentation, etc.) and analyze the gaps.

   — Existing operating and manuals
   — Ad-hoc databases
   — Electronic drawings
   — Hard-copy drawings
   — Employee knowledge

2. Survey and audit the facility to close the gaps.

3. Centralize all information in a common portal as 'master' documents.

4. Work to ensure contribution from the team.

5. Develop processes by which all users become contributors for managing updates to all "master" documents.

6. Use the information to operate the facility and plan for new construction.

7. Apply learning from the implementation to other buildings and facilities.

A3.6 PROJECT SCHEDULE

Period	Activity
1999	Alpha product chosen for planning at GRH
2000	Alpha product implemented across GRH property for planning
2000	New directors at SMGH
2002	Emergency project completed SMGH
2003	REMCC project completed GRH
2003	GRRCC project completed GRH
2004	Pilot project initiated at SMGH
2005	Pilot project success guides future work
2006	GRH seeks product similar to SMGH
2007	Mass deployment at GRH for key systems
2008	SMGH completes 100,000 square feet addition
2009	GRH completes 30,000 square feet of renovations and major infrastructure project
2009	GRH begins $67 million in construction projects
2010	GRH completes 25,000 square feet of long-term care renovations

A3.7 RESULTS AND LESSONS LEARNED

The key to success in the implementation of a project such as this is to work diligently both to leverage the value of the initial investment and to invest in the maintenance of the solution. At SMGH and GRH, the team has been challenged in two ways to support these goals. First, they have been participating in an incentive-based program that rewards contribution to the base system. Second, the team is encouraged to collaborate with the management team to develop new ideas of how a new feature and/or document set could improve the efficiency of their day-to-day operations. This implementation process is continuing as they discover new CAFM requirements that development their system and protect their investment and the hospital.

Finally, there are some unforeseen interactions that have been facilitated by the implementation project. Effectively, SMGH and GRH have changed the way they do business with third-party service providers, and many of these have either agreed to or are required to (and most prefer to) use these new systems as their primary information source. Also, should their work impact the systems, the third-party service providers are contractually required to provide updated documentation. The number of this type of user continues to grow.

APPENDIX 4:

CASE STUDY HERMAN MILLER

Marty Chobot

A4.1 CORPORATE OVERVIEW

Herman Miller creates great places to work by researching, designing, manufacturing, and distributing innovative interior furnishings that support companies, organizations, and individuals all over the world. The company's award-winning products, complemented by primary furniture-management services, generated nearly two billion dollars in revenue during fiscal 2000. Herman Miller is widely recognized both for its innovative products and for its business practices, including the use of industry-leading, customer-focused technology. Herman Miller has been headquartered in Zeeland, Michigan, since its founding in 1923. Its employee-owners place high value on and foster good design, participative management, and environmental responsibility.

A4.2 REAL ESTATE RELATED DATA

Herman Miller's west Michigan facilities encompass ten buildings, totaling 2.6 million square feet. The five campuses house diverse office, warehouse, and manufacturing functions. The corporate headquarters in Holland is called the Design Yard, with unique groupings of buildings reminiscent of American barn design. Not only does the Design Yard house office space, it is also where Herman Miller concepts are designed and products are tested. Another unique building is the Green House; its sustainable architecture reflects Herman Miller's commitment to protecting the environment.

A4.3 THE INITIAL SITUATION

Prior to implementing a solution, Herman Miller used three different processes to manage workplace information—a work order system, a real estate system, and paper floor plans for space management. The systems did not "talk to each other," making workplace information difficult to gather and share.

A4.4 THE CAFM/IWMS PROJECT

With the initial implementation of FM:Systems solutions thirteen years ago, Herman Miller addressed these challenges. Over time, Herman Miller has continued to expand its implementation to address new business problems and create a comprehensive Integrated Workplace Management System (IWMS).

In 1996 Dave Kuiper, corporate workplace strategist for Herman Miller, and his team reviewed several CAFM systems, evaluating them for capabilities, ease of operation, and cost. After deciding on FM:Interact, Herman Miller's in-house team proceeded with implementation. The team prepared CAD drawings, imported data from human resources, tested, and then launched the system.

Herman Miller implemented a workplace management suite with the hands-on support of a consulting services team. Now that implementation is complete, all departments in the west Michigan facility use the expanded system—from site coordinators to project managers to workplace strategists.

With its IWMS solution, the company benefits from enterprise-wide access to drawings and reports, stacking and strategic planning capabilities, and continued productivity improvements.

A4.5 RESULTS AND LESSONS LEARNED

Significant benefits have been realized as a result of implementing the IWMS technology:

- *Reduced annual move spend:* Herman Miller cut move costs from 2 million dollars per year to less than 250,000 dollars per year. It realized move spending reductions by enabling the use of space standards to simplify the move process, eliminating unneeded reconfiguration projects, and reducing warehousing of furniture and related assets.

- *Increased productivity of the workplace strategies group:* Since using its IWMS solution, the company has been able to implement more efficient and automated workplace processes. This has directly resulted in enormous savings in time and effort, enabling Herman Miller to reduce move times by 85 percent. The tools helped improve planning and coordination, and as a result, the company can complete moves in one day as compared to seven days before implementation.

- *Improved customer service with enterprise access to facility information:* Since implementing the IWMS, all employees have benefited from web-based access to employee information, floor plans, and views of move or service request status. Enterprise access to its facility data has helped Herman Miller improve customer service. The customer satisfaction score went from 90 to 97 percent during a three-year period.

- *Improved accuracy of facility data:* Better visibility into space and occupancy has helped Herman Miller improve utilization of space and served as the foundation for move and service request process improvements.

- *Automated publishing to CAD drawings:* With the drawing component, Herman Miller is able to automatically show updated information on CAD drawings in a web browser. In the past, the organization was publishing this information manually three times per week. Now end users are able to get real-time, visual displays of move plans, vacancies, etc.

In addition to the benefits listed above, Herman Miller's latest expansion of the IWMS solution will continue to improve productivity. The CAFM/IWMS integration with Crystal Reports gives Herman Miller the capability to do better reporting and make reports available online. Right now, there are several different areas of the company that are interested in getting access. IT is interested in having this information as well as telecom. In the past, there was a manual process to generate a Crystal Report, and then it had to be emailed to the individual or department. With the CAFM/IWMS software, a lot of time is saved by letting employees view real-time workplace reports from their Web browsers.

Also, the stacking and strategic planning module is used extensively. The robust feature allows Herman Miller to determine future space requirements better, helping to best utilize the available space and reduce churn rates—an important factor considering the nearly 50 percent churn rate manufacturing companies endure.

Additionally, the company plans to expand its use of the asset module beyond artwork in order to track telecom and IT resources, and plans to deploy its IWMS internationally when its new U.K. facility opens.

APPENDIX 5:

CASE STUDY MUNICH AIRPORT

Michael May, Geoff Williams

A5.1 CORPORATE OVERVIEW

Civilian aviation in Munich has over 110 years of history. Flying operations in Munich began in 1890/91 with the first Royal Bavarian Army balloon flights at the Oberwiesenfeld, which is currently the site of the Munich Olympic Stadium. In 1909 engine-based aviation began on the same site. Until 1931, the airfield was further expanded and thereby became Munich's first fully functional airport.

Shortly thereafter it became evident that the Oberwiesenfeld would not be sufficient for the increasing air traffic. In 1936 an area to the south was chosen as new airport location, and one year later the ground-breaking ceremony took place. On October 25, 1939, the first airliner landed, after the opening of the airport for civilian traffic was delayed due to the German invasion of Poland. After the collapse of the German Reich in

1945, 70 percent of the previously ultramodern airport was destroyed, and flying operations were no longer possible.

After a provisional structure was completed, the first postwar airliner landed in Riem in April 1948. Gradually the reconstruction progressed, and in 1951 a large arrival hall was opened. Until the mid-1970's Riem was continuously redeveloped and added onto until it outgrew its site. Due to an acute lack of space and changes in the aviation industry, a petition was filed with the aviation authorities on August 14, 1969, for the permission for construction and operation of the airport Munich II (Erdinger Moos).

After long negotiations with the government, the authorities, and communities, construction work for the new Munich Airport began on November 3, 1980. Meanwhile, passenger traffic numbers in Riem rose to over 6 million. Disputes in the policy, particularly because of the ever-increasing awareness of the environmental impact of airports, led to the halting of construction six months after it had started. This stoppage of construction continued until March 8, 1985. After a seven-year construction period, the Munich Airport (Franz-Josef-Strauss) was officially opened May 17, 1992, and after fifty-three years, the existing airport (Munich Riem) was closed.

The new airport (see figures A5.1 and A5.2) lies in the middle of the Erdinger Moos (28.5 kilometers northeast of the Munich city center) and covers over 15 square kilometers of property. The operator is the Flughafen München GmbH (Munich Airport GmbH) with its three shareholders Freistaat Bavaria (51 percent), Federal Republic of Germany (26 percent), and the city of Munich (23 percent).

Fig. A5.1: Aerial view of the Munich Airport

Fig. A5.2: View of the Munich Airport's Terminal 2

In 2007, this air traffic hub in the south of Germany had approximately 430,000 flights, and passenger traffic had grown to 34 million. Thus the Munich Airport ranks as the seventh-largest airport in Europe.

Technically the conditions necessary for such a high utilization were accounted for in the planning phases of the airport. The two runways are each 13,000 feet long and 196 feet wide and are designed for a constantly increasing traffic volume. A third runway is currently in the planning stage. The passenger aprons cover 1,350,000 square meters. For maintaining the airplanes, a 230,000-square-meter apron is at their disposal. It also has one of the largest hangars in Europe offering space, large enough for six Boeing 747 aircrafts.

To handle the logistics resulting from rising passenger loads, Terminal 2 (see figure A5.2 and Hofmann 2002) was added in June 2003. This was a joint project between the Flughafen München GmbH and Lufthansa AG, with a combined investment of approximately 1.25 billion euros. The new terminal allowed the airport to increase its passenger capacity to 50 million passengers.

In support of both the core business of air traffic (aviation) and real estate management (non-aviation) the FM team (Haller 2002; May 2002b) fulfills important tasks for the airport operator. The organizational structure was adapted to support the delivery of services to both. It administers approximately 300 individual above-ground structures that cover more than 2,000,000 square meters.

A5.2 REAL ESTATE RELATED DATA

A large airport like Munich's can be compared in size and number of inhabitants to a small town. Similarly its infrastructure requirements are likened to a small town. There are presently 28,000 people employed across 1.560 hectares. Following is a view of the real estate data as it pertains to the FM functions outlines the challenges faced by the Munich Airport.

Technical Building Management

■ Central control system with 220,000 data points

■ 242 escalators and moving walkways

- 285 elevators

- 9 combined heat and power station generation (18 MW)

- 95 fire reporting centers, 48,000 fire alarms

- 3,550 electrical distribution panels

- 15,000 telephone connections and terminals

Commercial Building Management

- Administration and management of 27,000 rooms

- Support for 350 tenants

- Marketing of 550 advertising surfaces

Infrastructural Building Management

- Administration of over 38,000 mechanical and 87 electronic locking systems

- Winter services for 400 hectares of air traffic area (per winter 30,000 tons of snow)

- Administration of 30,000 parking bays

- Organization of fairs

Site Management

- Documentation of and site planning for 1,560 hectares of airport areas

- Documentation of and space planning for 330 buildings

In addition table A5.1 gives a rough overview of the kind, quantity, and degree of detail that the FM function is responsible for at the Munich Airport. The variety and complexity of the data suggest a strong need for IT-based facility management. In the database there are 1,830,706 point objects, 272,681 line objects, and 53,698 surface objects.

Table A5.1: Type, quantity, and degree of detail of the facilities/tasks recorded

Facilities/Tasks	Number and type of the data to be recorded
Surveying	996,167 points (surface and underground)
Groundwater	2,595 objects (e.g., levels, boreholes)
Road Signs	3,418 objects (mostly traffic signs)
Aviation Facing Signs	634 objects (runway sign-posting)
Beaconing	23,297 objects (e.g., fire, sensors)
Gates	475 objects
Cleaning	1,877 objects (e.g., containers, trash cans)
Doors	36,326 objects (doors in the building)
Escape and emergency routes	3,121 objects (e.g., locations, fire hydrant, fire extinguisher, fire alarm, collecting points)
Fire-brigade plans	19,711 objects (e.g., fire-hose cabinets, approach roads, fire-brigade key boxes)
Security	41,320 objects (locksets)
Emergency exit signs	3,638 objects (rescue cubes)
Heating/cold weather	2,004 objects (e.g., enclosures, heating element, circulating air coolers)
Fire suppression technology	7,543 objects (e.g., deluge sprinkler)
Electrical technology	360,355 objects (e.g., plug sockets, lights, tracers)
Communications technology	1,247 objects (e.g., antennae, WLAN)
Communications technology (2)	75,667 objects (e.g., junction boxes, distributers)
Information technology	5,849 objects (e.g., monitors, cameras)
Person and load-conveying engineering	892 objects (e.g., elevators, moving sidewalks, lifting platforms, window-cleaning lifts)
Doors and gates (electrical)	3,272 objects (e.g., automatic doors, folding gates, fire protection sliding gates)
Public-address systems	23,613 objects (e.g., loudspeakers)
Clock installations	512 objects (e.g., analog/digital clocks, time registration devices)
Control and IRC (individual room control) technology	15,955 objects (e.g., room control circuits, CO alarms)
Fire alarm system	69,321 objects (e.g., alarm devices, panels)
Smoke control	11,368 objects (e.g., fire protection dampers, smoke exhaust dampers, pushbutton devices)
Safety systems	9,135 objects (e.g., access control systems, alarm unit, substations)
Door safety engineering	1,114 objects (e.g., multifunction doors, substations, door lock cylinders)
Public parking spaces	11,663 parking spaces outside of buildings, airport-wide monitoring and connection to the management system
IT inventory	17,581 objects (e.g., PC, monitors, printers)
Fire separations	30,758 objects
Energy meters	2,213 objects

A5.3 FM GOALS AND POLITICS

The constantly growing requirements for efficient facility management at the Munich Airport mandate the constant renewal of the structures.

From the outset, it was decided corporately that FM would play a key role in the success of the airport as an enterprise. Under the project name M-Power, the entire corporation was restructured. As part of this restructuring, a new corporate service department "technology" was created to support all technical business units, including the range of activities known as "building management." This department also integrates other service elements such as cleaning management.

The new company structure was designed to align itself consistently with the customer. Internal as well as external customers would now be offered an equally reliable quality of service.

Basically, the Flughafen München GmbH has always been offering their facility management services both internally and externally. The core of these external activities are in the support of customers in the airport area, such as airlines, restaurants, shipping companies, authorities, and all the businesses based at the site.

Since 1997 the Flughafen München GmbH has also been managing facilities outside the confines of its own property. At first this was predominantly with its own personnel, where several assets were taken on and managed within the company. The expectation was to gain new insights for the self-owned properties and to benefit from synergy effects that could be applied both internally and externally.

In 2004, in joint venture with Bayerische Landesbank (BayernLB), a subsidiary company, "Bayern Facility Management GmbH" (BayernFM), was created to increase the management of external facilities. BayernFM offers its competence and experience in the management of more complex and technically demanding real estate properties.

The FM activities of the Flughafen München GmbH personnel since the establishment of the subsidiary company are primarily concentrated on the Munich Airport campus.

In June 2003, assuming responsibility for the new Terminal 2 represented a large challenge for the CAFM. Therefore the advancement of CAFM at the Munich Airport provides substantial support for the FM activities and plays an essential role for the Flughafen München GmbH.

A5.4 THE INITIAL SITUATION

In May 1992 the Munich Airport was opened as one of the largest building complexes in Europe from a land-area perspective. Due to the complexity of the airport and the associated data, it was clear that suitable
computer support would be essential to FM, with the focus on the visual
(graphic) information.

It ranks among the most modern international large airports, but
plans were drawn by hand by the architectural office Busse and partners
Blees, Büch and Kampmann. This was because CAD was still in its infancy within their offices and wasn't ready for such a large undertaking.
Digital collection of airport drawings was therefore limited to exterior
installations and underground supply lines. The absence of substantial
digital building and space data was very problematic and was considered
to be crucial during the introduction of a CAFM system.

Also, crucial for initiating the CAFM project was the collection of
current basic data. Two years before opening the Munich Airport, the
Technical Documentation department began with the entry of building
drawings into a CAD system using the GDS software. In addition, an
alphanumeric room equipment catalog was developed.

A5.5 THE CAFM PROJECT

A5.5.1 REQUIREMENTS OF THE CAFM SOFTWARE AND ITS ARCHITECTURE

By the end of the 1990s, the most important FM processes were presented in different IT tools, which individually looked at only the por-
tions of the airport that they were responsible for. These tools included,
among others, the systems for maintenance, cleaning management, lock
and key management, cable administration, safety engineering, fire alarm
systems, call center, room equipment catalog, and SAP. Munich Airport
sought a solution that made data centrally accessible to the different systems without impacting the functionality of the individual systems. The
predominating IT structure, which in the beginning was held within the
Facility Management Department of the Flughafen München GmbH, was
oriented toward the organizational structure of the company. Thus a much
broader scope of interests including other independent organizational
units had to be considered for the implementation of a CAFM solution.

Due to the numerous airport-specific requirements and the extremely large dataset, no standard software could meet the needs of the organization. The IT philosophy that a running system should never be changed thus formed the criterion for the search for a new CAFM software.

The initial ideals for the CAFM solution were based on the following:

- Integration of the existing systems and the use of a central database

- Design of an efficient graphic component

The first step in the integration of the existing systems, and thus the cornerstone for the implementation of its own CAFM solution, was the installation of a metadatabase. It was crucial that all subsystems could access a central database—the central room and object book (ZROB). This is a collective relational database, based on Oracle, that all existing FM subsystems could be linked into both currently and in the future.

Each system is independent and holds its own data and then provides a copy to the central database. Once the data is stored, centrally different applications can access this data for their own uses. This approach shows similarities with data warehouse concepts, which are, as they relate to FM, only at the beginning of their development. All applications used for FM (see figure A5.3) are based already on one of the three (de facto) standards: Oracle, SAP, or AutoCAD. On the one hand, in-house tools were developed based on Oracle and/or SAP for the following"

- Room equipment catalog with OMS (Object Management System)

- Cleaning management with CMS (Cleaning Management System)

- Administration of telecommunications with KOLA

- Documentation of the groundwater levels with a customized SAP module

On the other hand, other vendors' systems are used for these:

- Real estate management and leasing with the SAP-RE FX

- Maintenance management with SAP-PM

- Locking asset management with Key Access

- IT call center management with ARS (Action Request System)

- Document management with ELO

- Cable management with C6000

The visualization of data was realized by VisMan. VisMan is a graphic information system that connects CAD, CAFM, and GIS (Geographic Information System). The VisMan system (Visualization and Management of Buildings, Surface Areas, Technical Facilities) was developed together with the Stuttgart Airport GmbH and is now also used at the Hanover Airport.

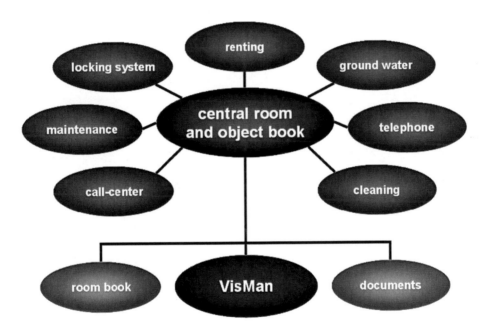

Fig. A5.3: Integration of the FM subsystems at Flughafen München GmbH

The following premises were fundamental in defining this graphic component of the CAFM solution:

- A standard system must be used that operates on Microsoft Windows. This way, in case of technical difficulties, the airport's own Windows specialists can provide support onsite.

- The use of standard software decreases the operating cost due to a simplified administration.

- With the selection of applications, one does not want to be dependent on relatively small, niche vendors.

- All FM tools already used are to be able to make use of the graphic component through a central database.

- Graphic data should be made accessible to as many users as possible in a simple and cost-effective manner.

AutoCAD is used for the CAD system. Figure A5.4 gives an idea of the variety of the drawings managed via VisMan. Through the central space and object book, VisMan has access to all of the airport's relevant data pools.

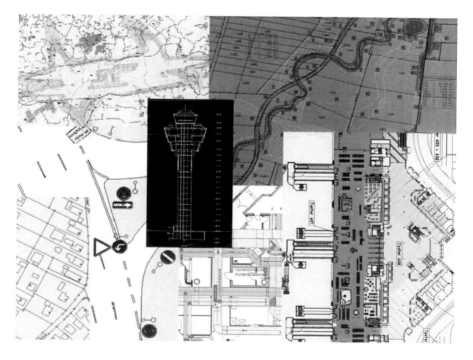

Fig. A5.4: Graphic documents handled by VisMan

A main goal concerning the supply of graphic information was to provide users with a very simple and inexpensive portal to support their business processes effectively. This was attained by using the VisMan Web solution.

VisMan Web is based on intranet technology and uses MapGuide software tools. Over-a-web browser drawings of the airport can be opened and database information retrieved. The key advantage is that the software is very user-friendly. Also, since no CAD system licenses are needed for individual users, the cost impact was more directly related to the implementation of the system and not to the purchase of additional CAD licenses. At present VisMan Web is installed and internally supported for over seven hundred users in the Munich Airport, representing over twenty different user departments. Approximately five hundred users regularly use the system.

For the administration of documents, the document management system was assigned to ELO. The extent of the documents contained in the system covers 500,000 drawings and 4,000 technical manuals.

A5.5.2 PROJECT SCHEDULE

Period	Activity
1990-1995	Preliminary work: Entry of Munich Airport planning documents into the GDS CAD system Collection of room equipment catalog
1992	Opening of the airport
1997	Termination of the GDS development
1998	Concept of a CAFM solution (list of requirements) Search for a suitable solution and decision for own development
1999-2002	Conception, development, and gradual implementation of VisMan and VisMan Web Development of the central room and object book ZROB as metadatabase
2000-2002	Import of the graphic data in VisMan
2001	Introduction of the document management system Business Flow
2001	Introduction of SAP-PM
2002	End of project
2002	Development of Miet-SAP (SAP for leasing) (ABAP programming)
2002	Introduction of the cable management system C6000
2002	Investigation regarding use and efficiency of mobile computers (PDAs, pocket PC, Pen PC) for FM tasks (Location Based Services)
2003	Productive use of tablet PCs to support processes locally
2008	Introduction of SAP-RE FX and conversion of the document management to the system ELO

A5.6 EXPERIENCES AND LESSONS LEARNED

The intention for the implementation of CAFM lay in the support of the FM business processes. With the processes documented, many users were looking for a method of graphically illustrating these processes. The information created by the Flughafen München GmbH by using VisMan and VisMan Web provided each individual with relevant airport data. Space allocation, cleaning, and maintenance plans belong likewise to the scope of service along with the display of the mobile radio supply, the air flight routes, or the groundwater lines.

The system is now being used for multiple applications within the Munich Airport. This includes the following application types:

- Electro-technology
- Energy management
- Energy and supply engineering
- Fire brigade
- Building engineering
- Above-ground construction
- Civil engineering
- Communications networks
- Person-conveying engineering
- Cleaning

- Key administration
- Safety engineering
- Sprinklers
- Technical documentation
- Environmental protection
- Leasing
- Public relations
- Water management
- Winter services

Flughafen München GmbH specialists look after the full-service spectrum from master planning of a department right down to the individual workplace layout. In the context of site management, the Flughafen München GmbH provides planning for optimal use of the site and designates areas for special requirements. The visualization and management system VisMan provides visibility to all conceivable spaces, building, and plant data for analysis in the requested format.

Commonly, an enterprise-wide CAFM implementation takes off-the-shelf CAFM software and customizes it to the individual requirements of the user. The alternative way builds on the existing IT structures and tools. The goal is to let the existing database applications continue as such but to interface them in such a way that the data is made available in different forms depending on the need of the CAFM tool. In the interests of Munich Airport, this second approach proved to be correct. A general preference for one of the two possible ways or for combinations of the two cannot be given, because the needs of individual organizations differ.

Also, this application shows that the postulation that the value of visual data is declining is frequently not applicable. In many FM functions, plans in either electronic form or as hard-copy are indispensable. AutoCAD had some struggles initially as files were being transferred from GDS to the new CAD system.

The experiences with VisMan and VisMan Web can be summarized as follows:

- Both tools are structural, process-oriented, and entirely fulfill the demands made on them.

- Due to the simplicity of the operation and the usefulness of the available demonstration tools, the software was quickly accepted by the users.

- The adjustment of the solution to new requirements essentially can be accomplished by Flughafen München GmbH's own personnel. For special tasks, external programmers are used.

Thus, for the Flughafen München GmbH, the in-house development of CAFM tools proved to be more practical than customizing an off-the shelf product.

By now, the developed toolkit made it possible to show and work on FM data with mobile devices such as tablet PCs (Haller 2004). For this, pilot projects were utilized to prove the concept. A further efficiency increase is expected with the use of the CAFM solution.

APPENDIX 6:

CASE STUDY BAYER SCHERING PHARMA AG

Michael May, Geoff Williams

A6.1 CORPORATE OVERVIEW

Until December 2006, Schering AG was a German, independent pharmaceutical research company. Bayer Schering Pharma AG was formed in 2006 as a result of the acquisition of the Schering AG by the Bayer AG, including the following four divisions: Animal Health, Consumer Care, Diabetes Care, and Bayer Health Care AG. In 2011 the name Bayer Schering Pharma was changed to Bayer HealthCare Pharmaceuticals. Since the case study dates back to 2005 (May 2006) and was updated in 2008, we will continue to use the name "Bayer Schering Pharma" in this chapter.

The enterprise created in 1851 by the pharmacist Ernst Schering is still active worldwide today. Bayer Schering Pharma has become a market leader in specialized areas. By growing its innovative ability and by acquiring high-tech support, it is now one of the top ten manufacturers of special pharmaceuticals internationally.

The enterprise presently has more than 150 subsidiaries and holding companies worldwide, in over 100 countries. In 2007 the transaction (Bayer Schering Pharma) amounted to approximately 10.267 billion euros and included 40,000 employees.

Bayer Schering Pharma AG concentrates on the following four strategic departments:

- General medicine

- Specialty medicine

- Women' s health care

- Diagnostic imaging

A6.2 REAL ESTATE RELATED DATA

Since properties and buildings consume a large portion of its balanced material assets, it is not surprising that the concepts of facility management represented a high value to the enterprise.

Bayer Schering Pharma is headquartered at the Berlin Wedding location, which was built in 1864 (see figure A6.1). The FM team is responsible for approximately 5,000 staff across a building area of approximately 1,970,000 square feet along with approximately 3,600,000 square feet of gross floor area and approximately 2,070,000 square feet of net usable area. This portfolio contains, among other things, the following building functions:

- Office space: 1,100,000 square feet

- Laboratory space: 1,000,000 square feet

- Multipurpose space: 1,100,000 square feet

- Other buildings: 200,000 square feet

- Outdoor property: 1,400,000 square feet

Fig. A6.1: Aerial view of the Bayer Schering Pharma AG (now Bayer HealthCare Pharmaceuticals) in Wedding, Berlin

A6.3 FM GOALS AND POLITICS

The goals of facility management are to make available and optimize the buildings and open spaces as much as possible for the respective users. Thereby the FM functions for each space are effectively location-oriented. The divisions present at a location are cared for by their respective "building management" (Reichenberger 2003).

The customers of the FM team are presently the company organizational units but will also provide support in the future for new subsidiaries.

In order that the value proposition for FM in the enterprise can be kept as efficient as possible, Bayer Schering Pharma defines the major task for facility management as "To guarantee the economical operation of buildings that deliver a high level of customer satisfaction." This definition clarifies the high value of FM in the enterprise. It concerns not only the cost side of space management and technical building management, but also the satisfaction of the customers who benefit from the achievements of FM. This presupposes a tight integration between customer needs and

FM. All FM activities are based on the satisfaction of the customers and thus the staff at the Wedding location. The fundamental premise of the FM department reads: "All users rent their space and pay for it!"

The FM must also meet the competition-driven economic requirements in order to make a business case for all initiatives. FM projects require an ROI on their investments of between one year and five years.

The FM charges back its services to the internal customers. The accounting of services for the FM costs (housekeeping, maintenance management, move management, telephone directory, etc.) are weighed against occupied floor space and according to types of space use. These costs already contain specific object services such as small renovations and renewal projects, security, cleaning support, waste management, and facility consultancy. To be able to benchmark values, the above values must be converted to net usable area.

A6.4 THE INITIAL SITUATION

The first FM concepts were started at Schering AG around 1990/91 after the establishment of the space management specialist role (May 2002a). This task was to develop a methodology for building management. In addition, there were already some subfunctions, such as support for housekeeping, for building maintenance, and in parts for space management.

The Building Management (BM) department got the task of introducing and coordinating FM at the Berlin location. The department merged with scarcely forty staff to complete the job function alignment and brought with them both the Schering internal services and also external suppliers.

Since this time, the BM department has experienced several reorganizations through the integration and centralizing of specialty functions in 2005 and also by the acquisition of Schering by Bayer in 2006.

The tasks of today's FM team are divided into five processes and/or subranges (see table A6.1) and are managed by specialized teams.

Table A6.1: Organizational structure and tasks of facility management

Process	Tasks/Subprocesses	#Empl.
Asset Management	• Customer service (as a core task) • Facility consulting, planning, and realization • Relocation planning and realization • Housekeeping management • Inventory management, HVAC distribution and control • Coordination of maintenance (planning, changes, project control) • Industrial safety • Documentation of allocation changes • Technical object management • Maintenance management	27
Commercial FM	• Contract management • Budget planning and controlling • Energy supply and cost controlling • Benchmarking	2
Space and Site Management	• Allocation concepts and planning • Concepts for use and adjustment of buildings • Production and care of work layout plans • Work structure planning • Support of the CAFM system	7
FM Services	• Care of the exterior installations • Waste disposal • General services • Central purchasing management • Conference services • Equipment technology • Electromagnetic reflection/instrumentation • Service workshop • Assignment management	64
Technical FM	• Operations • Maintenance • Realization of change and modernization projects • Energy management	12

At the Berlin location, for the planned tasks in 2007, there was a budget of about 45 million euros available plus 9 million for large-scale projects.

The operational budget is broken down in figure A6.2. When large-scale projects are removed, the largest expenditures are on technical equipment, equipment depreciation, and energy consumption.

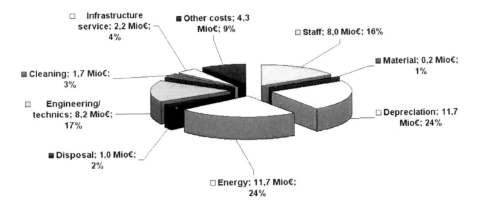

Fig. A6.2: FM budget overview of the building management for the Berlin location

IT support for FM at Schering was available until the mid-1990s only on selected application fields. In 1990 the IT infrastructure was still housed on mainframe computers. In about 1992 this central data administration was abolished in favor of a decentralized, interconnected administration. Different IT islands emerged, such as those for sales and marketing as well as for research and development and for technology.

The tasks of the FM department were only marginally supported at this time. The starting point for the realization of an electronic catalog for room and equipment data in SAP had been rejected at that time, since they could not find a suitable development partner. At the same time, there certain FM-relevant information already existed, which naturally should also be further utilized. For instance, there was an extensive cleaning surface file on PC that had been available since 1987. Also in 1992 the first pilot project was completed for the introduction of a CAFM system for space management. Using a computer-generated forecast to add the entire location, it turned out that the solution would have been far too expensive. Additionally the system provider disappeared from the market shortly thereafter.

The various solutions thus led to a dead end and could not meet the new requirements any longer. These requirements resulted from the increased mandate to manage the buildings efficiently and the fast-growing development of the intranet.

A6.5 THE CAFM PROJECT

A6.5.1 REQUIREMENTS OF THE CAFM SOLUTION AND SYSTEM SELECTION

The requirements of a future IT solution for the facility management of Schering resulted from building management tasks at that time and the modern IT infrastructure.

The solution needed to possess the usual CAFM functionalities and also needed to integrate with different IT systems on the company-wide intranet. Thus it was necessary to introduce both standardized CAFM software and also a web-based EAI solution (Enterprise Application Integration).

The requirements of CAFM functionality were as follows:

- Assumption and addition of the existing room equipment catalog
- Ability to interface with existing systems, software, and databases
- Structure of both relocation and allocation management
- Expandability of the system
- Production of reports (benchmarking)
- Production of cost transparency

The substantial requirements of the EAI solution were as follows:

- Possibility of the integration with the CAFM software
- Possibility of the integration with SAP and other database systems
- Smooth integration into the Schering Intranet
- Organization of the solution with pure HTML clients using standard web browsers (without additional plug-ins)
- Possibility of the integration of internal and external suppliers
- Expandability of the system

After the requirements were fixed in the form of simplified product requirement specifications, the selection process began. Three systems were chosen for detailed scrutiny. Finally the system BuiSy client server (conjectFM since 2008) of agiplan TechnoSoft AG (conjectAG since July 2003) was selected. The decision was not only based on functionality but also on the fact that the acquisition of aged datasets was guaranteed by the system provider. In addition, within its own research department, Schering was using the same development platform (PowerBuilder) as the CAFM system supplier.

The choice for realizing the technical helpdesk solution (EAI solution) was the Berlin-based company Axentris Informationssysteme GmbH. At the same time, as part of the reorganization in 2005 (noted above) this solution was replaced by Loy & Hutz's more complex VisualFM work-order management system.

A6.5.2 PROJECT SCHEDULE

Schering decided that the introduction and integration of a CAFM solution should take place via the current BM staff. From the outset, the possibility of translating the existing, aged datasets into the new system was flagged as being very important. Also, the solution had to integrate itself into the existing IT infrastructure and be expanded to all buildings quickly after a pilot project was used as proof of concept.

The priority list during the conversion was as follows: data transfer, space management, allocation scheme, move management, and housekeeping management. In the meantime, further tasks were added. For the conversion of the project, a multilevel plan was set up. In table A6.2, the major stages of the CAFM project are listed briefly.

A basic system for building data had been started in 1997 with the introduction of the conjectFM (formerly BuiSy) CAFM software. In the first two years, the system was filled with the basic data. These datasets included the room equipment catalogs, the CAD drawings and personnel location data. Parallel to the first data capture the necessary interfaces for translation were developed. Thus over a batch input procedure, the data was transferred to cost centers and staff (departments) by SAP on a daily basis to conjectFM.

Table A6.2: Stages of the CAFM project at Bayer Schering Pharma AG

Period	Activity
1990/91	First ideas for the introduction of FM with Schering; structure of FM knowledge within property management
1992	Conversion of the central, large computer technology to decentralized IT islands for the solution of selected singular tasks of FM (e.g., cleaning surfaces)
1992	Execution of a first pilot project for cataloging room equipment
1994-1996	Definition of a requirement profile for the CAFM solution; generation of product requirement specifications; selection of the CAFM software.
1997	System decision
1998	Introduction of the CAFM software conjectFM (formerly BuiSy)
1998	Importing/capturing the basic data (room equipment catalog, floor plans, space allocation, etc.)
1998	Development of an interface to SAP and other IT systems; assumption of FM-relevant data (e.g., cost centers, personnel, departments of, addresses)
1998	Gradual development of the CAFM solution around new modules.
1998	Development of an intranet directory solution and coupling with the CAFM system.
1999-2000	Development and introduction of intranet-based technical support.
2001	Introduction of an Internet-enabled tool for space management
2002/2003	Project "Plant Maintenance"; planning room book (requirement specifications); realization/illustration of exterior installations; dynamic user information via intranet
2004/2005	Introduction web application for cleaning inquiries; migration of the access control (key) management
2006	Replacement of the EAI solution by the work-order management system VisualFM
2007	Migration of the commercial interfaces into the Bayer SAP system P2R (CO, MM, etc.)
2007	Realization of KPIs for the building form of a pilot project
2008	Introduction of a solution to manage the inventory of the furniture by bar-code scanners and PDAs
2008	Migration of the HR interface into the Bayer SAP system P2R

The following modules were introduced gradually and are used on fifty CAFM workstations:

- Space management (see figure A6.3)

- Personnel management

- Relocation management

- Cleaning management

As a consequence, an important decision was made that selected FM functionalities should be accessible also over the enterprise's intranet by each employee:

- Technical support

- Electronic directory (ETB)

- Conference room reservation

These tasks were not covered by the standard functionalities of the CAFM software and required additional development costs.

In the case of the room reservation tool, the selection went to a system called Prequest specifically developed for this task. The reason for choosing Prequest was that the CAFM system had one drawback: it did not allow for block reservations, for instance reserving room 27 each Monday between 1:00 p.m. and 6:00 p.m.

An extension of the existing system concerning central key administration is also intended.

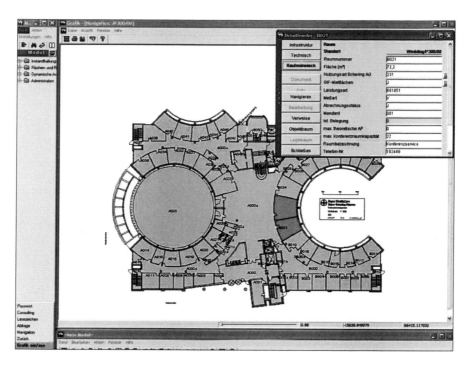

Fig. A6.3: *Building floor plan with room equipment catalog information*

A6.5.3 COLLECTION AND STRUCTURING OF THE FM DATA

An important criterion during the introduction of CAFM was the assumption of existing data sources that contained FM-relevant data. Unfortunately these sources were not completely up-to-date and had to be updated before the data was transferred. For the assumption of alphanumeric data from SAP and other enterprise applications, special interfaces were developed.

The CAD data (predominantly building floor plans) were exported from an old system (Canvas) into DXF format. In a second step, these plans were updated in AutoCAD. At the same time, a strategy was developed for drawing requirements for new buildings, including file and data acceptance procedures for new plans including layer definition.

This process of the data transfer and/or actualization was done by the existing personnel within the enterprise. This procedure took nearly three years, but with it came a substantial information gain and a clear increase in the acceptance of the new CAFM system.

A6.5.4 STRUCTURE OF A WEB-BASED INTEGRATION SOLUTION FOR FACILITY MANAGEMENT

The increasing impact and requirement of using the intranet within the Schering Company required an efficient integration of facility management into this new communication medium.

A first step in this direction was made with an intranet directory (see figure A6.4). ConjectFM provided the data for the directory, which is then made available via intranet. Information can be retrieved using different search fields. The functionality goes far beyond those of a traditional directory; persons can not only be located by their name but also filtered by cost center, building, location, or area. These possibilities were, as expected, very quickly used and valued by the staff. This comparatively simple add-on application was developed with support from HTW Berlin and contributed substantially to the acceptance and visibility of FM in the company.

The second, more complex task, fault reporting (work-order management) was then integrated into the intranet (see figure A6.5). Four functional groups participated in the completion of the processes:

- Those who can report a fault (approximately five thousand employees)

- Those who qualify and distribute a fault report (technical support staff on the hotline)

- Those who clear a fault (internal and external services)

- Controllers (those responsible for the cost centers)

This entire process of communication is completed using Internet browsers. The IT systems used in the background are transparent and insignificant to the user. The technical advantage is that no software needs to be installed on the users' computers. In addition, personnel are comfortable working with a web browser.

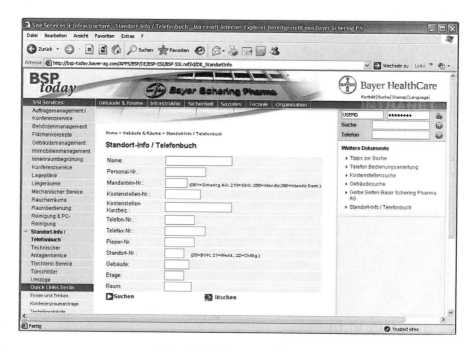

Fig. A6.4: Intranet directory

This solution was implemented through the introduction of a web-based EAI solution. The intranet-based fault reporting solution was migrated to VisualFM in 2006.

This system is used by the FM department to coordinate numerous tasks. The acceptance of this kind of this tool is evidenced by a continuing increase in corrective work-order requests. At present, an average of 500 intranet and approximately 2,500 telephone messages are worked on monthly. The range of "genuine" requests is anything from complaints over cleaning to the desire for a picture to be hung.

For the use of the system in the intranet, its own user administration solution was introduced. Many users find the system to be customer friendly, and they are able to remain anonymous, except when they use the hotline or the call center.

According to the roles and access rights, the system allows each user only his or her data (see figure A6.5). For instance, the electrical workshops see only the work planned for them.

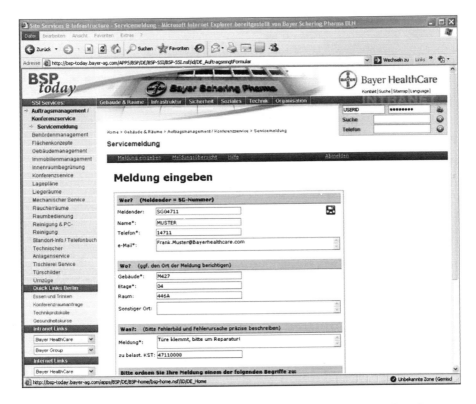

Fig. A6.5: Display screen mask from the intranet-based work-order management

A6.6 RESULTS AND LESSONS LEARNED

Bayer Schering Pharma succeeded in implementing an efficient holistic CAFM solution through the leadership of the FM department. The following points must be emphasized:

- Clear, basic concept

- Strong customer orientation and thus customer satisfaction

- Gradual IT introduction and integration

- Use of the cost-saving potentials already in the introduction phase

- Smooth integration of the CAFM into the intranet

- High degree of acceptance, including the web-based tools

- Inclusion of efficient EAI techniques

- Continuous extension of the entire software solution

A clear differentiation between classical CAFM projects and this approach (client focused and web based) can be made. When comparing this project to other CAFM approaches the effort invested and the existing immaterial advantages of user orientation and web-based technology must be considered. The intensified inclusion of users into the FM processes by means of easily operable intranet solutions turned out to be efficient and trend-setting. For example, the intranet directory improved the visibility of the FM department. Up to then, few had knowledge of any of the facility management's activities.

In addition, it led to more involvement by the users during development of new requirements. The introduction of the intranet-based, work-order management tool led to staff dealing more with the responsible manager and with facility resources. In addition, apart from qualitative improvements in the control and completion of the FM processes, a number of quantitative effects were obtained, such as savings of approximately 10 percent in cleaning costs. Also, moves and hiring new staff can be accomplished more economically and in a shorter time.

The integration of the CAFM system into the spreading EAI solutions is a major improvement over the typical IT silo situation in facility management.

APPENDIX 7:

CHECKLIST FOR THE IMPLEMENTATION OF A CAFM SYSTEM

Michael Marchionini, Michael May

The following checklist is intended to assist facility managers in developing a clear strategy for a CAFM implementation project. It provides a basis for monitoring the progress on a project's schedule, and it provides a rough estimate of the necessary expenditures and costs. The related activities should not start before the management has decided in principle on a CAFM deployment and before it decides to provide the necessary financial support. For explicit information on the CAFM implementation process, see chapter 13.

The most important activities are summarized in table A7.1. For the purpose of illustration, some data based on a fictional case are filled in. The assessment of the expenditures and periods are based on the assumption of the following case:

The property managers of an office building with about 1,000,000 square feet of gross area want to introduce a CAFM system to support the current FM processes. They are limited in the staffing that they can afford in the preparation and implementation of the project. As a result, external knowhow needs to be included. The external consultant takes the role of a moderator who accompanies the project and supports the project team. The consultant summarizes the results of the conception phase in a product requirement document and a functional specification including the contract details for a tender.

A client-server system with five workstations is the favored solution. Additionally, web access for additional users, including FM service providers, is to be examined.

Accordingly, the requirements for the administration and flexibility of user access are high.

Graphical data (floor plans and interior designs) are available in the form of CAD drawings and textual data (e.g., room information, list of employees, inventory data) in the form of up-to-date Excel sheets. Sufficient IT knowledge is present in the company.

The related expenditures (time and costs) are displayed in table A7.1 and exemplify the approach. They neither claim universal applicability nor are they intended to be transferred simply to similar projects. Even if the requirements seem to be very similar in two projects, the expenditures can differ due to the specific situation in each case. The general procedure and the necessary activities are valid in general. Users only have to check the listed activities they really need in the project.

Table A7.1: Prototypical approach for a CAFM implementation

Specification, Activity	Required Y/N	Capacity Projected (PD)	Cost Projected (T$)	Deadline (M)	Capacity actual (PD)	Cost actual (T$)	Completion date
Advance information							
Information on the topic of CAFM (guidelines, special literature, etc.)	Y	2					
Information on typical performance indicators of CAFM software (visit of exhibitions, conferences)	Y	10					
Project start							
Formation of a project group with a management-appointed leader	Y			X			
Decision on employing an external consultant	Y		20	X+1			
Initial workshop with the project group communicating the goals and next steps	Y	10		X+1			
Conception							
Clarifying qualification requirements	N			X+1			
Analysis							
Analysis (organizational and operational structure, FM processes, IT, information requirements and sources, cost estimation, etc.)	Y	20		X+2			
Weak points	Y	5		X+2			

Specification, Activity	Requi-red Y/N	Capa-city Projec-ted (PD)	Cost Projec-ted (T$)	Dead-line (M)	Capa-city actual (PD)	Cost actual (TS)	Comple-tion date
Goal							
Definition of target processes	Y	4		X+3			
Detailed project goals	Y	2		X+3			
Specify resources	Y	1		X+3			
Data Model							
Definition of necessary data and level of detail	Y	8		X+4			
Definition of classification/ID scheme to be used in documentation	Y	4		X+4			
Clarifying missing and/or imprecise data	Y	8		X+4			
Strategy and methods of data acquisition	Y	2		X+4			
Data maintenance concept	Y	2		X+4			
Data backup and data security concept	Y	2		X+4			
Rough specification of necessary interfaces	Y	5		X+4			
Requirements specification							
Efficiency analysis (cost/benefit) and decision proposal for project continuation	Y	10		X+5			
Creation of a schedule for the implementation with consideration of priorities and costs	Y	2		X+5			
Completion of concept (requirements specification) and presentation to the management, decision for continuation	Y	8		X+5			
Sum expenditures in the conception phase		105	20				

Specification, Activity	Requi-red Y/N	Capa-city Projec-ted (PD)	Cost Pro-jec-ted (T$)	Dead-line (M)	Capa-city actual (PD)	Cost actual (T$)	Comple-tion date
Selection and purchase of CAFM software							
Information concerning the CAFM market (market surveys, Internet, etc.)	Y	4		X+6			
Visit of reference projects and customer information days	N			X+6			
Pre-selection of CAFM software and/or provider	Y	2		X+6			
Pre-selection of service provider for data acquisition and inventory data	N			X+6			
Definition pilot project	N			X+6			
Software presentation with customer data by provider	Y	10		X+6			
Preparation bidding and assignment	Y	5		X+6			
Test installation and evaluation	N			X+7			
Decision for CAFM software and purchase	Y	2	80	X+7			
Sum expenditures of selection and purchase of the CAFM software		**23**	**80**				
Implementation/Deployment							
Decision to work with an external consultant	N			X+8			
Installation of hardware and software	Y	2	2	X+8			
Training administrator	Y	2	3	X+8			
Training user	Y	15	5	X+8			
Realization pilot project	N			X+9			
Input of the available data by the user	N						

Specification, Activity	Required Y/N	Capacity Projected (PD)	Cost Projected (T$)	Dead-line (M)	Capacity actual (PD)	Cost actual (T$)	Completion date
Input of the available data by external implementation partner (e.g., software provider)	Y		5	X+9			
Update/addition of existing data by the user	Y	40		X+10			
Update/addition of existing data by external service provider	N						
Comprehensive data acquisition by the user	N						
Comprehensive data acquisition by external service provider	N						
Realization of interfaces to other systems (ERP, BMS, etc.)	Y	4	15	X+10			
Evaluation of pilot project	N			X+10			
Realization of target system (training on the installed functionality)	Y	30		X+11			
Acceptance and rollout of the CAFM system	Y	2		X+11			
Sum expenditures of the implementation phase		95	30				
Project closure							
Final presentation by project team	N			X+12			
Sum expenditures of the entire project		**223**	**130**				

Specification, Activity	Required Y/N	Capacity Projected (PD)	Cost Projected (T$)	Deadline (M)	Capacity actual (PD)	Cost actual (T$)	Completion date
Utilization phase							
Routine use and quality control	Y						
Decision on future extensions of the CAFM system	Y						
Key: X — Point of project start PD — Expenditure in person days M — Months							

APPENDIX 8:

GEFMA-IFMA SURVEY ON INFORMATION TECHNOLOGY IN FM

Michael May, Geoff Williams

AUDIENCE

This survey was aimed at both the current and future users of IT tools within facility management. These tools include CAFM, IWMS, and facility automation. The survey was conducted in 2008 by GEFMA's CAFM Working Group and IFMA's ITC. Of those sixty-four organizations who have responded, about two-thirds are already using a CAFM system.

PURPOSE

The purpose of this survey was twofold. First, it sought to gain a better understanding of the challenges of current CAFM and IT approaches.

Second, it was aimed at supporting GEFMA and IFMA in assisting IT providers and FM users with setup guidelines and recommendations for future development. These guidelines and recommendations come from data gathered by GEFMA and IFMA's ITC.

RUNNING THEMES IN THE SURVEY

There are a total of twenty-six survey questions that begin by gathering baseline data about the facility, including the number of employees (inside the FM department and total employees), facility locations, and the context of the FM department inside the greater organization. The body of the survey seeks to understand the value that is placed on the FM department within the overall organization and also the level of automation/IT support it provides. Finally, specific questions relating to how and why respondents use their IT tools were asked. This included discussion questions on how they were implemented and customized.

RESULTS

The following is a breakdown of the results of the survey:

- The numbers of employees of the participating companies varied between 1 and 350,000 with no tendency that would suggest an average.

- Employees in the FM departments varied between 1 and 1,500. In this case, there was a clear tendency toward a department of fewer than ten employees.

- The number of facilities managed was up to 2,800, but a single location was most prominent, with 23 percent of respondents responsible for only one facility.

- More than 67 percent of the respondents were using some form of FM/IT tool. Of these, most had purchased standard FM/IT (CAFM) tools instead of completing their own development. Of those that were not using CAFM tools, most responded that an implementation would be "soon."

- The reasons for an affirmative decision to implement FM automation were usability and costs. A sum of more than 44 percent of the respondents chose all seven listed reasons for implementation.

- When asked how the staffing was affected after an implementation, the answer provided by most was that they had not changed their staffing levels after implementation.

GRAPHICAL REPRESENTATION OF THE RESULTS

Figure A8.1 shows the responses of the participants by market segment. Note that the heaviest response representation was by Financial Services/ Research and Public Sector.

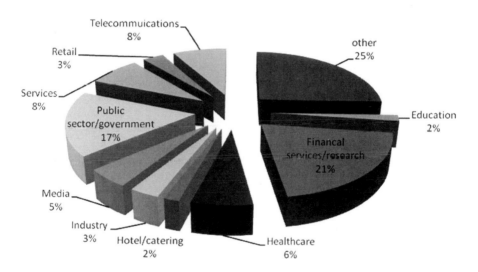

Fig. A8.1: Responses by market segment

Figure A8.2 illustrates that "efficiency" and "improvement of FM processes" were among the most important factors for implementing CAFM.

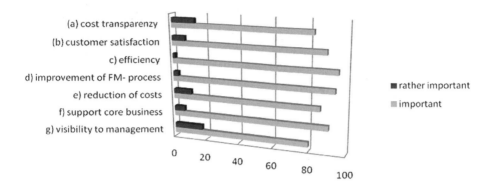

Fig. A8.2: Importance of reasons for CAFM

Figure A8.3 shows that in the majority of projects, it is the FM department and not the management that is pushing the CAFM project.

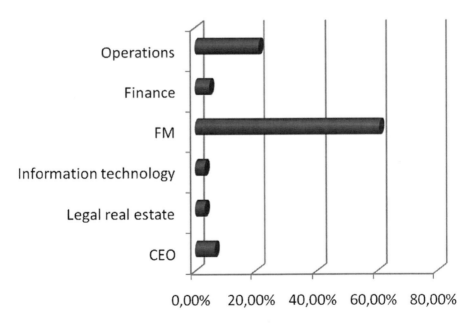

Fig. A8.3: Organizational units that push CAFM implementation

Figure A8.4 shows the distribution of already existing FM/IT tools. Maintenance management and building control systems were the most common. These software components can be stand-alone systems or can be part of a more complex (e.g., CAFM) solution

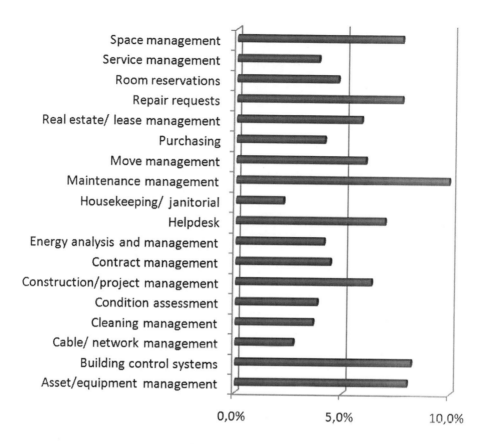

Fig. A8.4: Already used FM/IT tools

Figure A8.5 shows a balanced combination of the hurdles to a successful CAFM implementation, with "Duration of Implementation" being the greatest obstacle.

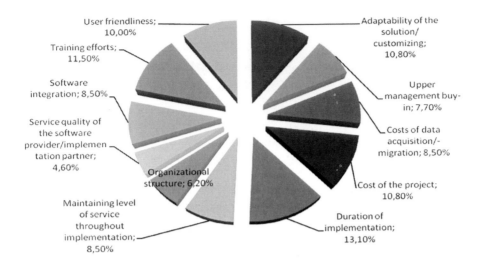

Fig. A8.5: Hurdles to a CAFM project

Figure A8.6 gives an interesting overview of the amortization period of the CAFM projects with an average of about two years, showing that quite some projects are not run efficiently enough. Furthermore, it is interesting to note that about 1/3 of the participants could not specify an amortization period showing the importance of ROI considerations in FM.

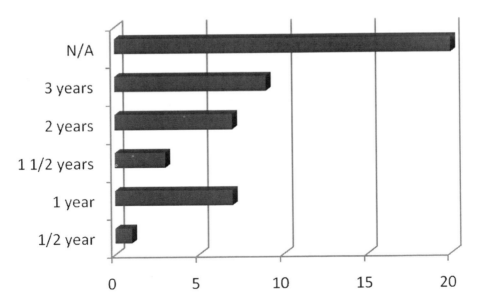

Fig. A8.6: Amortization period of the CAFM projects

APPENDIX 9:

SOURCES OF FIGURES

Figures	Source
3.4	2K Systems
7.1-7.3, 7.6, 7.11	Graphisoft Deutschland GmbH
7.4, 7.10	zeit + raum
7.7-7.9	EuSIS Europäische Standort Informations Service Gesellschaft mbH
8.8-8.16	Axentris Informationssysteme GmbH
10.4-10.7	1000hands AG
11.10-11.18	KORASOFT GmbH
11.20	IC information company
A2.1-A2.3	General Dynamics C4 Systems
A5.1-A5.4	Flughafen München GmbH
A6.1-A6.5	Bayer HealthCare Pharmaceuticals (former Bayer Schering Pharma AG)

The rights of all other figures stay with the author(s) of the corresponding chapters.

Authors

MICHAEL MAY

Michael W. May has been a Professor of Computer Sciences and FM at the University of Applied Sciences Berlin (HTW Berlin) since 1994 and the head of the Competence Center FM (CCFM) at HTW Berlin. His current research and lecturing (including abroad) is in the field of IT and FM. He earned his PhD in Mathematics in 1981 and his Habilitation in Information Technology in 1990 at the German Academy of Sciences Berlin. Prior to 1994 he worked for the German Ministry of Research and Technology.

He is a board member of the German Facility Management Association (GEFMA). He represents GEFMA at the international level. He is the founder and since 2001 the head of GEFMA's Working Group on CAFM and a member of IFMA. Michael has been a member of the program committee and/or a speaker at many national and international conferences.

Michael is the publisher of the German *CAFM Handbook*, at Springer Publishing House—the first German IT textbook for FMs, which provided the basis for the current English edition. He established contact with IFMA's ITC and initiated the publication of the current textbook *The Facility Manager's Guide to Information Technology*.

GEOFF WILLIAMS

Geoff Williams is currently Facilities Director at Centre for Health & Safety Innovation in Mississauga, Ontario where he is responsible for its day-to-day operations, business development and corporate strategy development. Prior to joining CHSI, Geoff oversaw the development, implementation, and marketing of a web-based CAFM solution that is currently assisting the day-to-day operations of a wide variety of health-care facilities in managing more than 10 million square feet of property.

Geoff is also the past president (and current secretary) of the IT Council of IFMA and the past president of the Toronto Chapter of IFMA. In all of these roles, he supports the FM industry at large. Geoff is a graduate of the University of Waterloo's School of Architecture, holding degrees in both Architecture and Environmental Studies.

Geoff resides northeast of Toronto, where he lives with his wife, Laurie, and their two children, Claire and Lauren.

RUSS BERLEW

Russ Berlew, CFM, has been in the facilities field for more than twenty years, the last ten plus with Experian, a credit services and information technology company with global reach. He has held varying facility positions within Experian and is currently the facilities manager of the Experian Americas Data Center, which houses one of the operation centers for the global monitoring of Experian IT sites.

Russ graduated from LeTourneau University in Longview, Texas, with a bachelor's in Business Management. In addition to the CFM credentials earned through IFMA, he is a member in good standing on IFMA's Technology Council. Russ is also certified in Ergonomics through the National Association of Safety Professionals

ROBERT BURNS

Robert Burns, CFM, CFMJ, is an FM consultant for FacilityNow, Inc., where he works with customers who need to bridge the gap between a box of software and a meaningful solution. He brings an extensive background in day-to-day facility and maintenance operation skills and combines it with deep IT knowledge and an engaging personal style.

Alongside his duties at work, Robert also acts in a leadership capacity for anniversary celebrations at the Harley-Davidson Motor Company, most notably for the planning and execution of huge motorcycle parades. The recent 105th parade featured 7,500 bikes running smoothly through the heart of downtown Milwaukee.

MARTY CHOBOT

As VP of Product Management and Strategic Alliances, Marty helps FM:Systems better understand the needs of its customers and bring new products to market. His primary roles include working with others on the management team to set the strategic direction for the company, helping align product direction with market needs, and communicating the company's offerings and values to customers, prospects, and partners.

Marty's current focus is the convergence of BIM and the operation of sustainable, cost-efficient buildings. Key activities include leading the FM-BIM Working Group and conducting customer and market research on the application of BIM models and data in the operational phase of the building life cycle.

Marty has more than eighteen years of experience with enterprise software. Prior to joining FM:Systems, he served in a number of roles for enterprise software companies and founded two consulting firms focused on serving technology companies.

Marty has a degree from North Carolina State University with studies in Computer Science, English Literature, and Graphic Design.

KEVIN FOLEY

Kevin Foley (CFM) has background as a practicing facility manager at several major U.S. corporations.

This gives him unique insight into the many challenges facing FM personnel. In addition to his real-world experience, he has over fourteen years of experience focusing on FM technologies and software.

RITA GOERZE

Rita Goerze holds a master's in Computer Science from Technical University Dresden, where she graduated in 1992.

Her career started in 1992 in one of Germany's largest construction companies, HOCHTIEF. In the software development department, she was significantly involved in the development of database-oriented CAD applications, later called FM. From 1994 to 2001 she was with HOCHTIEF Software AG where she was responsible for the product management in the Facility and Real Estate Management division. After the acquisition of the Facility and Real Estate Management division by the agiplan Technosoft in 2002, she was significantly involved in the process of merging the two CAFM systems. In addition she managed strategic development projects.

In 2004 Rita assumed the position of the CTO of the Kopernikus Software GmbH. There she was responsible for development and product management.

In 2005 she moved to KORASOFT to accept a new challenge and provide her experience in facility and real estate management. She has a long-term experience in interfacing CAD and CAFM systems to RE and PM as well as other IT systems.

JOACHIM HOHMANN

Joachim W. Hohmann, CFM, PhD, is a professor at the Technical University Kaiserslautern, Germany, teaching Foundations of FM and Information Technology. He holds a bachelor's degree in Electrical Engineering from the Technical University Darmstadt, a master's degree in Computer Science from the Karlsruhe Institute of Technology (KIT), and a PhD from the Technical University Darmstadt. As a cofounder and CEO of Consultants Circle, he provides consultancy in FM technology to major European companies and federal agencies as well as state and local governments. He is a chartered surveyor of the European Patent Office and an author of numerous of books and articles on IT in facility and real estate management.

Joachim earned his CFM designation in 2002. Joachim represents Germany in IFMA's European Strategy Task Force and is a founding program committee member of the EFMC. He also has been an active member of the IFMA FMCC since 2004 and serves as its global liaison for Central Europe.

As a founding member of GEFMA's (German FM Association) Working Group on CAFM, is he one of the coauthors of the original German CAFM Handbook edition of the FM IT book. Together with Michael May, he established contact with IFMA's ITC to publish this text. In 2010 he became a member of IFMA's board of directors.

ROGER HOLLISS

Roger Holliss currently is the Integrate Engineering Director for two distinct hospital systems: Grand River Hospital and St. Mary's General Hospital. This unique organizational arrangement between two hospitals arose from the recognition that both organizations would benefit from a unified strategic management approach to deal with current and future infrastructure needs.

Roger brings to these organizations the academic qualification of a combined Mechanical Engineering and Management degree from McMaster as well as a master's in Engineering from the University of Western Ontario. Upon receiving his P. Eng designation for the Province of Ontario, he has learned and applied optimization and change management techniques though a number of both private and public industry sectors, ranging from highly customized electronic filter manufacturing to high-volume printing, logistics, and now health care.

KEVIN JANUS

Kevin Janus, CFM began his professional career in the automotive field and moved from retail automotive management to the facilities field in 1996. He currently is the principal of his own consulting company, where he works with government and commercial clients developing effective procedures and business models designed to enhance the operational productivity of the facility enterprise through the use of process and technology. Prior to his current position, Kevin was the Vice President of Operations and FM Services for Integrated Data Solutions.

Kevin's facilities management experience began as the director of facilities for a 630-location, multibillion-dollar corporation with a budget for repair, maintenance, and capital expenditures totaling over 100 million dollars. He was a leader in implementing green projects when they were still just about money. He has over a decade of experience in all aspects of the facilities industry with focuses on process analysis, software development, and hardware solutions.

Kevin is a member of IFMA and just completed his second term as president of the Information Technology Council.

BILL JORDAN

Bill Jordon, director for AMS CAD + CAFM Solutions, is responsible for pre- and post-sales support of CAFM systems for AMS's client base of pharmaceutical, technology, government, and other organizations. He also oversees project management, consulting, and implementation of CAFM technology for AMS's diverse client base. Prior to joining AMS, Bill was executive vice president of FM Innovations, the FM division of Tecton Architects,  Inc., in Hartford, Connecticut, where he was responsible for the group's vision, development, growth, and operations. Bill has also held management positions at a national Steelcase dealership, a global insurance company, and with Autodesk resellers.

Bill has a strong background in various CAD products, CAD management, project management, and CAFM implementation and management. He also has extensive experience in CAFM programs and is approaching 100 million total square feet of space managed within CAFM products.

CHRIS KELLER

Chris is a recovering and reformed architect. He has worked with CAD systems since 1983 and has been implementing FM automation for more than fifteen years.

In 1988, while setting up a CAD system, Chris perceived the need for implementation services to help integrate CAD with business and business with CAD. In 1993, he formed Integrated Data Solutions,  a consulting firm specializing in the synthesis of FM, technology, and business process.

In 2006 Chris merged his company with Facilities Solutions Group, LLC, and was appointed the managing director. Facilities Solutions Group works with government and commercial clients, developing effective procedures and business models designed to enhance the operational productivity of the facility enterprise through the use of process and technology.

JULIE KNUDSON

Julie Knudson is a consultant and writer based in Seattle. She has over fifteen years of experience in facility and technology management, with a strong focus on the biotechnology industry. She founded Olympic Bay Management to provide highly specialized support to small and mid-sized companies undertaking facility and technology projects. In addition, Julie uses her experience as a facility manager to help industry vendors strengthen and improve their client relationships and communications, streamline operations, and increase profitability.

Julie also writes articles, white papers, and other material for clients in the facility and technology industries. She has been an IFMA member for more than five years.

STEFAN KOCH

Dr.-Ing. Stefan Koch is managing partner of the IT company Axentris Informationssysteme GmbH. Axentris is an IT service provider for FM tasks with offices in Berlin as well as in Wettingen, Switzerland. Driven by innovative technologies, Axentris develops middleware-based IT-solutions for FM applications. Stefan's main activity lies in the coordination of the product development in accordance with the demands of IT solutions for customer projects.

Since 2001 he has been a member GEFMA's CAFM Working Group. He is also a member of the board of directors of the Society for the Promotion of Applied Computer Science (GFaI) in Berlin.

Stefan studied mechanical engineering at the Technical University of Berlin. From 1986 to 1994 he was a scientific assistant at the Fraunhofer-Gesellschaft (FhG), where he contributed to and coordinated several international research projects. In 1993 he received his PhD at the University of Berlin.

GARY KROPP

Gary Kropp, CFM, MCSE, is a facilities management professional with over thirty years of experience in applying information technology solutions to facility management. With a unique background in both facilities and IT, he has worked for architects, contractors, real estate developers, facility services providers, and facility owners applying the use of technology to improve facility operations.

Gary holds a BS degree in Business Administration from the University of Nebraska. He is a member of IFMA and the IFMA Information Technology Council. He is a board member of the Oklahoma City Chapter of IFMA, serving as co-chair of the Education Committee. He lives in Oklahoma City and is currently working with a leading Oklahoma City-based energy company.

EBERHARD LAEPPLE

Eberhard Laepple has a degree in Architecture from Stuttgart University and a PhD in Architecture from Texas A&M University with a certificate in FM. He has over eight years of project and teaching experience in the areas of architectural design, master planning, urban planning, strategic planning and technology development, and facilities planning in Europe, North America, and the Middle East. He has extensive experience and has led and assisted in facility planning, market analysis, workplace standards, and developing database systems for industrial, corporate, institutional, governmental, aviation, and private-sector clients, as a senior programmer or project manager.

Eberhard has established and facilitated approval of major, complex facility programs beginning with a land-use model down to a detailed room level of over 30 million square feet. This expertise spans critical and industrial installations, airports, leading science and technology facilities, and communities.

NICOLE LOBB

Nicole holds a diploma in Advanced Interior Design from Georgian College. She is currently responsible for managing Seawood Solutions and Services (a member of MMM Group Limited) Facility Management team, in Thornhill, Ontario. The SeawoodFM team assists facility managers across Ontario, primarily in the healthcare industry, with the ability to effectively manage their facility by creating reliable, comprehensive and timely knowledge of that facility. This  is accomplished through a variety of methods including documentation, analysis and investigation, with the end result delivered to clients in real-time through Seawood's web-based visualization tool.

Prior to joining Seawood, Nicole consulted Royal Victoria Hospital, providing documentation support for the existing facility, and renovations required, in preparation for the hospital's 500,000 square foot expansion.

Nicole is also active in the facility management community where she currently sits on the IFMA Toronto Chapter board of directors.

MICHAEL MARCHIONINI

Michael Marchionini holds a degree in Mathematics. He is the managing director of the ReCoTech GmbH in Berlin. He has been involved with FM since 1994. The emphasis of his work during the last years lies in the conceptual preparation and implementation of IT projects in FM. Currently he works intensively on projects that focus on strategic space utilization optimization by innovative IT technologies.

Furthermore, he made significant contributions to GEFMA 400 guidelines on IT in FM and the *CAFM Handbook*. He teaches FM and CAFM at several Universities of Applied Sciences, among them, HTW Berlin.

PATRICK OKAMURA

Patrick Okamura, CFM, LEED AP, has been working in facilities for nearly thirty years and is currently the facility manager for General Dynamics C4 Systems in Scottsdale, Arizona. He facilitated and co-ordinated the LEED EB certification of the first industrial site in the world—achieving LEED EB for the Roosevelt Building in 2005 on the Scottsdale site. Four years later, the site's second main building achieved the LEED EB/OM. Patrick holds certifications in Indoor Air Quality and Safety Administration. He also holds graduate degrees in Business Administration, Organizational Management, and Construction Science.

MARKO OPIĆ

Marko Opić, Dipl.-Ing. (graduate engineer, University of Applied Sciences), was born in 1974 and studied Utility Engineering at the Georg-Simon-Ohm-University of Applied Sciences in Nuremberg. During his time at the university, he was already involved in projects at Ebert-Ingenieure in Nuremberg, focusing on integrated supply systems, energy technology, and FM. Since 2001, he has been a member of Ebert-Ingenieure, and since 2008,  he has been an FM consultant at makon GmbH (a consulting firm of the Ebert-Group). His areas of expertise ranges from FM-oriented project planning and construction, to concept development and tender processes for FM services, to the implementation of CAFM systems. Since 2006, he has also been the quality management representative of the Ebert-Group.

Marko Opić is editor of *Marktübersicht CAFM-Software*, the most comprehensive product survey on the German-speaking market, which is published annually in collaboration with GEFMA and the magazine *Der Facility Manager*.

PETER PRISCHL

Peter Prischl, born in 1953 in Austria, studied international business administration in Vienna. He then worked in functions dealing with management consulting, heating systems, building management and costing systems as well as building automation systems in Austria, Sweden, and Germany, always with an international business focus.

Since 1996 he has been the managing director of Reality Consult GmbH, an international management consultancy for real estate and FM. In this field, Reality Consult focuses on competencies in strategy, organization, controlling, and IT. Reality Consult has contributed to the improvement of real estate productivity through more than four hundred projects in over 150 companies and organizations.

Peter is a member of GEFMA and of its Guidelines and Real Estate Asset Management committees. He is a member of gif German Society for Real Estate Research and deputy chair of its FM committee. He is active in the Austria FM Association and the Austrian Association of Real Estate Managers. He is a lecturer in real estate and FM at several German and Austrian universities. He has lectured and chaired at many congresses and seminars in Europe and the United States.

DIRK RANGLACK

Having graduated from the Technical University of Dresden and the Bauhaus University in Weimar, Dirk Ranglack started his professional career in the early nineties in one of Germany's largest construction company's IT department. He was responsible for database oriented CAD applications, later called CAFM systems. Leaving the then-outsourced company, he was a member of the board and responsible for the FM department.

In 2000 Dirk founded an SAP consulting company with three partners. Responsible for the product management, he designed and implemented a CAD integration platform for the maintenance and real estate modules of SAP. His growing experiences with different FM-relevant modules of the SAP system caused him to look for new ways of approaching the FM market. He set up KORASOFT Corporation in 2006, which became a preferred vendor of SAP. To serve the North American market better, Korasoft, Inc., was set up as an Illinois company with him as the president in early 2010.

TED RITTER

Ted Ritter has over twenty-five years of experience in facility operations and project management. He has supported a wide range client projects with local, regional, and global focuses. He is the current president of the Greater Phoenix Chapter of IFMA and President of the Information Technology Council.

In addition he is the cofounder of the Facility Managers Green Peer Group based in Phoenix, which has a national following on LINKEDIN. He has published multiple articles and has been a presenter at over forty regional and national industry events

DAN RUSCH-FISCHER

Dan Rusch-Fischer, CFM, LEED-AP, currently works for FM Solutions in Phoenix, Arizona, providing facility consulting/assessments/evaluations/reporting, architectural design, LEED consulting, and code compliance services to corporate and government clientele. He has over thirty-five years of facility, maintenance, and operations experience. He has managed the facility growth of a pharmaceutical company in developing the anti-viral medications Tamiflu and Vistide—from medical research, through FDA drug approval, to drug manufacturing facility construction, test, and startup.

He has implemented numerous CMMS systems, including the first in use by the federal government at the U.S. Geological Survey. In addition, Dan has assisted numerous clients with detailed studies on operational issues, including benchmarking studies, best-management-practice operating programs, facility life-cycle assessments, facility budgeting, ADA assessments, emergency power maintenance evaluation, and site security assessments.

Dan has also served on the Development Advisory Board for the City of Phoenix for life safety, ADA, and building code adoption and amendment.

ALWIN SCHAUER

Alwin Schauer, Dipl.-Ing., studied architecture at the University of Applied Sciences in Augsburg, Germany. During his studies he was already interested in FM. That's why he established the EuSIS Europaeische Standort Information Service Gesellschaft mbH. Since his graduation, he has been teaching real estate and FM at different universities of Applied Sciences in Germany, including those in Dessau/Anhalt and Berlin.

Due to his work at EuSIS, he has been more and more involved with IT-based process optimization for FM, maintenance, and time recording. Based on his IT focus, he created the sMOTIVE product line—a web-portal-based CAFM and Business Process Integration Framework for the implementation and control of management processes. As acting partner of EuSIS, Alwin is responsible for the sMOTIVE product line. EuSIS is an active member of GEFMA. In addition, Alwin is an active member of GEFMA's CAFM Working Group and IAI's working group on FM.

MAIK SCHLUNDT

Maik Schlundt, Dipl.-Inf. (FH), studied Applied Computer Science at the University of Applied Science in Berlin. He started to work as a trainee in FM at BSR, and that enabled him to get to know FM processes from a user's point of view. Since 2006 Maik has been team leader in information and knowledge management at BSR and has focused on topics such as CAFM and data integration.

For several years, he has worked as a lecturer for CA(A)D, database, and FM automation at several universities. He is a member of GEFMA's CAFM Working Group.

DEBORAH SCHNEIDERMAN

Deborah Schneiderman, RA, LEED AP, is Director of Sustainable Initiatives and Assistant Professor in the Herberger Institute for Design and the Arts at Arizona State University. Her current research interests are in sustainable built environments, sustainability, and prefabrication, and in the integration of sustainability into design curriculum. Currently she teaches advanced Interior Design studio and sustainable materiality. Her firm, deSc Architecture, focuses on new, alternative, and ecologically sound building materials.

IFMA ITC and GEFMA

IFMA ITC

The International Facility Management Association (IFMA) is the world's largest and most widely recognized international association for professional facility managers, supporting more than 19,500 members in seventy-eight countries. The association's membership includes 125 chapters and sixteen industry councils worldwide.

The Information Technology Council (ITC) of IFMA is dedicated to the continuous improvement of the facility management profession through the exploration and analysis of technology tools, solutions, and methods and through educating and communicating these findings to the profession.

Striving to utilize technology to support our work and our profession we, through the Information Technology Council, share triumphs as well as lessons learned and information on new technology initiatives. The council also supports IFMA in its information technology initiatives and the introduction of the technology competency.

GEFMA AND THE CAFM (IT) WORKING GROUP

GEFMA is the German network for executives in facility management. With more than eight hundred corporate members, GEFMA represents providers and users of a broad range of facility services, including commercial, technical and infrastructural, real estate management, consulting, financial, and information technology. In-house facility managers as customers, investors, property owners, and increasingly the public sector with its municipalities are also part of the association. In Germany, GEFMA is the leading representative of both FM clients' and FM suppliers' interests.

In 2001 established members of FM research and education, CAFM software developers/providers, users, and consultants within GEFMA formed the CAFM (IT) Working Group. It pursues the following goals:

- Popularization of (CA)FM

- Knowledge dissemination

- Clarify potentials and benefits of CAFM

- CAFM market research

- Provision of guidelines and support of the CAFM community

- Quality control (CAFM certification)

- Identify and initiate new trends

The support of GEFMA members is manifested in the CAFM Working Group's broad library of guidelines and white papers. The experiences of the Working Group have been culminated in the *CAFM Handbook*, which was the major source for this publication.

References

Anderson R (2008) Security Engineering: A Guide to Building Dependable Distributed Systems. 2nd edition, Wiley Indianapolis, April 2008

Bagadia K (2006) Computerized Maintenance Management Systems Made Easy: How to Evaluate, Select, and Manage CMMS. McGraw-Hill New York, June 2006

Bell, M. A. 2005. Magic Quadrant for Integrated Workplace Management Systems, 2005. Gartner RAS Core Research Note G00135917, 20 December 2005.

Brauer RL (1992) Facilities Planning—The User Requirements Method. amacon, New York, 1992

Brown D E (2006) RFID Implementation. McGraw-Hill New York, September 2006

Brugger R (2005) Der IT Business Case. Springer-Verlag Berlin Heidelberg 2005

Buettner B, May M, Bernhold T, Riemenschneider F (2008) FM Implementation Processes Supported by IT. In: Alexander K. (Ed.) EuroFM Research Monograph "Facilities Management Processes", Salford, June 2008, pp 56-66

Chamoni P, Gluchovski P (1999) (Hrsg.) Analytische Informationssysteme—Data Warehouse, On-Line Analytical Processing, Data Mining. 2. Auflage, Springer-Verlag, Berlin Heidelberg New York et al., 1999

Corsten H (1997) (Hrsg.) Management von Geschäftsprozessen— Theoretische Ansätze—Praktische Beispiele. Verlag W. Kohlhammer Stuttgart Berlin Köln, 1997

Disterer G, Fels F, Hausotter A (2003) Taschenbuch der Wirtschaftsinformatik. 2. Auflage, Fachbuchverlag Leipzig, 2003

Eastman C, Teicholz E, Sacks R, Liston K (2008) BIM Handbook—A Guide to Building Information Modeling. John Wiley & Sons, Inc., Hoboken, New Jersey, 2008

Eppenberger S, König T (2003) Data Warehouse im strategischen Facility Management. In: Proc. Facility Management 2003, Düsseldorf, 20.-22. Mai 2003, pp 207-216

Essig B (2002) Kennzeichnungssystematik als Basiskonzept für das Informationsmanagement im Facility Management. In: Proc. Facility Management 2002, Düsseldorf, 11.-13. Juni 2002, pp 124-132

Haller W (2002) Grafische Informationssysteme zur Unterstützung von Facility Management am Flughafen München. In: Proc. Facility Management 2002, Düsseldorf, 11.-13. Juni 2002, pp 287-293

Haller W (2004) Orientierung auf dem Vorfeld. Autocad-Magazin (07/2004)

Hillier B (1999) Space is the Machine—A Configurational Theory of Architecture. Press Syndicate of the University of Cambridge, 1999

Hofmann S (2002) Ein Hub für München. Terminal II—das Gemeinschaftsprojekt der Flughafen München GmbH und der Lufthansa nimmt Gestalt an. Der Facility Manager, 9(2002)1/2, pp 20-22

Hohmann J (2002) A ROI-Model for the Implementation of CAFM-Systems. In: Proc. IFMA World Workplace Conference & Expo, Toronto, 2002

Hohmann J (2003a) Die ROI-Treiber lassen sich identifizieren. Immobilien Zeitung (11/2003) p 12

Hohmann J (2003b) Ist CAFM zu kompliziert für den Facility Manager? In: Proc. Facility Management 2003, Düsseldorf, 20.-22. Mai 2003, pp 181-188

Hohmann J, Janus K, May M (2008) Facility Automation—Between Myth and Methodology. Proc. World Workplace 2008, Dallas, October, 2008, 13p

Hohmann J, Marchionini M (2006) Auswahl und Einführung von CAFM nach einem standardisierten Verfahren. In: Proc. Europ. Facility Management Conf. 2006, Frankfurt, 7-9 March 2006, pp 211-215

Hoppe A, Marchionini M (2002) Unterstützung bei der Vorbereitung der Einführung komplexer CAFM-Systeme durch die GEFMA-Richtlinie 400—Computer Aided Facility Management

(Begriffsbestimmungen, Leistungsmerkmale). In: Proc. Facility Management 2002, Düsseldorf, 11.-13. Juni 2002, pp 295-300

Johnson M (2011) Mobile Device Management: What you Need to Know for IT Operations Management. Emereo, Brisbane, May 2011

Kaplan RS, Norton DP (1997) Balanced Scorecard—Strategien erfolgreich umsetzen. Schäffer Poeschel, Stuttgart, 1997

Keller F, Kruse K (2005) Konzeption und Realisierung eines CAFM-Online-Systems. Diplomarbeit an der FHTW Berlin, Mai 2005

Keller F, Kruse S, May M (2005) Open.FMgate—Eine Open-Source-Premiere auf dem CAFM-Softwaremarkt. Der Facility Manager 12(November 2005)11, pp 24-25

Koopmans TC, Beckmann MJ (1957) Assignment Problems and the Location of Economic Activities. Econometria, Vol. 25, pp 53-76

Lassmann W, Picht J, Rogge R (2001) Wirtschaftsinformatik Kalender 2002. IM Marketing-Forum GmbH, Ettlingen, 2001

Lunn S D, Stephenson P (2000) The Impact of Tactical and Strategic FM Automation. Facilities 18(7/8)2000, pp 312-322

Mahnke W, Leitner S-H, Damm M (2009) OPC Unified Architecture. Springer-Verlag Berlin Heidelberg, 2009

Marchionini M, May M (2008) Neue Technologien zur Optimierung einer strategischen Flächennutzungsplanung. Der Facility Manager, Vol. 15, No. 5, pp 28-31

May M (1999) Studienschwerpunkt Facility Management an der FHTW Berlin. In: Lutz, W. (Hrsg.): Handbuch Facility Management—Gebäudebewirtschaftung und Dienstleistungen. Ecomed Verlagsges. (Losebl.-Ausg.), Landsberg/Lech, 1996, 11. Erg.Lfg. 11/1999, 8p

May M (2001a) CAFM—eine Bestandsaufnahme. Gebäudemanagement (7-8/ 2001) pp 42-43

May M (2001b) CAFM in Deutschland—Erfahrungen, Erfolge und Perspektiven. Proceedings Facility Management 2001, Düsseldorf, 20.-22. März 2001, pp 93-102

May M (2002a) Zufriedenheit ist das Ziel. CAFM—Success Stories (IV): Schering. Gebäudemanagement (6/2002) pp 56-58

May M (2002b) Orientiert am Bedarf. CAFM—Success Stories (V): Flughafen München. Gebäudemanagement (9/2002) pp 30-33

May M (2005) CAFM-Einführung—(K)ein Buch mit sieben Siegeln—Tipps zur CAFM-Einführung. Facility Management (6/2005) 2-5

May M (Ed.) (2006) IT im Facility Management erfolgreich einsetzen—Das CAFM-Handbuch. 2nd edition, Springer Berlin Heidelberg New York, 2006

May M, Deininger J, Marchionini M (2009) Strategic Space Optimization by an Innovative IT Technology. Proc. 8th EuroFM Research Symposium, Amsterdam, 16-17 June 2009, 10p

May M, Lost T (1998) Optimierte Raum- und Belegungsplanung—eine CAFM-Herausforderung, Proc. INFO'98. Potsdam, pp 375-380

May M, Madritsch T, König T, Meier J, Scharer M (2007) Computer Aided Facility Management im deutschsprachigen Raum—CAFM-Praxiserfahrungen aus Deutschland, Österreich und der Schweiz. BoD, Norderstedt, 2007, 313p

May M, Marchionini M, Schlundt M (2007) CAFM—Status Quo. Facility Management Praxis, No. 12, pp 1-33

May M, Müller B (2002) Kosten- und Nutzenbetrachtung im CAFM. In: Seminarbeiträge CAFM—von der Projektidee bis zum Echtbetrieb. Frankfurt/Main, 07.11.2002, 29p

May M, Nehrlich W, Weese, M. (Ed.) (1988) Layout-Entwurf—Mathematische Probleme und Verfahren, AdW/ZKI, Berlin, 396p

Merz H, Hansemann T, Huebner C (2009) Buildung Automation—Communication Systems with EIB/KNX, LON and BACnet. Springer-Verlag, Berlin Heidelberg, 2009

Milbach K (2002) Datenerfassung für FM. In: Seminarbeiträge CAFM—von der Projektidee bis zum Echtbetrieb. Frankfurt/Main, 07.11.2002, 15p

Müller B (2003) Der schnellste Weg zu aktuellen Bestandsdaten und CAD-Plänen für Architektur und Facility Management, 1000hands AG Berlin, http://www.1000hands.com, Dated: Januar 2003

NN (2002) Web Services Architecture, W3C Working Draft 14 November 2002, http://www.w3.org/TR/2002/WD-ws-arch-20021114/

NN (2004a) GEFMA Richtlinie 100-1: Facility Management—Grundlagen, 2004

NN (2004b) GEFMA Richtlinie 100-2: Facility Management—Leistungsspektrum, 2004

NN (2005a) Normenausschuss Bauwesen im DIN Deutsches Institut für Normung e.V.: DIN 277 Grundflächen und Rauminhalte von Bauwerken im Hochbau, Teil 1 und 2, Februar 2005

NN (2006a) http://de.wikipedia.org/wiki/swot_analyse (Dated: 24.04.2006)

NN (2006b) BSI—Bundesamt für Sicherheit in der Informationstechnik: Handbuch IT-Grundschutz, http://www.bsi.bund.de/gshb (Dated: 04.05.2006)

NN (2006c) http://www.ogc.gov.uk/prince2/ (Dated: 08.06.2006)

NN (2007a) GEFMA Richtlinie 410: Schnittstellen zur IT-Integration von CAFM-Software, 2007

NN (2007b) GEFMA Richtlinie 400: Computer Aided Facility Management CAFM—Begriffsbestimmungen, Leistungsmerkmale, 2007

NN (2007c) GEFMA Richtlinie 430: Datenbasis und Datenmanagement in CAFM-Systemen, 2007

NN (2007d) GEFMA Richtlinie 420: Einführung eines CAFM-Systems, 2007

NN (2008a) A Unified Approach for Measuring Office Space, IFMA/ BOMA, 2008

NN (2008b) Facilities Management Action Agenda—Managing the Built Environment. Third Year Implementation Report, FMA, Melbourne, 2008

NN (2009) Space Utilization Optimization, ESRI White Paper J-9780, June 2009

NN (2010) GEFMA Richtlinie 460: Wirtschaftlichkeit von CAFM-Systemen, 2010

NN (2011) GEFMA 940: Marktübersicht CAFM-Software. Sonderausgabe von Der Facility Management, März 2011

Olfert K (2001) Investition. 8. Auflage, Friedrich Kiehl Verlag GmbH, Ludwigshafen (Rhein), 2001

Opic M, Hohmann J, May M (2011) CAFM-Zertifikat will Orientierung geben. Der Facility Manager 18(März 2011)1/2, pp 34-37

Pyzdek T, Keller P (2009) The Six Sigma Handbook, 3rd edition, McGraw-Hill, 2009

Reichenberger D (2003) Aktueller Stand der FM-Anwendung bei Schering. In: Beiträge facility world Kongress, Berlin, 15. Mai 2003

Richter P (2000) Informationsmanagement als Basis des Facilities Managements. In: Schulte KW, Pierschke B (Hrsg.): Facilities

Management. Immobilien Informationsverlag Rudolf Müller, Köln, 2000

Sabol L (2008) Building Information Modeling. In: Teicholz E (Ed.) FM Technology Update. IFMA Foundation, Houston, 2008, pp 18-26

Scharer M (2002) Wirtschaftlichkeitsanalyse von CAFM Systemen. Diplomarbeit, Wirtschaftsuniversität Wien, April 2002

Schauer A, Marchionini M (2006) RFID im Facility Management. Der Facility Manager 13(September 2006) pp 36-39

Scheer AW (2001) ARIS—Modellierungsmethoden, Metamodelle, Anwendungen. 4. Auflage, Springer-Verlag, Berlin et al., 2001

Stahlknecht P (1998) Einführung in die Wirtschaftsinformatik. Springer-Verlag, Berlin Heidelberg, 1998

Stern J (2001) The EVA Challenge: Implementing Value-Added Change in an Organization. Wiley & Sons, 2001

Stewart GB (1991) The Quest for Value. Harper Collins, 1991

Tsai H-L (2003) Information Technology and Business Process Reengineering: New Perspectives and Strategies. Praeger Publishers, Westport, 2003

Wöhe G (2002) Einführung in die Allgemeine Betriebswirtschaftslehre. 21. Auflage, Vahlen, München, 2002

Zehnder CA (1998) Informationssysteme und Datenbanken. B.G. Teubner, Stuttgart, 1998

Index